JA
MICHAEL MANLEY:

THE GREAT TRANSFORMATION (1972-92)

Jamaica's Michael Manley:

The Great Transformation (1972-92)

David Panton

With a Foreword by Rex Nettleford

LMH LMH Publishing

© 1993 by David K. Panton
First edition 1993

10 9 8 7 6 5 4 3 2

Published by LMH Publishing Limited
7-9 Norman Road, Kingston CSO
Email: henryles@cwjamaica.com

ISBN 976-610-156-6

Cover illustration: Errol Rhule
Typeset by: Karen Holloway

Photographs courtesy of: The Gleaner Company Limited; London Pictures Service
Poster courtesy of: Jamaica Information Service

NATIONAL LIBRARY OF JAMAICA CATALOGUING IN PUBLICATION DATA

Panton, David

  Jamaica's Michael Manley: the
  great transformation (1972-92)

      Bibliography : p.

  1. Jamaica - Politics and government - 1962 -
  2. Manley, Michael Norman, 1924 -

  I. Title

  972.92'06 - dc 20

Printed by Lightning Print, USA

*This book is dedicated to the people of Jamaica,
in the hope that one day they will enter the promised land
for which they have laboured so hard and suffered so long.*

Supporters have referred to Michael Manley as 'Joshua' for the past 25 years. Manley's father, Norman Washington Manley, was popularly known as 'Moses' because he forged Jamaica's 1962 independence but was unable to lead his party into the promised land by serving as Prime Minister. The story goes that in 1964 his son Michael, then a popular union organizer, was leading a strike against the state television company. In a speech, Manley said he would lead the workers in a march around the company headquarters, which he called the 'walls of Jericho'. Someone in the crowd called out 'Joshua! Joshua!' The name stuck.

—Julia Preston, "Letter from Jamaica"

And Moses gave Joshua a charge, and said, be strong and of good courage; for thou shalt bring the children of Israel into the land which I swore unto them.

—Deutoronomy 31: 23, The Holy Bible

CONTENTS

PART III - JOSHUA'S EXILE, RETURN AND LEGACY: EVOLUTION AND CHANGE

Arguably the most internationally acclaimed political leader Jamaica has had in its modern history, Michael Manley invites continuing analysis and comment from students of politics worldwide as well as in his native Jamaica. David Panton, the author of the essay which follows, grew up in the period when Manley flourished as change-agent, guru to his people, inspirer of new thinking on economic growth and development, and living embodiment of the contradictions, complexities and, if one likes, the chaos of a still fledgling nation in groping quest for form and purpose in a changing global setting. Panton has clearly been affected by the "noise" emanating from the turbulence of the desperate search for solutions by a society in transition.

His response in the form of this study may well be posing more questions than it is able to answer at this time. Happily, they are the sort of questions that can help the reader to meaningful participation in what I suspect will be a continuing discourse about shaping a society emerging from a sustained period of slavery which underpinned a protracted colonial relationship between itself and imperial Britain, as much as about the continuing dependency re-inforced in an increasingly economically globalised world that is determined to have power concentrated in the North Atlantic with headquarters in Washington, D.C.

In such a situation, the problematique remains the same. It is the strategies for dealing with the stubborn reality that must change. Mr. Manley's dramatic switch on return to power in 1989 from a passionate embrace of democratic socialism in the seventies to "radical economic liberalisation" in the late eighties and early nineties has been cause for speculation, if not for anguished concern, among supporters and detractors alike. Far from serving as an apologia for what to some may be regarded as chameleon-like indulgences, what follows **attem**pts to place into perspective the "break from the state-driven aspect of the socialist path to...a market-driven impulse". As is to be expected, there are different views explaining that "break". They include those of Mr. Manley himself who, in the search for a serviceable scaffolding to repair the building, seemed to have had no intention of abandoning the building itself.

Issues of poverty, unemployment, social justice, equality, accessible primary health-care, education for all, *inter alia* are, after all, still on the agenda. Perhaps, neither statism nor a *laissez-faire* dispensation can provide the total answers to these intractable problems of the human condition. But as Mr. Panton tells it, the perceived extensive state interventionism of the seventies did not succeed. Nor did the partial attempt to liberalise the Jamaican economy during the 1980's as antidote to the socialist preoccupations of the preceding decade. Mr. Edward Seaga, the then Prime Minister, "was [in fact] forced to re-evaluate and reformulate his structural adjustment and stabilisation reform agenda", the reader is reminded from the outset.

The triumphalist stance of economic liberalism, worldwide, has undoubtedly impacted on the Manley decision to embrace the new strategy. Was this a mere tactical pragmatic response to inescapable pressures in order to meet inescapable ends? Mr. Panton insists that "the book does not attempt to address the normative question regarding the wisdom of economic liberalisation for Jamaica". Yet the reader will be forced to contemplate this very question in plotting what he/she reads against the lived reality of a Jamaica which has been shaped in large measure by the vision of Michael Manley himself—what with his gift of persuasion, the credibility of his advocacy for justice and equality locally and internationally, and the political pedigree he has enjoyed at home as charismatic, icon among not only "the poor Jamaican masses" but also the "crucial interest groups" in the private sector who were to welcome his market-forces embrace with the same enthusiasm and passion they brought to their denunciation of his socialist rhetoric at an earlier period of political stewardship.

In this, there may well be an indication of a growing maturity shared by protagonists and antagonists of this or that ideology in Jamaica. This author even speaks of the existence of a consensus between the Jamaica Labour Party and the People's National Party, the fiercely contending forces since 1944 in Jamaica's robust and vibrant competitive electoral politics. The private sector, by 1989, may well have come to understand the importance of the state in economic development—as in the case with the much admired Asian tigers in the Pacific Rim; and political directorates have themselves come to appreciate the pivotal role of the private sector in nation-building. The leadership of both the PNP and JLP have at different times declared the Jamaican private sector an"engine of growth".

Another dimension of the Manley phenomenon, manifested in his dramatic change from one strategy to a diametrically opposed "other", is the pluralist imperative of the Jamaican reality. Jamaicans are said to be a people of options: they never seem comfortable putting all their eggs into one basket. Rather, there seems to be an unending attempt to navigate all possible routes to a destination not only sequentially but also simultaneously.

David Panton gets the message loud and clear, and presents it thus in describing the actions of his protagonist, Michael Manley: "He effectively abandoned a central tenet of his earlier beliefs *(stated socialism)* and adopted a strategy he had opposed vigorously *(free-market liberalisation)* while maintaining a general philosophical framework *(democratic socialism)*". The author reinforces his insight into Jamaicans' seeming ease with dialectical discourse (and action?) with the further observation that "throughout the process of his transformation, [Michael Manley] was driven by a burning desire to improve the social and economic conditions of the Jamaican people" —the regulative principle underlying Mr. Manley's change of direction. The reader is wisely left to make what he or she will of all this. Mr. Panton's essay deserves more than passing attention.

PROF. THE HON. REX NETTLEFORD O.M.

PRO VICE CHANCELLOR AND
DIRECTOR OF SCHOOL OF CONTINUING STUDIES
U.W.I. MONA

In the February 1989 national election, Michael Manley became Prime Minister of Jamaica for the third time when his People's National Party (PNP) emerged victorious over the Jamaica Labour Party (JLP) led by Edward Seaga. Between 1972 and 1980 Manley had embarked on a democratic socialist path and had risen to international prominence as a vocal spokesman for the Third World. In the three years after his return to power in 1989, Manley surprised the Jamaican people by furthering the market-led strategy adopted by the JLP in the preceding decade. Prior to his return, Manley had clearly moderated his radical democratic socialist image, but no one—including himself—had predicted the massive ideological shift that Manley underwent during his three-year tenure in office.

In many ways, Manley's transformation reflected the radical changes that have occurred globally in the past decade. Since the late 1980's, "liberalisation" and "structural adjustment" have become the popular buzzwords and dominant economic agenda throughout much of the developing world. As previously communist and authoritarian regimes have fallen in the former Soviet Union and throughout Eastern Europe, Latin America, and Africa, many of these nations have moved toward unshackling the massive apparatus of the state and opening up their economic systems to free market forces.

"Liberalisation" and "structural adjustment" refer to a wide range of economic and political tools that generally involve a reduction in the restrictiveness of government controls—either their complete removal, or the replacement of restrictive controls with less restrictive ones. The extent and degree to which controls are removed vary from country to country and depend upon a variety of economic and political factors.

A critical component of this transformation in these ·

developing states has involved the role of leadership in the implementation and continuation of these reforms. The reforms in the Commonwealth of Independent States (CIS) are closely associated with the President of Russia, Boris Yeltsin and, before the disintegration of the Soviet Union, reform was dependent on the fortunes of former Soviet leader, Mikhael Gorbachev. Similarly, the economic liberalisation programme in Poland depended in large part upon the personal capabilities and capacities of the President, Lech Walesa.

Although liberalisation occurs for a variety of reasons depending upon specific political and economic circumstances, committed leadership has usually been the necessary, but not sufficient, variable for economic reform. The introduction of liberalisation measures has frequently depended upon the strong support of national leaders (usually prodded by western nations and international agencies such as the International Monetary Fund and the World Bank). Examples include Rajiv Gandhi in India, Carlos Menem in Argentina, and Carlos Salinas in Mexico. In most cases, these leaders have represented either a new political elite that hoped to erase the socialist history of the past, or former socialists who had abandoned socialism for a capitalist path. But strong leadership in support of liberalisation has been the exception throughout the so-called Third World. Political leaders in most developing countries are normally wary of liberalisation and structural adjustment because these policies represent a limit on the politician's ability to direct resources to clients.

Although Jamaica serves as a typical example of a nation moving toward increased liberalisation of its economy, it differs radically from most developing nations pursuing economic reform in at least two important regards. First, Michael Manley remained firmly committed to his socialist past and synthesised his socialist beliefs with the "new thinking" of economic liberalisation during his term in office. Manley was not a member of a new political elite providing hope or a former socialist who had "seen the light" as is the case in other countries. Instead, he was a committed socialist who rejected the methodology of the past and replaced it with the popular agenda of the future, liberalisation.

Second, and paradoxically, Manley's reforms were extremely radical and even surpassed the basic demands and expectations of the IMF, the World Bank, and the local private sector. Indeed,

Jamaica is one of very few developing nations that has dismantled most significant state controls over the economy (although many still remain). Unlike most nations that grudgingly and reluctantly accept IMF and World Bank dictates, Jamaica has gone above and beyond these terms in the implementation of major market reform. This book critically examines Jamaica's historical and contemporary development from both a political and socio-economic perspective. More specifically, it analyses the role of political leadership and management in the economic liberalisation of Jamaica using Michael Manley as a focal point. Manley is chosen because he represents the most prominent political figure in Jamaica's post-independence history. His impact on the nation has been significant, largely because he has spearheaded two crucial ideological and economic turning points in the island's development. In order to examine the effects and impact for Jamaica's future economic and political development, particular emphasis will be placed on Manley's recent transformation toward market reform and liberalisation (1989-92).

Toward this latter objective, this book will address two general questions. First, the question of why Michael Manley decided to break from the state-driven aspect of the socialist path and to replace it with a market-driven impulse. By understanding the motivation and reasoning behind Manley's shift, we can then analyse the possibility that these reforms will succeed in their goals and objectives. The book will argue that a confluence of three factors serves to explain Manley's transformation. These include (1) the limited options available to Manley as a result of the nature of the Jamaican economy, (2) the significant changes in the international environment, and (3) Manley's pragmatic re-evaluation of his past efforts and possible development strategies for Jamaica's future.

It will argue that in his first year of office, Manley remained wary of extensive economic reform. International changes and the stark reality of the Jamaican economy thwarted Manley's plans for a limited social welfare programme, however, and forced him on a path of radical economic liberalisation and structural adjustment. When Manley recognised that reform represented his only serious option, he provided an ideological justification for it consistent with his democratic socialist ideals, and thus embraced it.

The second question addresses the issue of how Michael Manley implemented his liberalisation package. Historical experience has demonstrated the political problems associated with economic liberalisation and stablisation measures. The strength of political opposition has led to the slowing down or, in some cases, complete derailment of the reform process in various countries. Indeed, Seaga's partial attempt to liberalise the Jamaican economy during the 1980's led to massive national riots and strikes. Political pressures became so intense that throughout his term in office, Seaga was forced to re-evaluate and reformulate his structural adjustment and stabilisation reform agenda.

This book will argue that Michael Manley possessed significant "political capital" derived from his populist socialist image that appealed to large segments of the populace. Manley successfully used this political capital to mitigate many of the harsh effects of his economic programme and thus facilitated the initial stages of its implementation. In addition, Manley's attempts at wooing various class and social groups initially resulted in a loose national consensus that proved critical in his ability to soften the impact of interest group opposition to liberalisation.

One caveat is in order before proceeding. This book does not attempt to address the normative question regarding the wisdom of economic liberalisation for Jamaica. Rather, this book focuses on how the Jamaican government has attempted to implement the broad liberalisation strategy given that both the JLP and PNP have generally accepted the philosophy of economic liberalism. Most analysts seem to agree that extensive state controls and protectionist policies during the first decades of Jamaica's industrial development hindered the island's economic productivity and growth. It does not necessarily follow, however, that less state intervention is the necessary prescription for reform. Indeed, the remarkable success of various East Asian nations such as Singapore, South Korea, and Japan, demonstrates that state intervention can serve as a critical factor in generating economic growth and development. The debate over the type and extent of state intervention that Jamaica needs falls outside the scope of this study.

Economists and political scientists alike have often criticised national leaders in developing countries who succumb to overriding political constraints in economic reform. Yet, in three years, Michael Manley translated his massive personal popularity and his overtures to crucial interest groups into a significant adjustment of the Jamaican economy. This process did not come without major short-term economic and social costs. In the three years of Manley's rule, the Jamaican economy suffered from a substantial decline in the standard of living, massive price increases, and seemingly uncontrollable devaluation. The economic crisis became so severe prior to Manley's exit from office that his political capital had effectively dissipated, and when he did demit office, in March 1992, the political future of the PNP seemed uncertain (at best) under the stewardship of his successor, the experienced, yet controversial, P.J. Patterson. However, in the year since he has been in power, Patterson has assumed a low-key and quiet leadership posture that has increasingly "grown" in its appeal to the Jamaican populace. Initially, critics questioned his ability to unify the PNP and lead the party to victory in the next general election which must be held by February 1994. Patterson has defied his detractors, however, and has proven to be an astute and shrewd political strategist who, through his "Live and Direct" programme (where he has been meeting and dialoguing with Jamaicans in their communities across the island) has garnered tremendous national support. Indeed, Patterson's personal popularity ratings have surged to levels unprecedented in Jamaica's history, and the PNP has recaptured the lead in the polls from the JLP in a dramatic and surprising turnaround.

With a burst of social spending over the 1992 Christmas holiday period, coupled with significant economic measures designed in part to bolster government support (such as the recent reduction in the personal income tax rate from 33.3% to 25%), general elections seem imminent—an event whose outcome will be critical in determining the road Jamaica takes into the twenty-first century.

The material in this work is presented in three parts which follow fairly closely the subject matter of the seven chapters of the book:

Part I Joshua's History and Origins: The Historical Context

Part II Joshua's Ascent and Fall: New Development Paths – Strategies and Outcomes

Part III Joshua's Exile, Return and Legacy: Evolution and Change

Part I, which groups Chapters 1 and 2, examines Jamaica's political and economic history, with particular focus on the building of a democratic tradition in the context of the legacy of British colonialism.

Part II (Chapters 3 and 4) takes its central theme from the seemingly contrasting experiments by Michael Manley with democratic socialism (1972-1980), and Edward Seaga's structural adjustment (1980-1989)—both of which failed to address successfully the critical twin issues of social equity and economic growth.

Part III spans the last three chapters and adds to the debate of the PNP and Manley in opposition, in a climate of structural adjustment and, on Manley's return to power, his "dramatic switch" to economic liberalism. Chapter 7, in particular, examines the theories behind Manley's transformation and identifies his commitment to the new path. Further, it addresses that leader's use of political capital and relationship with social groups in the application of the liberalisation process, and concludes by evaluating the political and economic ramifications of the Manley rule.

ACKOWLEDGEMENTS

This book, a revised version of my senior thesis prepared for the Woodrow Wilson School of Public and International Affairs at Princeton University, represents the culmination of over three years research. Over that period, I accumulated a tremendous burden of debt to many individuals for their kind support and assistance. I am particularly grateful to the following people and organisations:

• To the numerous government officials, businessmen, trade unionists, journalists, and academics who generously gave of their time to share their thoughts with me in personal interviews. I am particularly grateful to those who spoke with me candidly and in full confidence. To many of these people, I have respected their wishes to remain anonymous.

• To the hundreds of Jamaicans with whom I spoke on an informal basis who provided me with valuable perspectives and viewpoints. Although their names do not appear in the reference list, their voices can be heard on every page of this book.

• To the numerous agencies and organisations that generously allowed me to utilise their resources to conduct primary research. Thanks in particular to the PNP National Archives (especially Olga Hammond), The Jamaica Information Service, the Bank of Jamaica, the Statistical Institute of Jamaica, the Planning Institute of Jamaica, the *Daily Gleaner*, and the *Money Index*. I sincerely thank former Prime Minister Michael Manley and his Special Assistant Tony Bogues, who provided me with numerous unreleased drafts of party documents as well as personal speeches and essays.

• To Professor Gerald Meier at the Stanford Business School for stimulating my intellectual appreciation for economic development. I am also grateful to the Ford and Mellon Foundations which granted me a six-week Research Fellowship Award to

Stanford Business School where I conducted invaluable research for this book.

- To Jean Pitter and Thyra Hudson who served as a continual source of support in helping to coordinate my travelling arrangements and interviews.
- To Professor Paul Sigmund and Professor Atul Kohli of Princeton University who both provided many valuable comments on the book.
- To Mike Henry of Kingston Publishers, to Pansy Benn and to Rex Nettleford for their commitment and enthusiasm.
- To Coleman, Daniel, Fadil, Karen, Lisa, Liz, Julie, Peter and Sharon, thank you all for your encouragement and assistance. Special thanks to Ted for helping me to retain my sanity.
- Finally and most importantly, to my parents and family, for their patience, love, and limitless support.

Despite these kind contributions, all errors and omissions remain my own.

Author's note: This book is based on numerous secondary sources and materials. Although most references and citations have been removed from the original academic thesis (available from the Woodrow School of Public and International Affairs at Princeton University), the complete bibliography is included herein.

PART I

Joshua's History and Origins: The Historical Context

CHAPTER 1

THE SOCIO-ECONOMIC AND HISTORICAL SETTING

Joshua said unto all the people, "your forefathers dwelt on the other side of the flood in old times and served other gods."
—Joshua 24: 2.

When Michael Manley became Prime Minister in 1972, he inherited an economy which had been shaped by over three centuries of English colonial rule and domination. The growth of sugar and banana exports had relied on quotas and protective legislation by Britain. This colonial regime had created a structural dependence in Jamaican agriculture on protected markets and reduced incentives for agricultural innovation or efficiency. In addition, the British had actively worked to prevent local production. This action increased the island's dependence on imports and weakened Jamaica's potential for developing a local productive capacity.

Import substitution and the rapid expansion of the mining and tourist sectors contributed to significant economic growth during the 1950's and 1960's. Most of the businesses created under import substitution, as well as the bauxite and tourist sectors, lacked significant linkages, made minimal contributions to employment, continued dependence on imported inputs, and relied extensively on capital for output. In addition, the government had essentially neglected the agricultural sector. This neglect contributed to that sector's rapid decline in efficiency and ability to produce.

Most importantly, successive governments between 1944 and 1972 had established an apparatus of state centralisation and control by creating numerous government organisations and boards, imposing quantitative restrictions on imports, passing legislation to actively intervene in the productive process, and, after independence, placing restrictions on foreign capital. With the growing economic crisis during the 1960's, political pressures (in the form of calls for social redress and employment) increased. Given the centralising state apparatus left by the import-substitution model, it was not only very tempting, but indeed extremely easy, for Manley to respond to these social demands by pushing the state to play an even more active and dominant role in the economy.

European Colonisation and the Plantation Economy (1494-1900)

The Plantation System, Sugar Export, and the Slave Trade (1494-1838)

Christopher Columbus' visit to Jamaica in 1494 marked the beginning of an era of Spanish colonisation that officially ended with the capture of the island by the English in 1655. Although almost all impact on Jamaica's economy developed later under British control, the Spanish created the plantation system and started the African slave trade, both of which dominated Jamaican society for centuries. The Spanish first attempted to force the indigenous Tainos Arawak Indians to work on the plantations, but the brutality of this exploitative process led to a substantial reduction in the local Arawak population and eventually resulted in its complete extermination.

Under British rule, the Jamaican sugar trade became so large that by the mid-eighteenth century, Jamaica was the most prized possession of the British Crown, far exceeding in importance and value any of the other British Caribbean or American mainland colonies. British authorities fostered a structural dependence on sugar exports as part of the larger economic relationship England shared with her colonies. England imported raw materials from Jamaica (and other colonies), processed and refined them, and then sold back the final products at inflated prices. The plantation system thus created a structural import bias in Jamaica that reflected the desires of the British to expand their export market by restricting domestic production in the colonies. The sugar plantation's emphasis on large-scale production also created a bias against small-scale agriculture which had long-term detrimental effects upon employment and income distribution in the Jamaican economy.

The Banana Industry and Infrastructure Growth (1838-1900)

The emancipation of slaves in 1838 and the international movement toward free trade in the 1850's led to a fall in sugar input costs and a resultant decline in sugar production. In 1846, Britain passed the Sugar Duties Act which called for a gradual abolition of all preferential duties on sugar. By 1852, Jamaica was competing—without the benefit of protective tariffs—against other British colonies. In addition to these setbacks, the planters also faced stiff competition from sugar beet production as well as a severe capital shortage as most available capital was being sent back to

Britain to finance the rapidly expanding industrial revolution occurring there. Between 1832 and 1910, the value of sugar exports declined from J$2.6 million to J$418,400.

In the wake of the sugar industry decline, many planters shifted their efforts from sugar cultivation to banking and the import-export trade. At the same time, most freed slaves migrated from the plantations to small plots of land although some remained on the plantations to work for wages and others migrated to "free villages" set up by missionaries. Those former slaves who took up peasant farming produced primarily for the local economy which led to the development of market towns and to the creation of a dual economy. Distressed planters turned to Chinese and Indian immigrants to fill the demand for labour. Between 1838 and 1917, over 33,000 Indians migrated to Jamaica, while nearly 5000 Chinese arrived between 1860 and 1893. These migrants assimilated well into Jamaican culture and many engaged in merchant trading and distribution and later became crucial actors in the Jamaican economic and social structure.

The development of the banana trade after 1869 helped to rescue the ailing Jamaican economy. By 1912, bananas accounted for 55% of the total value of exports, while sugar and rum combined had fallen to 8%. This trend continued until the 1940's when Panama disease dealt a crippling blow to banana production. For seventy years, between 1870 and 1940, banana export dominated the Jamaican economy. During that period, banana boat voyages also provided many Jamaicans with the opportunity to migrate. Between 1885 and 1935, an average ten thousand Jamaicans left the island each year.

The banana trade instigated the shift from British dominance over the Jamaican economy to the United States as American banana multinationals bought large land plantations previously owned by English sugar planters. A landed plantation elite did not survive, therefore, into twentieth century Jamaica. This differs significantly from many Latin American countries where wealthy aristocratic landowners (*latifundistas*) have played a crucial role in enacting or hindering economic reform. In Latin America, multinationals co-existed with (and, in some cases, co-opted) the landed class, whereas in Jamaica, they displaced the plantation-owning elite.

With the decline of British planters, local ownership in the banana industry also increased. Unlike the harvesting of sugar, banana cultivation increased small farmer involvement in agriculture because banana estate workers also engaged in independent hill-side production and sold their produce for cash. This activity increased the flow of money in small-scale farming and contributed to its subsequent growth. In 1929, six thousand small holders banded together to found the Jamaica Banana Producers' Association which aimed to sell and market their fruit in the United States and Europe. This action represented the first major organisational effort of local economic actors and foreshadowed the emergence of an active and well-organised economic interest group community that would come to play a crucial role in later development.

As the fortunes of the local plantation elite declined, the British government began to take a more active role in Jamaica's governance. As such, the colonial authorities embarked on a major infrastructure development scheme during the late nineteenth and early twentieth centuries which was concentrated in the capital city of Kingston. Between 1871 and 1943, the population in the island increased by 44%, while Kingston grew by 120.9% and St. Andrew grew by 204.5%. Many new jobs were created in infrastructure construction, secondary industries, and the civil service. This led to a sharp increase in rural to urban migration (as the number of urban-based jobs increased) and reflected the relative decline in agriculture (table 1.1). Although infrastructure expansion benefited primarily the (largely white) expatriate community in Kingston, the rural areas—where most of the poor black population lived—remained neglected.

Table 1.1   Labour Force Participation by Industry (%) (1844-1921)

Industry	1844	1861	1881	1911	1921
Agriculture	71.5	69.6	67.5	58.5	55.3
Industry & Construction	11.4	16.9	16.8	18.1	17.6
Commerce	3.0	2.2	3.0	5.9	5.9
Profession	1.3	1.3	1.9	2.7	3.3
Domestic	12.8	10.0	10.8	14.8	17.9

Source: Eisner, Jamaica 1830-1930, 163.

ECONOMIC CRISIS AND THE BEGINNING OF INDUSTRIAL GROWTH (1900-1952)

Economic Instability and Social Unrest (1900-38)

In the early twentieth century, Jamaica began to face a severe economic crisis. Although urban growth expanded throughout this period, the decline of agriculture and the dislocation of World War I had serious negative impacts on the economy. Initially, World War I created a rise in the international price of sugar, which provided hope for sugar planters, but by 1920, the prices fell rapidly, and once again, the sugar industry fell into massive decline. Only the restitution of quotas by Britain in 1934 saved the sugar industry from complete collapse. In addition, while the population expanded in this period, the safety valve of migration closed with the onset of the great depression during the early 1930's. Indeed, major recipient countries of Jamaican migrants all closed their borders during this period in response to the international economic recession.

Between 1929 and 1934, the rapid decline in Jamaican exports resulted in a significant drop in real per capita income, despite efforts at stimulating domestic production. At the same time, unemployment and underemployment, which had been adversely affected by the decline in migration, only grew worse. Estimates of employment figures for urban workers (wage earners in the non-agricultural sector) range from 25% to 33% during the late 1930's. By 1937-38, there was wide-spread malnutrition, inadequate housing, few educational opportunities for the average Jamaican, widespread poverty and unemployment, as well as spreading resentment, discontentment, and agitation among the Jamaican working classes.

These conditions served as the primary causes for the various disturbances and riots which broke out across the island between 1935 and 1938. Resistance to stagnant economic conditions spread throughout the island and, in 1938, the colonial authorities called out troops to quell the uprisings. In response to these disturbances, the colonial office commissioned an Englishman (Lord Moyne) to investigate the reasons for the riots, which resulted in the Moyne Report, published at the end of the Second World War.

The Moyne Commission report was important for several reasons. First, the Commission recognised for the first time the failures of the colonial office in adequately dealing with economic conditions on the island. Citing low income earnings and increased unemployment as the two reasons for social unrest, the report recommended the implementation of various social welfare measures to provide long overdue social services, but it fell short of calling for significant structural economic transformations.

In addition, although it made references to the importance of small, local industry, the overall tone of the report was unenthusiastic about the development of domestic industry. This bias against industrialisation in the colonies stemmed from the early days of British control when colonial authorities had discouraged industrialisation fearing that it would damage the interests of British exporters. Moreover, the commission reaffirmed the historical British attitude against government intervention in the local economy. For example, the report rejected the submission that the government should establish a cement factory and instead recommended that a British firm should be invited to perform that task.

The Birth of Nationalism and the Seeds of Industrial Growth (1938-51)
     Despite the bias against government involvement and local industry development, the advent of universal suffrage and other political changes instigated a shift in these directions between 1938-51. In 1944, local political parties led by Jamaicans competed for and assumed leadership in the island's first election under universal adult suffrage. This election initiated the process toward national independence which occurred in 1962. Although government decisions remained under the auspices of colonial control, nationalist impulses among the new local leadership created a critical shift in economic direction. Recognising the vast opportunities for British private investment with the industrialisation of the island, the colonial authorities eventually decided to pursue an industrial path of development.
     In 1945, the government passed the Colonial Development and Welfare Act, the extension of a 1940 act of the same name. The new act provided capital for roads, housing, water systems, and schools, all of which formed the infrastructure development for later industrial growth. In addition, two government committees, the Economic Policy Committee and the Agricultural Policy Committee, tabled reports for long-term economic growth in 1945. Two years later, the government passed the first Ten Year Development Plan. Both the policy committees and the Ten-Year Plan emphasised agricultural growth as the primary government objective, placing industrial investment as a secondary priority.
     The Ten Year plan did make reference, however, to measures which the government had under consideration for the encouragement of industry through tax relief and temporary protection to infant industries. In 1949, the government passed the Pioneer Industry Encouragement Law, the first of a series of

legislative efforts to stimulate industrial development. The revision of the Ten Year Plan in 1951 formally marked the government's shift to the adoption of an official industrial policy. In that year, the government created the Industrial Development Corporation and charged it with coordinating and promoting the island's industrial policy. In 1952, the government formally invited the World Bank to make an independent and objective study of the industrial development requirements of Jamaica. In addition, the government invited a team of British industrialists to Jamaica and retained the services of an American consulting firm for the primary purpose of recommending specific industrial projects and promoting foreign investment in Jamaica.

IMPORT SUBSTITUTION AND THE RISE OF BAUXITE AND TOURISM (1952-1972)

Import Substitution: Origins and Implementation
 Influenced by the writings of economist and later Nobel Laureate Sir W. Arthur Lewis, the Jamaican government embarked upon an ambitious industrialisation campaign. After World War II, the Caribbean Commission asked Lewis to prepare a study for the future of the British West Indies, in which Lewis recommended that the English-Speaking Caribbean industrialise as quickly as possible. Although his suggestions were initially rejected, nationalist pressure reversed this decision and Jamaican policymakers embraced Lewis' recommendations. Many of these policymakers ignored significant elements of Lewis' industrial strategy although Lewis himself later played a more direct role in the direction (and particularly the financing) of Jamaican industrialisation when he served as president of the Caribbean Development Bank.
 Lewis argued that the government needed to restrict imports, focus on domestic production, and actively encourage the development of secondary industries (especially those industries that processed raw materials with relatively low capital and labour skill inputs). Lewis believed that industrialisation in the "capitalist" sector would eventually absorb the surplus labour found in the agricultural "subsistence" sector and thus lead to increased employment, an objective which he repeatedly stressed.
 The Lewis model differed somewhat from the traditional Raul Prebisch/ECLA import substitution model in its heavy emphasis on foreign capital and in its call for long term export development. The

emphasis on foreign capital as the primary catalyst of development instigated the use of the term "industrialisation by invitation" to characterise this era. Between 1950 and 1968, one scholar estimates that foreign capital accounted for 35% of total net investment in the Jamaican economy. Despite his emphasis on foreign investment, Lewis recognised the limitations of the Puerto Rican model ("Operation Bootstrap"), and thus he stressed the need to customise the import substitution model to the Jamaican context.

The government import substitution programme rested on three platforms. These were (1) the creation of government agencies to stimulate industrial development, (2) the enactment of legislation to encourage industrial production, and (3) the implementation of quantitative restrictions on imports to protect domestic industries.

The government created a number of agencies to direct the import substitution model and to provide financial and technical support to export-oriented, labour intensive, low-import content industries. These organisations included the Industrial Development Corporation (1951), the Central Planning Unit (1955), the Small Business Loans Board (1956), and the Development Finance Corporation (1959). Incentive Legislation either targeted specific industries or emphasised general industrial development through the Pioneer Industries Law, the Industrial Incentives Law, and the Export Industries Law. In addition, the government imposed a series of quantitative or absolute import restrictions on a number of consumer, capital, and intermediate goods (table 1.2).

Table 1.2   Number of Items under Quantitative or Absolute Restriction (1961-73)

	Consumer goods	Intermediate goods	Capital goods	Total
1961	44	3	3	50
1964	58	5	9	72
1968	128	15	15	158
1973	164	16	21	201

Source: Bonnick, "Jamaica: Centralization to Liberalization, and Back?" 273.

Import Substitution: Impact and Effects on the Economy
    The import-substitution strategy succeeded in transforming the Jamaican economy and in generating substantial economic growth

(Appendix C). Gross Domestic Product (GDP) increased during this period by an average annual rate of 7%. However, real per capita GDP increased at less than 5% during the same period, reflecting the rapid growth of the population. Manufacturing increased from 6.8% of GDP in 1938 to 13.2% in 1960, and thus replaced agriculture as the leading contributor to the GDP. Nearly 60% of the industrial expansion in this period resulted from the import substitution initiative.

The industrialisation process generated significant production increases in secondary and some primary manufacturing industries. As such, producers in these industries formed the core economic elite in the island, a position they would hold for the next three decades. Powerful families which engaged in construction, food processing, pharmaceuticals, and other related forms of manufacturing, made large profits throughout this period. Industrial firms that these families controlled dominated the local manufacturing industry.

As these manufacturing firms grew increasingly wealthy, small farmers, rural labourers, and the urban unemployed suffered from a decline in income. After centuries of colonial rule, income inequality had become a striking feature of Jamaican society. In 1958, the top 20% of households controlled 61.5% of income in the island (table 1.4). This severe income inequality increased dramatically during the period of import substitution, with most of the income earned in the creation of GNP accruing to the owners of local manufacturing firms (table 1.3). Between 1958 and 1968, the income share of the poorest 40% of the population (in personal earned income) declined from 7.2% to 5.4%.

Table 1.3 Distribution of Income Earned in the Creation of the GNP (1953-59)

Income Shares	1953	1954	1955	1956	1957	1958	1959
Earnings of Employees	50.4	49.6	50.3	50.8	49.1	49.9	49.9
Earnings of Resident Corporations	2.8	3.2	3.4	4.7	6.8	6.8	6.7
Earnings of Property and Self Employment	33.2	33.2	32.4	30.4	29.8	29.0	28.9
Net Indirect Taxes	7.6	6.6	6.4	6.3	7.0	7.2	7.2

Source: Munroe, *The Politics of Constitutional Decolonization,* 203.

Despite the significant economic and industrial growth, the import-substitution strategy had several negative effects on the economy. Although the government imposed numerous restrictions, imports rose rapidly during this period. Imports grew from 32.5% of GNP in 1950 to 51.6% in 1968, while exports grew from 26% to only 40% over the same time frame. The rapid growth in imports reflected the growing demand for imported food, consumer durables, and manufacturing inputs generated by the import-substitution model. Moreover, despite its contribution to national income, the import substitution strategy failed to reduce the sectoral pattern of import coefficients.

Table 1.4   Percentage of Income of Deciles of Households (1958)

Decile		% of Income
1st	10%	2.2
2nd	10%	
3rd	10%	2.5
4th	10%	3.5
5th	10%	4.7
6th	10%	6.1
7th	10%	8.3
8th	10%	11.2
9th	10%	18.0
10th (first 5%)	5%	13.3
10th (second 5%)	5%	30.2

Source: Ahiram, *Income Distribution in Jamaica*, 337.

In addition, despite efforts to the contrary, most of the new industries created during this period were extremely capital intensive and thus contributed little to local employment. Between 1956 and 1968, firms established under import substitution provided direct and indirect employment for 26,000 persons, as compared with an annual labour force increase of 25,000 in the years preceding this period. Indeed, the number of workers employed by the manufacturing sector under the Incentive Programme over a ten-year period was less than the growth of the labour force in a single year. Excessive migration rates in the post war period led to a reduction in the size of the labour force and thus postponed an inevitable unemployment crisis. Between 1953 and 1957 the economy grew by 11.5% per annum, but unemployment remained constant at around 18%. As migration rates slowed, the situation became even more severe. Between 1960 and 1972, unemployment increased beyond 20% despite a real growth rate of 5% annually. The new industries started during this period did not create significant inter-sectoral backward or forward linkages. Most of these firms engaged primarily in assembly or finishing operations—so-called "screwdriver" operations—and therefore did not contribute to other aspects of the local economy. The firms were heavily dependent on imports for raw materials and partly finished components. In addition, the nature of the employment created under the import-substitution model was biased toward unskilled labour. Local firms thus had little incentive to develop training facilities for the growing working force. This lack of training establishments created a largely unskilled labour force that later posed a major obstacle to effective employment creation.

In macroeconomic terms, the contribution of new manufacturing firms to employment and income generation did not justify the substantial loss of revenue caused by government incentive programmes. Tax breaks and other economic incentives to production were unnecessarily excessive in many instances and only led to increased profits for local merchants and producers. Although economic production increased during this period, government revenues were substantially lower than they could have been. Jefferson calculates that between 1959 and 1969, the funds flowing out of the Jamaican economy actually exceeded all the incoming investments attracted by official incentive policies.[1]

The Further Decline of the Agricultural Sector

The governmental emphasis on import substitution also led to neglect and subsequent decline in the agricultural sector. Significantly, few linkages occurred with the agricultural sector, which contributed to its relative stagnation. Although agriculture employed more than one-third of the Jamaican labour force between 1950-1968, agricultural production increased at a rate of only 2% in that time, compared to a 6.7% increase in real GDP over the same time period. Over these years, export agriculture fared the worse, although livestock and crop production for domestic consumption expanded at a faster rate.

The plantation system had created unequal land distribution

exacerbating agriculture's problems.   In 1954, 1300 farms of 100 acres or more accounted for nearly half of the island's total farm acreage, while 43,000 farms of under one acre in size accounted for less than one percent of total farm acreage. More than one quarter of the land suitable for continuous cultivation was lying idle in 1961. Although successive governments expressed a commitment to improvements in agriculture, no major land reform programme was instituted during this period.

The sugar and banana export industries deteriorated even further during the late 1950's and 1960's, especially under the weight of colonial neglect. In the sugar industry, the technological capabilities of the factories had declined substantially, input costs were increasing, investment was low, and cane yield per acre had fallen. Only extensive tariff and quota protection from Britain kept the industry alive. Poor management of sugar plantations in Jamaica led to a further decline in production and by 1969, Jamaica could no longer meet its protected markets quota. Banana output during this period also fell short of its quota as a result of inefficient spraying, labour shortages, and rigid quality controls on bunches for export. Banana farmers faced particularly difficult conditions such as expensive transportation costs, difficult access to credit, poor storage and distribution facilities, and the high cost of imported inputs such as fertilisers.

The Rise of Bauxite/Alumina Production and Tourism

The mining industry was the primary contributor to the structural transformation which occurred in the Jamaican economy during the 1950's and 1960's. Mining for bauxite—the ore which is the base mineral in the production of aluminum—first began in 1952 under the control of privately-held American and Canadian companies. The American declaration that bauxite was a "strategic resource", demand from the Korean War, and worldwide economic boom conditions contributed to the rise of the industry. In addition, the industry received significant government funding through the Marshall Plan in the United States and the Economic Co-operation Administration in England. The mining companies in Jamaica also received substantial encouragement and support from the Jamaican government, primarily through the 1950 Bauxite and Alumina Industries Encouragement Law, which provided a tax relief on mining inputs.

By 1957, Jamaica had become the world's leading bauxite producer and the primary supplier of bauxite to the United States, a position it held for nearly fifteen years, until 1971. The bauxite companies were all foreign-owned and all exported the mineral ore without processing it into aluminum. Only one bauxite company, Alcan Jamaica Company, converted bauxite into alumina locally (the first part of the process of converting bauxite into alumininum). This fact would later prove critical, as bauxite-producing firms could easily leave the island to other countries (which almost all of them did), while Alcan was one of only two companies that did not leave the country despite adverse relations with the government during the 1970's.

The expansion of the tourist industry represented further diversification of the Jamaican economy. Active government participation played a critical role in the growth of the tourist industry. This government participation included legislation—such as the Hotel Aid Encouragement Law of 1944—and the reconstitution of the Tourist Board in 1955. Although tourism had made a small contribution to the economy preceding the Second World War, Jamaica was transformed from a vacation spot for the relatively wealthy to a mass tourist destination during the 1950's. Between 1945 and 1969, the number of hotels increased threefold, and in the latter year, there were 95 hotels with 4,352 rooms and a guest capacity of 8,413.

Unlike the bauxite industry, tourism offered significant opportunity for local participation (largely confined to a wealthy local elite). In 1968, 53% of hotels on the island were in local hands compared to 39% for foreign owners (9% belonged to both). Although Jamaican-owned hotels existed, the industry depended to a great extent upon North American tourists (primarily Americans) for its survival. For example, American visitors made up 66% to 81% of visitors during the 1960's. In 1966, 345,000 visitors spent approximately J$90 million on the island. Tourism's contribution to national income increased from 4.4% to 6.5% between 1959 and 1969, and its contribution to total retained foreign exchange earnings moved from 10% to 17% during the same period. By 1970, tourism had become one of the most important sources of government revenue, second only to the mining sector.

Bauxite and Tourism: An Evaluation of their Impact on the Economy
Both the mining and tourist sectors contributed to the significant diversification and growth of the Jamaican economy during this period. Despite their income contributions, they made only minimal contributions to employment, largely because of their exceedingly high capital-intensity and import content. Bauxite production requires little labour and instead depends on large machinery to facilitate the process. Although the industry contributed 17% of Jamaica's retained foreign exchange earning and 14% of GDP in 1968, it provided only one percent of total employment in the same year.

In addition, the mining industry paid extremely high wages and exacerbated the severe wage dualism characteristic of the Jamaican economy. Tidrick posits a provocative thesis that wage increases in the high-wage mining sector reduced employment directly because these wage increases tended to "spill over" and create unemployment elsewhere in the economy.[2] High wages induced unemployment because they drew large numbers of workers from rural into urban areas in search of high incomes. Tidrick argues, however, that the limited number of jobs available led to widespread open unemployment in urban cities.

More labour-intensive than bauxite/alumina production, tourism employed between 10,000-12,000 workers directly and an equal number in related sectors during this period. Most of this labour was seasonal and the industry was extremely vulnerable to international conditions. In addition, the tourist industry had an extremely high import content. Scholars estimate that for every dollar of tourist expenditure in Jamaica throughout this period, 34 cents was spent on imports. Many theorists conclude that the returned value to the Jamaican economy of both industries (including local purchases, salaries and wages, tax and royalty payments), was much less than possible. Between 1956 and 1967, the bauxite industry contributed between 36% and 43% of the total value of bauxite and alumina exports—the rest accruing as profits to the bauxite and alumina firms. In tourism, estimates of profit outflow during this time range from 70 to 77 cents per dollar. Both the bauxite/alumina and tourism industries made significant contributions to the Jamaican economy during this period, although the overall net impact on the Jamaican economy could have been greater.

The Expansion of the Informal Sector

In addition to the expansion of the bauxite/alumina, tourism, and manufacturing industries, the other significant aspect of economic growth during this period involved the informal, or hustling sector, primarily the export of marijuana ("ganja"). With the sluggish growth in traditional agricultural exports, many small farmers turned their interests toward the illegal production of ganja to supply the growing North American market. Although few studies exist on the extent or growth of the ganja trade during this period, subsequent studies estimate that ganja probably surpassed banana and sugar as the islands chief export crop.

For many of the farmers who did not engage in ganja cultivation, migration to urban areas became a major source of increasing their incomes. As numerous agricultural labourers migrated in the hope of finding high wage employment, many of them found few job opportunities available. Until these workers found formal employment, they engaged in small-time hustling, trading, and the provision of personal services outside of the official economy. Most remained unemployed, however.

Participation in the urban informal economy usually paid more than did agricultural production, although not as much as industrial employment. By participating in "casual employment," labourers earned at least as much or more over a year's time as full-time wage earners in agriculture. Between 1943 and 1960, the service sector experienced the largest gain in employment, second only to manufacturing, which clearly indicates the rapid expansion of the urban informal sector. Table 1.5 charts the levels of urbanisation that occurred between 1943 and 1970.

Table 1.5   Urbanisation, 1943, 1960, 1970 (thousands and %)

	1943	1960	1970
Total Population	1237.1	1609.8	1797.4
Urban Population*	236.8	519.5	751.2
Urban Population as % of total	19	32	42
Corporate Area**	201.8	376.5	475.6
Corporate Area as % of total	16	23	26

*Excludes places with populations of less than 5000.
**Urban population of Kingston and St. Andrew parishes.
Source: Stephens and Stephens, *Democratic Socialism*, 25.

The Influence of Nationalism on Economic Policy: Increased Centralisation
Although official government policy during this period was to actively pursue foreign capital investment, this policy did not supplant strong nationalist tendencies among various government administrations. For example, in 1957, the officially socialist People's National Party (PNP) under the leadership of Norman Manley, renegotiated the government contract with the bauxite companies, which led to a six fold increase in revenue. Indeed, this PNP government set the dominant economic agenda for the future by establishing numerous government bodies, statutory boards, and quasi-government authorities to regulate and play an active role in industry.

With official independence from England in 1962, nationalist fervour achieved new highs. The Jamaica Labour Party (JLP) won the first post-independence elections and, despite its overtly pro-Western capitalist leanings, embarked on a relatively ambitious "Jamaicanisation" programme to increase local participation in the economy. Using various tax measures and policy statements, the JLP government encouraged foreign businesses to sell shares on the local stock exchange, to increase domestic holdings of companies to 50%, and to establish local Boards of Directors. This programme targeted the financial sector where foreign control and ownership was exceedingly high.

In response to this "Jamaicanisation" drive, a number of financial and industrial firms divested partial ownership to local hands prior to 1972. The JLP regime also strengthened the import substitution industrialisation policy, increased public sector activity, and expanded domestic monetary and credit policies. The centralisation of the state and the increasing number of controls on production characterised the Jamaican economy which Michael Manley inherited when he assumed office in 1972.

CHAPTER 2

THE DEVELOPMENT OF A POLITICAL TRADITION

And when Joshua heard the noise of the people as they shouted, he said unto Moses, "there is a noise of war in the camp."
—Exodus 32: 14.

Jamaica's political history provides a valuable insight into the development strategies which were adopted by Michael Manley both in 1972 and later in the 1989. This chapter argues that political change in Jamaica until 1972 can be understood only within the context of English colonialism which sharply divided the Jamaican society. Local English authorities subjugated the black Jamaican underclass. Political and economic change occurred mainly as a result of rebellion and riots among this politically disenfranchised and economically exploited group. Local authorities did not implement this reform in direct response to class agitation but were forced to do so by the English parliament.

This "benevolence" on the part of the English led to an increased respect for colonial authority among most Jamaicans. As such, the move for self-governance was delayed for several years and led to division among the local populace, with many loyal to Britain and others adamant in their call for national control over political decision-making. This sharp division helped to foster the two-party political system in Jamaica.

The lack of national unity among the local political elite also led to political tribalism that later erupted into violence. Jamaica thus established a democratic tradition, but a democracy tainted by violence, tribalism, and patronage. By 1972, although the government had achieved self-governance and full independence, years of English control had left a political legacy of sharp social inequality that easily fell for the persuasive rhetoric of egalitarianism and social justice espoused by Michael Manley.

LOCAL PLANTOCRACY DOMINATION VS. ENGLISH CONTROL (1655-1900)

Local Plantocracy Domination and Popular Unrest (1655-1866)
Until 1865, Jamaican society could best be understood by

using the "conflict pluralist" approach put forward by Smith.[1] The conflict pluralist approach presupposes the existence of differing cultural groups with one dominant group ruling through coercive and regulatory institutions. Political change usually follows changes in the social structure and is often accompanied by violence. Under British colonial rule, these two striking patterns emerged in Jamaican society.

Effective political control and power over the island rested not in England, but in the hands of local wealthy plantation owners intent upon furthering their own economic interests. Consequently, almost all significant political change that occurred during this period did so in direct response to resistance from the oppressed black population.

The local plantation elite maintained strict control over the island and brutally suppressed all acts of revolt among slaves. A major rebellion in 1831 played a crucial role in quickening the emancipation process that occurred in 1838. Even after emancipation, the local authorities used their legislative and political power to restrict the rights of freed slaves and limit their economic and political mobility. In response, angered blacks, with the support of sympathetic freed coloreds, rose up in the Morant Bay Rebellion of 1865 which was brutally suppressed by the local authorities.

The Rise of the Colonial Office (1865-1900)

The post-rebellion repression by the local planters led the English Parliament to reassert a dominant role in Jamaica's affairs. To facilitate this new role, the English implemented the Crown Colony system of government in 1866 which created a non-elected Legislative Council and strengthened the position of the Governor. From this time onward until independence in 1962, English authorities played a dominant leadership role in the governance of the island. Prodded by England, successive governors embarked on social reform and infrastructure growth programmes that improved the plight of the black underclass by creating employment and providing welfare relief. These reforms were limited, however, and many Jamaicans, especially those in rural areas, remained unaffected by them.

In 1884, English authorities allowed unofficial members of the Legislative Council to be elected. For the next fifty years, the English slowly facilitated increased representation into the political process, including the extension of suffrage to women in 1919. Although the British increased political representation among the local populace, the Governor still retained executive control over the affairs of the island and the Legislative Council still served in an advisory capacity, as a vocal but largely ineffectual group.

POLITICAL ORGANISATION: SEARCHING FOR AN IDEOLOGY (1900-44)

Increased Political Awareness and Participation (1900-38)

This period witnessed the rise of organised black leadership both inside and outside of the formal political process. During the 1900's, as the black population expanded, so did their participation on the Legislative Council. In 1900, the first black was elected to the Legislative Council. By 1910, there were five brown members and one black member of the Legislative Council out of the fourteen elected members. By the 1920's there were more black members than white and by the 1930's the membership was almost entirely black. Criticism of the island's political structure by these new entrants often led to initial response from the colonial office but not to subsequent action. For instance, colonial authorities formed a committee in 1921 to examine government structure in response to a call from J.A.G. Smith, but nothing arose of it. Members of the Legislative Council were forced to form their own political organisations to lobby for reform. Although vocal, these organisations failed to achieve any meaningful success as the colonial office remained intent upon preventing substantial change.

Outside of government, various leaders had began to press for change in a variety of fora. In the religious arena, Alexander Bedward, a prominent evangelist with a mass following, called for black people to rise up against white oppression. His anti-government message led him into difficulties with the authorities and, after he declared himself to be Jesus Christ, the government locked him up in the insane asylum.

Marcus Garvey, a black nationalist, also rose to prominence during this time. In 1928, Garvey founded Jamaica's first black political party, the People's Political Party (PPP). Garvey's party resulted in failure, however, largely because of the limited political enfranchisement for blacks and harassment by government authorities. Despite efforts to restrict his political participation, Garvey was elected as councillor of the Kingston and St. Andrew

Corporation. Like that of Bedward, Garvey's message consisted of a call for political redress that reflected the growing dissatisfaction among the black underclass with their conditions.

Despite the rise in political awareness and organisation, the extent of popular participation still remained abysmally low. In 1930, only eight percent of the population was eligible to vote and in 1935, that number had fallen to six percent. More importantly, material conditions had deteriorated rapidly. The great depression in the United States affected Jamaica significantly, thus driving up unemployment. This resulted in numerous labour riots and protests that spread throughout the island between 1935 and 1938. The Moyne Commission examined the reason for the disturbances and suggested several constitutional changes; this resulted in the establishment of limited self-government in 1944 based on universal adult suffrage.

The Organisation of the Labour and Political Reform Movements (1938-44)

The 1938 disturbances marked the birth of the modern trade union movement. The Jamaican Legislature first granted legal status to officially registered trade unions with the passage of the Trade Union Law in 1919, which was passed in response to widespread labour restiveness and the pressures of the liberal-leaning Governor. It deliberately denied the right to picket and placed numerous restrictions on the right to strike. In subsequent years, various unions were formed but none laid claim to substantial membership. In 1936, the Jamaica Workers and Tradesmen Union (JWTU)—the island's first union representing workers of all occupations—was founded and became the bedrock of all later unionism.

Alexander Bustamante, a near-white money-lender of a formerly wealthy Jamaican family, became the treasurer and eventual president of the JWTU. Bustamante, who had changed his name from Alexander Clarke, had left Jamaica at an early age and had gained initial prominence during the 1930's by writing a series of letters to the *Daily Gleaner* criticising the colonial office and decrying the conditions on the island. When he became president of the JWTU, Bustamante traveled across the island delivering speeches and holding rallies in which he displayed fiery oratory that made him extremely popular among the working class. Although he frequently criticised the colonial office, Bustamante's agenda called for improved labour conditions and not major political change. By 1938, Bustamante had emerged as the unofficial leader of the labour movement in Jamaica.

Between 1936 and 1938 the call for political and economic reform had reached a fevered pitch. As such, a diffuse political and reform movement began to grow to parallel the growth in trade union activity. Several left-leaning intellectuals formed organisations dedicated to securing self-government and founded journals dedicated to the cause of political reform. Four expatriate Jamaicans in New York formed an organisation called the Jamaica Progressive League (JPL) in 1936 committed to securing self-government for Jamaica and in 1937, three left-leaning middle class intellectuals in Jamaica founded a new journal, *Public Opinion*, dedicated to the cause of political reform throughout the colonies. In the same year, the most prominent and well-respected barrister on the island and Bustamante's cousin, Norman Washington Manley, started an economic organisation designed to promote community development in rural areas (Jamaica Welfare Limited). A few months earlier, various middle class political activists had approached Manley to lead a new organisation (the National Reform Association) designed to unify the several forces seeking change, an offer which Manley refused. By 1938, many Jamaicans began to recognise Manley as the unofficial head of the movement for political and economic change in Jamaica.

The 1938 riots brought these two forces—labour and political—and particularly these two men—Bustamante and Manley—to the fore of the reform cause. Bustamante's decision to intervene on behalf of rioting sugar workers by organising a demonstration led to his arrest. Norman Manley, who had previously represented sugar estates as a barrister, acted as a negotiator on the worker's behalf and attempted to secure Bustamante's freedom. The workers conceded to company demands only on the condition of Bustamante's discharge from prison. Manley had to vouch for Bustamante's subsequent release, an act which formally signified the beginning of a long professional relationship between the two men.

The disturbances came to an end when the employers agreed to wage increases and when the government announced a land-settlement programme to benefit peasant farmers. Prodded by authorities in England, the Legislature also instituted various working condition reforms. The Moyne Commission report played a significant role in enacting these changes and also laid the groundwork for the island's first election under universal adult suffrage in 1944.

In the wake of the 1938 riots, Bustamante went on to form his own trade union, the Bustamante Industrial Trade Union (BITU), over which he exercised dictatorial control by declaring himself President-General for Life. In September of the same year (1938), Manley was asked by O.T. Fairclough, a prominent middle class leftist, to head Jamaica's first mass political party, the People's National Party (PNP), dedicated to securing self-government for Jamaica. Initially, Bustamante supported the PNP, but he did not support the party's primary objective of self-government. Eventually, Manley's support for the BITU-rival Trade Union Advisory Council threatened Bustamante's stranglehold on labour leadership in the country. In addition, Manley's declaration of the PNP as a socialist party in 1940 further estranged Bustamante, which led to Bustamante's break with the PNP in 1942. Bustamante's departure from the PNP and his subsequent formation of the Jamaica Labour Party (JLP) in 1943 to contest the election devastated the grass root support base of the PNP.

The 1938 labour disturbances therefore signified a crucial turning point in Jamaican politics. Several dominant trends emerged out of this period. First, the powerful trade union movement established itself as a vital component of politics. Trade unions came to exercise significant control over both political and economic decisions. As such, mass political parties based on labour support dominated Jamaican politics. Labour support became especially critical as other parties later failed because they lacked this strong labour base. Second, members of the middle class (primarily intellectuals) came to dominate party politics. Most political activity not related to the labour movement came from left-leaning middle class intellectuals committed to improving the lives of the poor.

Third, a charismatic/personalist political tradition emerged out of this period. Bustamante derived most of his power from his magnetic personality which was able to win over most crowds. Although Manley possessed less personal charisma, his ability to command respect and his personal convictions earned him tremendous admiration from the Jamaican people. Through their dominant personalities, these two figures contributed greatly to a personalist legacy that intensified under Michael Manley during the 1970's.

INDEPENDENCE, DEMOCRACY, AND SOCIAL UNREST (1944-1972)

Forming a New Nation: Grappling with Ideology (1944-55)
In 1944, the new government structure consisted of a bicameral legislature with a lower house elected on the basis of universal adult suffrage, a Legislative Council with nominated members, and the Executive acting as the chief instrument of policy. Ultimate authority remained with the colonial office. Numerous parties contested the 1944 election, including the Federation of Citizen's Association, The Jamaica Liberal Party, the Jamaica Radical Workers' Party, the J.A.G. Smith Party, and the Rent Payer's Party. The most prominent party apart from the JLP and PNP was the Jamaica Democratic Party, formed in 1943 by urban representatives of the wealthy business class. All these parties lacked a labour base or grassroots support and thus the two primary contenders in the election were the JLP and PNP. In the election, the Bustamante-dominated Jamaica Labour Party (JLP) won an overwhelming majority of seats (23 of 32 compared to 4 for the PNP) and Manley failed even to win his seat. Importantly, five independent candidates won seats while all of the other parties failed to win even one seat.

Bustamante's campaign consisted of labour legislation and social welfare reform. The widespread popularity of the wage labour movement under Bustamante clearly appealed more to the Jamaican people than did the less attractive force of self-government which the PNP actively endorsed (Bustamante's campaign slogan was "self-government=slavery"). History explains the Jamaican people's initial aversion to self-government. Traditionally, most acts of welfare reform for the Jamaican people (such as the 1838 emancipation proclamation and the 1938 labour reforms) originated in the English Parliament only to face the resistance and hostility of local authorities. As such, Bustamante's opposition to self-government found support among a generally discontented, but essentially loyal, Jamaican people.

In preparation for the 1949 election, the PNP strengthened its labour support by creating a more overtly partisan organisation (the Trade Union Council) to replace the Trade Union Advisory Council. With this strengthened labour support, the party managed to win thirteen (13) seats in the 1949 election to combat the JLP's seventeen (17) seats. Ideological debate dominated in the 1949 election, more so than in the previous election. Bustamante repeatedly denounced the PNP's socialism and declared that "[t]he JLP dissociates itself completely with communism and socialism and other theories which lead to the domination of the individual and oppression of ambition under a soulless state machine."²

Manley's experiences in Britain had exposed him to the Fabian socialism popular among young intellectuals at the beginning of the century. In Jamaica, however, the general attitude toward socialist theory mirrored that of the United States to which Jamaica was becoming increasingly close. As such, socialist ideas fell into disfavour among the Jamaican electorate. Socialism was also viewed as similar to or the same as communism in the eyes of most Jamaicans, who were raised listening to the anti-communist message preached in Christian churches throughout Jamaica. Van Horne argues that the Church in Jamaica, "though split into several denominations, nevertheless exerts a strong influence on matters it perceives to be inimical to the moral foundation of Jamaican society."³ In Jamaica, the Church's "fundamental opposition to Communism" has fostered an anti-communist bias, especially given the extensive "power of the Church...in the culture of black Jamaicans."

Manley's interpretation of socialism rejected its violent or revolutionary streak and expressly rejected communism. However, Manley did advocate public ownership or control of "all the means of production" and called for a "vital transformation of the accepted actual existing organisation of society" along more egalitarian lines.⁴ The declaration of socialism in 1940 had occurred because Manley assessed the international environment (especially during World War II) and concluded that socialism was the ideological wave of the future. To Manley, the "world struggle was clearly between fascist Germany and socialist-oriented England" and since he was opposed to all totalitarian ideals, Manley felt obliged to side with socialism.⁵

Manley shied away from ideological extremism, however, and he chastised those in his party who became too embroiled with ideology. In 1952, Manley accused four Marxist members of the party who controlled the union organisation of 'subversive activity' and he expelled them from the PNP (the four were known as the four H's, Ken and Frank Hill, Richard Hart, and Arthur Henry). Manley did this both for organisational and political reasons. First, the internal power struggle threatened to destroy the party; to preserve party unity, one group had to go. Second, Manley recognised that four prominent Marxists in the party would serve as a liability in the next general election (which was held three years later), because the Jamaican people had a historical distrust for communism. Michael Manley, who had returned from England a few years earlier, heralded the move to expel the communist members of the party and declared that "the P.N.P. is not, and never can be, either wholly or in part, a Communist movement."[6]

The expulsion of the Marxists from the party signified a crucial shift in the ideological construct of the PNP. After 1942, the party abandoned the socialist platform of nationalisation and instead adopted a more centrist position that involved supporting the use of private capital to stimulate growth. Norman Manley explained that "as a socialist, I do not find it difficult or contradictory to invite capital to Jamaica and to help and to pledge the utmost good faith in our dealings with its enterprises."[7] As long as the government retained control over long-term development, Manley saw no problem with foreign capital financing that development. The departure of the Marxists also led to the exit of the union affiliate, which dealt a crippling blow to the party's labour support. The PNP quickly formed a new organisation, the National Worker's Union (NWU), which recruited Michael Manley to help the fledgling organisation grow. Manley proved particularly adept at this task and as the NWU made inroads into the sugar and bauxite industries, it began to erode the support of the old union. In the 1955 election, therefore, the NWU played a critical role in canvassing labour and grassroots support.

In 1953, a constitutional change made Bustamante Chief Minister of the island. This shift reflected Bustamante's realisation that Jamaica could indeed benefit from self-government and he thus abandoned his opposition to it. In the 1955 election, there was no explicit difference on self-government between the parties; the NWU had contributed to an increase in PNP labour support; and both parties had converged to the ideological center with the expulsion of the Marxists from the PNP. Bustamante could therefore find no major issue to rally the Jamaican people to his cause. In addition, after almost ten years of governance marred by several incidences of corruption, the complacent JLP could not stave off defeat against the aggressive and organisationally superior PNP. In the election, Manley assumed political power for the first time when the PNP secured eighteen (18) seats compared with the JLP's fourteen (14).

This election marked several important developments in Jamaican politics. First, it institutionalised the two party system that dominated Jamaican politics throughout the twentieth century. Since 1944, government control has shifted between the JLP and PNP consistently after every two-term period of rule, a pattern which continues to this day. In addition, the 1955 election saw a reduction in the number of independent seats from five in 1944 to two in 1949 to zero in 1955. In subsequent elections, no independent candidate would win a seat.

Second, the election marked the beginning of the Jamaican clientelist-patronage system, a striking characteristic of Jamaica's political culture. Close ties with labour coupled with the hostile divisions between the JLP and PNP led those leaders in power to concentrate economic benefits in the hands of party supporters. As the state expanded throughout this period, this system became increasingly important. The clientist state forms an integral and widely-practised component of Jamaica's political landscape. Although clientelism had played a role in the earlier 1944 and 1949 elections, the stakes became higher in the 1955 election leading to various instances of party-instigated violence and political intimidation of the electorate—another feature of Jamaican politics that became institutionalised by this election.

Moving Toward National Independence (1955-62)
The new PNP government introduced several major changes in the governance of the island. These reforms reflected in large part the desire of the colonial office to withdraw from British rule as the colonies had become a severe burden on English taxpayers. The British government slowly moved to shed its colonies. In 1957, the PNP implemented cabinet government which strengthened the role of local leadership in various aspects of the economy. In 1959, the PNP introduced full internal self-government where the Chief Minister became the Premier, and assumed responsibility for local affairs. In the 1959 election, Manley ran on his record of securing increased self-governance, while the JLP campaigned on the platform that the PNP had failed to live up to its promises. The PNP won the election and increased the number of seats to twenty-nine (29) (in a forty-five (45) member House) compared to the JLP's sixteen (16).

With the support and encouragement of the colonial office, the PNP led Jamaica into a West Indies Federation in January 1958.

This move reflected Manley's commitment to regional development through mutual cooperation, something he had advocated since 1945. In the Federal election, the PNP, which had allied with the Federal Labour Party, gained five (5) seats while the JLP, which joined the Democratic Labour Party, won twelve (12). Jamaica soon ran into conflict with the other islands in the Federation, primarily over the issue of sovereignty and the powers of the Federal government. In 1960, Bustamante declared his opposition to the Federation, insisting that Jamaica pursue independence alone. In response, Manley called a referendum on the issue, which resulted in a majority supporting withdrawal from the Federation (55% to 45%). In 1962, Manley announced the move toward independence and called an election. Although he had orchestrated the move to independence, Norman Manley and the PNP lost the election and Bustamante became Jamaica's first independent Prime Minister in 1962.

Before the 1962 election, the fever for full independence had peaked. The PNP had formed a small committee consisting of prominent local middle and upper-class Jamaicans to draft a constitution. Significantly, trade union membership was conspicuously absent from this committee, and because many members of the committee came from the nominated Upper House, the committee members were largely unrepresentative of the Jamaican population. The committee recommended that Jamaica adopt the British Westminster parliamentary system relatively unchanged. In newly-independent Jamaica, the Prime Minister received extensive powers and the Leader of the Opposition became a constitutionally-recognised position. The constitution also included a Bill of Rights as well as a compromise clause preventing government expropriation of property without adequate compensation as defined by the judicial system.

In the 1962 election, the PNP made a major shift back to the ideological left. In that year, the PNP founded the Young Socialist League (YSL), a group committed to advancing the cause of democratic socialism. Two years later, the party redeclared its commitment to democratic socialism by outlining a radical platform of nationalising the commanding heights of the economy, placing a 500-acre limit on the ownership of land, and eradicating illiteracy. In the snap election of 1967, the PNP realised that its platform was too radical for the Jamaican people and thus it dropped much of it.

Despite this, the JLP returned to power and increased its share of seats to thirty-three (33) of fifty-three (53) in the House (the PNP won twenty (20) seats). Prior to the election, Bustamante announced that he would resign as party leader after the election. In February 1967, Sir Donald Sangster, the Deputy Prime Minister became Prime Minister, but he died two months later. In April 1967 Hugh Shearer, the head of the Bustamante Industrial Trade Union, became Prime Minister. In 1969, Norman Manley resigned as PNP president and leader of the opposition. In a close election, Manley's son, Michael, defeated Vivian Blake for the post of PNP president—even though he had not received his father's official endorsement (Norman Manley was neutral in the election and supported neither candidate). Three years later in 1972, Michael Manley met Hugh Shearer at the polls.

Popular Discontentment and Social Unrest (1962-72)
        During the 1960's, a radical, unorganised black nationalist movement emerged which would play a significant role over the next two decades in affecting social change. This movement gained most if its support from four sources: the urban unemployed, radical intelligentsia, discontented students, and religious Rastafarians.
        With the influx of migrants from rural to urban areas during this time period, the number of poor unemployed increased rapidly. Rising income inequality from import substitution only made the situation worse. In addition, black intellectuals founded radical organisations such as the New World Group at UWI and started newspapers like *Abeng*, described as the official organ of the Black Power movement in Jamaica. Members of the Rastafarian faith (a syncretism of traditional African religions and Christianity which professes loyalty to Emperor Haile Selassie of Ethiopia) became increasingly vocal in their attacks against the government. The black reform movement manifested itself politically in organisations such as the People's Political Party (PPP), headed by a militant black nationalist, that unsuccessfully contested the 1962 election.
        Anger came to a head in 1968 when the government refused to allow Walter Rodney, a black nationalist lecturer at the University of the West Indies (UWI), to re-enter the island. This incident led to student riots which rapidly degenerated into sporadic and widespread looting and burnings throughout Kingston.
        The government responded to this rise in black nationalism

through both appeasement and repression. For example, the JLP government brought back the body of Marcus Garvey from England and also invited Haile Selaisse to Jamaica. More often than not, however, the government used oppressive and restrictive laws to ban and censor "subversive" literature and actions. This authoritarian response by the government only strengthened opposition to the JLP regime (and all forms of institutional authority) prior to the 1972 election. The resultant social unrest and widespread dissatisfaction formed the conditions under which Manley assumed power in the 1972 election.

Jamaica's Democratic Tradition: A Brief Comment

Just like that of other British dependents that achieved self-government, Jamaica's democratic tradition emerged out of the island's strong colonial legacy which had fostered a belief in and respect for democratic institutions. With some notable exceptions, almost all British colonies adopted some democratic basis for their political structure upon attaining national independence. In addition, the commitment to democracy held by the political and institutional leadership that rose to power during the 1944-72 period, helped to maintain this democratic tradition. Payne argues that "at independence, local leaders who genuinely believed in democracy took responsibility for its preservation...It was this élite, incorporating politicians, civil servants, judges, army officers, journalists, university teachers and others, which has been mainly responsible for the maintenance of that degree of openness and competitiveness which the Jamaican political system still possesses."[8]

But Jamaica's "democracy" requires several caveats. First, both political parties shared similar ideologies and could not be differentiated in any substantial way. Although the PNP had adopted a more progressive and socialist outlook, it abandoned this platform when in political office and instead adopted a more centrist political approach indistinguishable from that of the JLP. Hence, certain ideological viewpoints were not represented in political debate.

Second, the party leadership in both organisations possessed upper- and middle-class backgrounds, engaged either in elite professions (as lawyers, doctors, technical or managerial positions) or in white-collar jobs (such as teachers, ministers of religion, trade unionists), whereas party activists usually came form lower-class backgrounds. This party division led to the perpetuation of a patron-client framework which dominates Jamaican politics to this day.

Third, political tribalism between parties led to widespread instances of violence and political intimidation. In addition to this violence, instances of fraud and gerrymandering became widespread especially in safe-seat constituencies where one party predominated over the other. This political corruption, although practised by many, did not significantly alter election results. Indeed, "Jamaica can still count as a democracy especially when discussed in a Third World context. Elections have not been grotesquely rigged, as in Nigeria; former leaders have not been hanged by successor-regimes, as in Pakistan...All in all, given the pressures, it has been quite an heroic performance."⁹

PART II

Joshua's Ascent and Fall: New Development Paths - Strategies and Outcomes

CHAPTER 3

THE DEMOCRATIC SOCIALIST EXPERIMENT (1972-1980)

After the death of Moses, the Lord spake onto Joshua saying, "now therefore arise, go to Jordon with all my people, unto the land which I do give to them, be strong and couragous, turn not to the right hand or to the left."
—Joshua 1: 2,7.

Michael Manley's rise to power in 1972 must be understood within the historical context of popular social unrest and the widespread call for welfare reform in the decade preceding the election. Throughout history, the Jamaican people had consistently risen up in rebellion and revolt to increase political participation and improve their social conditions. Independence had not satiated these desires, however, and popular dissatisfaction reached new highs during the 1960's. The repressive and autocratic policies of various government administrations only intensified the general anger and desire for change. In many ways, this rise in popular unrest conditioned Manley's actions in government and provided the impulse for him to place a significant emphasis on social reform—as a means to pacify and quell discontentment.

This chapter will argue that Manley suceeded in enacting a psychological revolution by raising the political awareness of the populace and by incorporating previously neglected social groups into the political process. It also argues that Manley failed, however, to achieve economic growth both because of external shocks and internal mismanagement. As he himself later observed in the 1990's: "In the '70's, the government tried to tighten regulatory controls and entered into many areas of economic activity in the hope that this would ensure social justice and economic growth. We got some social justice, a lot of black market activity, and no economic growth."[1] Ultimately, Manley's rhetorical excesses and his failure to commit to a constant path of development led to his party's defeat in 1980.

Michael Manley won the 1972 election on a purely populist platform that lacked ideological substance. It was clear, however, that Manley was committed to the principles of international reform, social justice, the reorganisation of society along more equitable lines, and the extension of political participation beyond the middle and upper classes. He therefore passed legislation and created social programmes to remove the economic burdens on the disadvantaged and incorporate them into the political process. While he emphasised the need for the state to take the role in this regard, he viewed state power as a means to redistribute ownership among the people as opposed to being an end in itself. Although his rhetoric alienated business interests, Manley always maintained a commitment to a mixed economy and to active private sector participation.

After two years in office, Manley realised that his earlier populist appeal had created exceedingly high expectations among the populace which his social welfare programmes had not fulfilled. He also felt that while he was headed in the right direction, he lacked ideological focus and needed a unifying philosophy that would both clarify his long-term goals and motivate the public (especially since he would soon be facing an election). He therefore embraced democratic socialism as the guiding ideology of the party.

In theory, the socialist declaration served several practical purposes. Manley felt that it would mitigate opposition charges that he had embarked on a radical ideological experiment—because, technically, the party had always been socialist. Paradoxically, the democratic socialist label also provided substantial room to pursue a new development path. While the PNP was indeed socialist—it had never officially defined socialism and in fact explicitly clung to a vague conceptualisation of the ideology.

In reality, the attempts to define socialism led to fundamental questions about the reorganisation of Jamaican society that created intense internal factionalisation and debate. As left and moderate forces struggled for ideological control of the party, Manley vacillated between his idealistic aspirations for a society based on class consensus and his realistic assessment of the powerful capitalist forces opposed to this. Manley's indecision created an inconsistent policy direction that hindered successful policy making, reduced confidence in the government, and led to a rapid drop in the PNP's popular support. While Manley's personal popularity ratings fell between 1974-80, as we will see, he still remained the most popular political leader in the country.

Although the economy was adversely affected by several external factors, Manley's fiscal expansionism and restrictive controls on private sector production played the crucial role in the severe economic decline which characterised this period. On the positive side, the government managed to contain the trade deficit, improve domestic agricultural production, and provide incentives for informal opportunities, all of which prevented the total collapse of the Jamaican economy. Manley's relationship with the IMF—and his eventual break from the Fund—made him realise the tremendous power that capitalist forces in the international economy wielded over Jamaica's economic development, a fact that would have a tremendous impact on his later rethinking.

DEMOCRATIC SOCIALISM: POLITICAL AWARENESS AND ECONOMIC DECLINE

The victory of the PNP in the 1972 elections reflected widespread dissatisfaction with the status quo and a desire for economic and political change. Democratic socialism did not play a role in the PNP's campaign. Prior to the election, Manley declared that he rejected all forms of ideological "isms". Instead, Manley adopted a populist approach in an effort to win broad-based class support. His political agenda consisted of an end to political victimisation, the restoration of parliament to the center of political activity, voter registration reform, and various anti-corruption measures.

Manley's charisma and impressive oratory appealed to a wide-cross section of Jamaican society and thus contributed to his resounding victory. In contrast to the authoritarian response of the JLP to the rise of the black power movement, Manley openly courted black nationalists, Rastafarians, urban-youth, the unemployed, and the "sufferers" throughout the island. He used religious imagery by portraying himself as the biblical Joshua and labeling Prime Minister Shearer as pharaoh in his appeal to these groups. In addition, he captured support among Rastafarians and black nationalists by traveling with a "Rod of Correction" allegedly given to him by Ethiopian Emperor Haile Selassie. The Jamaican populace found renewed hope for the future in Manley's campaign slogans which argued that "Better Must Come," "It's Time for a Government of Love," and "Power for the People." In the election, the PNP captured 56% of the vote and thirty-seven (37) seats, compared to the JLP 43% and sixteen (16) seats.

In his first two years of office, Manley initiated various programmes and passed a series of laws designed to improve social welfare in the society. In his first budget debate speech, Manley outlined the four principles upon which his policies were premised: equality, social justice, self-reliance, and discipline. He also outlined his commitment to increasing employment, housing and nutrition and announced various programmes for addressing inequities facing women and youth.

The PNP declared a programme of democratic socialism in 1974. The democratic socialist declaration led to the formation of left and moderate ideological factions in the PNP that were divided on the exact meaning of democratic socialism. As political tensions heightened and as the economy worsened in response to the international oil shocks, violent activity escalated throughout the island. In response to these developments, the government declared a state of emergency in 1976. In the face of this extraordinary step and despite the decline in the island's economy between 1972 and 1976, the PNP won the 1976 election and increased its majority in the House from thirty-seven (37) to forty-seven (47) seats.

In 1977, the government attempted to avoid an imminent collision with the International Monetary Fund (IMF) by starting research to produce an alternative economic plan based on greater national self-reliance. With Manley's realisation that economic development without the IMF would be catastrophic for the country, the government halted this plan and eventually signed an agreement with the IMF in 1977.

Between 1977 and 1979, the IMF programme which Manley had delayed for years created deepening economic crisis. At the same time, vigorous opposition to the government by the JLP, the press, the bauxite companies, the private sector, and the US government led to charges of destabilisation by PNP supporters and others. By 1979, the crisis had become so severe that Manley decided to readopt his anti-IMF position. He called an election in 1980 and based his campaign on a break with the IMF. Widespread economic dissatisfaction led to the PNP's defeat in the extremely violent 1980 election. In the island's worst electoral defeat, the PNP managed to win only nine (9) seats, while the JLP won an overwhelming majority, with fifty-one (51) seats.

THE IDEOLOGY OF DEMOCRATIC SOCIALISM

Manley's Ideological Background
Michael Manley played a crucial role in the PNP's formal declaration of democratic socialism in 1974. As such, it is imperative that we discuss the ideological influences on Manley's life before examining the ideology of democratic socialism as manifest in the PNP political agenda. Four primary influences helped to shape Manley's ideological and political outlook: (1) his education at the London School of Economics (LSE) under the British socialist Harold Laski; (2) the political views of his father, Norman Manley; (3) the twenty years he spent representing labourers in the National Worker's Union; and (4) his work as a journalist for the left-wing reform journal, *Public Opinion*.

Manley studied politics and economics at the LSE, where he was greatly influenced by British Labour Party Chairman and LSE lecturer, Harold Laski. Manley later described Laski as "the greatest socialist thinker of our time."[2] Laski advocated socialism within the democratic framework, arguing that "liberty has no meaning save in the context of equality."[3] From Laski, Manley derived his sincere commitment to the application of socialist ideals within a democratic structure.

In addition, many of Manley's political views came from his father, Norman Manley, the former President of the PNP. Hoffman argues that "certainly, the elder Manley's commitment to Fabian socialism and his long association with members of the British Labor Party influenced his son."[4] In particular, Manley appreciated his father's broad view of socialism. The elder Manley's view of socialism allowed for substantial interpretation. When Norman Manley declared the PNP socialist in 1940, he explained that "[s]ocialism is not a rigid dogma...It is essentially a principle of social organisation which has to be applied to the particular place where you are trying to apply it because it must depend on the particular conditions which obtain from time to time in that place."[5]

As President of the National Worker's Union, Manley came face to face with numerous poor labourers whose interests he represented against wealthy employers. Manley developed a deep-seated commitment to social justice and equality from these experiences. In one of his first books, *A Voice at the Workplace*, he expressed these sentiments and argued against deplorable working conditions created by years of colonialism, slavery, and exploitative capitalism.

In the 1950's, Manley wrote a column entitled "The Root of the Matter" for *Public Opinion*, a nationalist, progressive, anti-establishment weekly sympathetic to the PNP. In his column, Manley was critical of the colonial government and repeatedly denounced imperialism and other forms of exploitation. In addition, following his father, he denounced communism as a political objective of the PNP: "The PNP is not, and never can be, either wholly or in part a Communist movement...Democratic socialism and planned economic progress for Jamaica are the bases of PNP political loyalty and integrity, the pillars of its existence."[6] From his work with the *Public Opinion*, Manley developed opposition to communist extremes and advocated instead a centrist viewpoint with mild socialist leanings.

The Decision to Embrace Democratic Socialism

Manley's book, *The Politics of Change*, was first published in 1973, the year after he had been elected Prime Minister. In that work, Manley outlined his view of Jamaica's past and laid out a philosophical agenda for future political change. He explicitly disavowed any particular political philosophy, however, and made only a few token references to democratic socialism. Instead, he focused on the broad principles of equality, social justice, self-reliance, and a commitment to democratic traditions. He used these ideals to justify his government's legislative reform in education, foreign policy, and various aspects of the economy. Because it focused solely on philosophical concepts, the book failed to provide detailed proposals for change.

The publication of this book was significant for two reasons. First, it reflected Manley's need for an ideological underpinning to explain and justify his actions. Second, it also highlighted Manley's tendency to avoid detailed economic or political plans. Manley soon developed an image for being a brilliant conceptualiser and thinker but for being less adept at implementing the concrete manifestations of his ideas and principles.

During his first two years in office, Manley implemented a number of social programmes. While these were generally well received, they failed to generate the broadbased support and consensus Manley desired. Indeed, certain of Manley's initiatives created widespread opposition. For instance, in May 1973, Manley announced that a levy would be imposed on landowners whose lands were not in full production. Within days after the announcement, "public opinion was ablaze throughout the country...common interest groups coalesced in public interest, sparking new groups of protesters into action. Never in Jamaican history was any Government bombarded, so quickly and completely." Eventually, the tax was watered down to the point where it became "largely emasculated."[7]

Manley's rhetoric in the election had created exceedingly high expectations which his limited social reforms could not fulfill. To further compound problems, the international economy began to decline and Jamaica began to feel the first effects of economic hardship. In just one year, from 1973 to 1974, Jamaica's oil import bill more than doubled from J$65 million to J$177 million. Between 1972 and 1974, Jamaica's public sector debt (used primarily to finance the government's welfare reform programmes) rose by 56.7% from J$332.6 million to J$520.8 million while the foreign component of the debt went up by even more, from J$117.3 million to J$206.3 million over the same period, an increase of 75.6%.

Manley recognised that he needed something more—something that could revitalise the disillusioned Jamaican people and inspire confidence in his government. The fact that he had to call an election within three years (with the economy on a downward slide) also convinced him of this need. In 1972, Manley had run on a platform lacking ideological substance. After two years in government, he needed something meaningful to compel the Jamaican people to believe in him (and to re-elect him). Consistent with his desire to justify his actions through philosophical underpinnings, Manley decided that a recommitment to democratic socialism was the answer.

In a speech before the PNP annual conference in 1974, therefore, Manley reaffirmed his commitment to democratic socialism. Manley made clear that he wished something profoundly new for Jamaica—a new socialist era. In his speech, he explained that historically, political parties in Jamaica had been comprised of "sordid...people who had particular interests that they wished to protect and promote."[8] Political parties had become "unclean...to be swept under the carpet on public occasions and to be trotted out when spoils are to be divided or candidates to be elected." He explained that the PNP needed to reject this view and strive for more noble goals.

Manley insisted that the party had to be organised around "ideals...to secure a national purpose." In the future, Manley promised that the PNP would be the "institution through which [to] organise the aspirations of the people." To accomplish this goal, Manley needed an ideological framework which socialism provided. For Manley, socialism was less of a policy directive and more of "an ideal, a goal and an attitude of mind that requires people to care for each other's welfare."[9] Manley felt that since the party was officially socialist, his actions would not seem too radical to skeptics. On the other hand, since the PNP had never really embraced its socialist past, socialism provided something profoundly "new". Payne concludes that "the direction of the government's policy was not noticeably changed by the declaration of support for socialism. The intention was rather to mobilise the people more actively behind the PNP's strategy of change...[T]he reaffirmation of socialism was conceived primarily as a piece of mid-term electioneering."[10]

With the announcement of democratic socialism, Manley assembled a team of young, bright leftists and a few moderate members of the party to draft a document defining socialism. This group "embarked on an exercise which went on for several weeks, exlusively at night, since the days were devoted to the running of the country."[11] Two months after Manley's speech, the PNP published "Thirteen Principles of Democratic Socialism," which reflected the work of this group. This document stressed general themes such as co-operation, but—reflecting the input of the moderates—it recognised the right to private property and called for a mixed economy.

Despite the publication of this document, the PNP failed to adequately define democratic socialism. In a variety of fora, Manley provided differing definitions of the political dogma. Socialism was defined as "Christianity in action," "love," and a system where "no man shall be allowed to exploit his brother." Eventually in a series of speeches and documents, the PNP slowly began to clarify democratic socialism.

As the excitement of ideological rebirth intensified, so too did the internal factionalisation within the PNP. Conflicts quickly emerged when the party attempted to define democratic socialism. With a deepening economic crisis in 1974 and 1975, and the election in 1976, the party could not adequately address the issue in a cohesive manner. In 1977, the left-wing of the party rose to prominence and the education efforts intensified. As a result the party published, in Manley's words, a "significant and extraordinary" document, "Principles and Objectives of the People's National Party" in 1978—four years after the socialist declaration. This document—which reflected months of extensive internal debate and dissent—finally clarified the party's socialist ideology.

The PNP and Democratic Socialism
Despite slight variances in how the party viewed socialism, certain basic principles quickly became evident. The PNP made its aim clear: "[t]he objective of the PNP is the construction of a socialist society."[12] This socialist society would rest on the two principles of social ownership over the means of production and societal equality of opportunity. *Principles and Objectives* therefore defines democratic socialism as "a political and economic theory under which the means of production, distribution and exchange are owned and/or controlled by the people...[and where] the opportunities of society are equally available to all."[13]

Although Manley quickly developed a close relationship with Cuba, he emphasised that his version of democratic socialism had "nothing to do with the Cuban model."[14] Indeed, Manley hoped to pursue an alternate "third path" between the so-called Puerto Rican model of dependent capitalist development and the Cuban model of dependent communist development. Manley stressed that while he hoped to find an independent and unique development path for Jamaica, he was interested in the "Scandanavian experiment. Norway and Sweden in particular" because of his interest in "co-operatives, mixed economy, [and a] strong state sector, working for industrial democracy through worker participation."

For Manley, social ownership did not necessarily mean state ownership, although it certainly meant that the state should take an active ownership role in certain industries. He proclaimed in a speech to his party, for example, that "we do not want more power for the state. What we want is more power for the people."[15] He felt that cooperatives were necessary for workers to have a "personal stake" but that the state needed to take the lead in providing services to the cooperatives and marketing their produce.[16] Although he encouraged cooperatives and "people" ownership, Manley argued that the state needed to maintain control over certain elements of the economy critical to national development. For example, he declared in 1973 that "land should be leased for specific development purposes, but never sold...nationals who hold land for speculative purpose should be required to develop what they own immediately or sell it back to government."[17]

The PNP hoped to build an alliance of all class interests in its pursuit of a socialist agenda. The party manifesto expressed this desire to formulate a broad-based consensus among "the working class, the small farmers, middle strata and reclaimed elements from the lumpen proletariat...[in addition to] capitalists who are willing and able to contribute to the building of the just society, which is the objective of socialism."[18]

With its firm commitment to a socialist path, the party explicitly rejected both communism and capitalism. Manley had long harboured an opposition to communism largely because its totalitarian tenets contradicted his deep respect for democracy. In the 1972 elections, Manley made it clear to the people that "I am opposed to communism, passionately. I am opposed...to all forms of subversion, passionately. Let us understand that it is not necessary to destroy to make change."[19] Although the party willingly accepted capitalists within its ranks as part of its desire to build national consensus, the PNP opposed "capitalism as the system upon which to base the future of Jamaica [because] this system involves the exploitation of people and obliges individuals to pursue private gain at the expense of their fellow citizens without regard to any other interest."[20]

Despite the strident rejection of a capitalist path, democratic socialist doctrine advocated a mixed economy in which the private sector would play a role. Manley emphasised that certain sectors, such as the manufacturing sector, naturally belonged in private hands, but that the state needed to control the commanding heights of the economy.[21] Specifically, the PNP felt that the state needed to establish sovereignty over the "national economy," defined as natural resources, financial institutions, and foreign trading relations.[22] To pacify local capitalists, the party re-emphasised its commitment to the right of every Jamaican to own private property.

To foreign capitalists, Manley stressed his opposition to government expropriation of property unless in the national interest and only with adequate compensation. In numerous speeches and in government documents, the party stressed that "wherever the

Government acquires assets in the national interest it will observe the principle of fair compensation. This Government rejects any form of expropriation."[23] Indeed, Manley made numerous references to the major role that both local and foreign capitalists should play in the economy. In an address to the National Executive of his party, he asserted that "[t]he socialist believes that private enterprise and economic activity can be a most efficient and effective way of producing the general run of goods and providing the general run of services in the country."[24] Manley also reiterated the need for foreign capital—"we need foreign capital and we need foreign technology"—but emphasised that this capital could operate only within a nationalist framework.[25]

Democratic socialism was therefore not as revolutionary as the rhetoric that accompanied it. Despite this fact, however, the PNP's ideological agenda created several problems that later caused severe strains and tension within the party. First, the excessive philosophical content of the ideology left substantial room for widely divergent interpretations of that ideology. As such, political factions within the party interpreted democratic socialism as they saw fit to suit their purposes. This led to intense internal strife which, in Manley's words "very nearly tore the party apart."[26] In addition, the tremendous emphasis on ideology and theory detracted from the technical and economic aspects of its practical implementation. Because the government focused so much of its efforts on political education and greater ideological clarity, it spent precious little time on the economic and bureaucratic realities of social reform.

POLICY INITIATIVES OF THE MANLEY REGIME

Following from the above ideological guidelines, the PNP's policy initiatives could be seen to fall into four categories: (1) independence from foreign control and an increase in the role of the state, (2) the pursuit of a more egalitarian society by increasing access to social benefits, (3) an increase in political awareness and participation, and (4) an alliance with other Third World nations in the pursuit of international economic reform. The government wavered between moderate and left ideological extremes during this period, but these goals remained basically constant.

Independence from Foreign Control and an Increase in the Role of the State
Although the PNP government supported foreign investment, it sought to reduce its dependence on foreign capital and control. Instead, the government encouraged a policy of national self-reliance through greater state ownership and an increase in domestic production. The most notable manifestation of this policy involved the government's relationship with the bauxite/alumina industry. Manley desired to play a more important role in the industry and to reduce the domination of foreign firms. The government therefore formed a National Bauxite Commission to investigate in what ways the government could participate more actively in the mining industry.

Eventually, the work of this commission led to the repatriation of lands owned by the bauxite companies, the acquisition by the government of fifty-one percent ownership in the bauxite mining operations, the establishment of the Jamaica Bauxite Institute (JBI), the formation of an international cartel of bauxite-producing countries (International Bauxite Association), increased revenues through a production levy imposed on the price of aluminum ingot, and the development of a smelter complex in cooperation with Venezuela and Mexico.

This increased government involvement in the industry led to a two-fold response by bauxite/alumina firms. On one hand, the companies filed suit with the World Bank's International Center for the Settlement of Investment Disputes contesting the legality of the unilaterally-imposed production tax, while on the other hand, they began to transfer bauxite and alumina production from Jamaica to other countries. Despite this hostile response, the introduction of the levy received widespread support from most of the local capitalist class and even from the *Daily Gleaner*, the island's largest newspaper which later became extremely hostile toward Manley.

Indeed, in terms of revenue generation, the government's actions with the bauxite companies proved relatively successful. The 7.5% tax on bauxite under the Bauxite Levy boosted Jamaica's earnings from its only exportable mineral from US$23 million in 1974 to US$195 million in 1979, but in the intervening years production was cut by approximately 50% because of the bauxite companies' reaction to the levy, as well as the loss of highly trained workers through migration.

In addition to the bauxite/alumina industry, the government

also increased its participation in various other aspects of the economy. The government nationalised the Jamaica Public Service (JPS) company, Jamaica Telephone Company (JTC), and the Jamaica Omnibus Service (JOS) as part of the strategy to control the "commanding heights." In trade, the government enacted a series of reforms that included restrictions on luxury imports, the implementation of import licensing, and the establishment of the State Trading Corporation (STC) to coordinate imports into the island.

In banking, the government nationalised Barclay's Bank and merged it with the Bank of Montreal to create the National Commercial Bank (NCB) in late 1977. In the same year, the government also nationalised a major radio station, Radio Jamaica (RJR), and in a move designed to spread ownership, the government divided shares in the station among the state, station employees, and the island's trade unions and professional associations. The government already owned the other radio station, the Jamaica Broadcasting Corporation. Evidence suggests that the PNP purchased Radio Jamaica "as part of a political education programme."[27] In manufacturing, which Manley had earlier proclaimed the "natural" domain of the private sector, the government purchased majority shares in the island's only cement company, an enterprise owned by the wealthy Ashenheim family.

In addition to these major nationalisations, the government increased the role it played in numerous other aspects of the economy including export agriculture, livestock, tourism, and general services. Consistent with its belief in a mixed economy, however, the state played little or no role in domestic food production, fishing, forestry, construction, distribution, and printing, leaving these areas to private sector control.[28] Manley only participated in industries that he felt were crucial to the national economy.

The Pursuit of a More Egalitarian Society By Increasing Access to Benefits
In Manley's first year of government, he announced various plans designed to increase the access of all members of society to certain social benefits. To address unemployment, the government created the Special Employment Programme (SEP) which emphasised jobs such as street cleaning and sanitation. Although the SEP reduced employment in the short-term, the programme created

little employment permanency and led to frequent incidences of idleness, absenteeism, and non-productivity. In addition, the government started a National Literacy Board later replaced by a Statutory Board for Adult Education (JAMAL) that launched a nationwide campaign to eradicate illiteracy. The JAMAL programme proved to be one of the government's most successful initiatives, where the government realised early potential implementation problems (with the National Literacy Board), took corrective action, and successfully introduced a replacement programme (JAMAL).

In agriculture, the government introduced a variety of schemes. Most importantly, the government started Project Land Lease, an agricultural programme designed to provide small holders and rural labourers with more land through tenancy. Other programmes included Operation GROW (Growing and Reaping Our Wealth), Project Food Farms, and Self-Help, all geared toward increasing domestic production for local consumption, creating jobs, and mobilising small farmers. The government also expanded sugar cooperatives by turning land over to sugarcane growers and strengthened the powers of the Sugar Industry Authority (SIA) to increase the role of small farmers in the industry.

These initiatives generated some success in increasing the number of small farmers and utilising idle land. Because the government did not institute a land reform package (out of respect for large landowners), no significant changes in land ownership structure occurred and only 14% of idle land was redistributed. In addition, these programmes suffered from extensive political patronage as the PNP distributed agricultural lands largely along party lines.

In education, the government made substantial reforms. In 1973, Manley announced free education for both secondary school and university education, free school uniforms for primary school children, and even a nutrition programme to provide lunches for students. Significantly, the government started a compulsory National Youth Service Programme for high school graduates to teach in schools, vocational training and the literacy programme (work in health, youth camps and civil service was an alternative).

Manley's introduction of free education highlighted one of his negative populist streaks—to introduce programmes based on principle but not on a realistic assessment of funding. In the announcement of free education, Manley introduced the proposal without the approval of the Ministry of Finance which had initially rejected the programme as too costly. The government had received an unexpected source of income from taxes which prompted Manley to announce the initiative anyway. But the programme led to a severe problem in long-term funding and served as a major drain on the budget.

In housing, the PNP created the National Housing Trust (NHT) to channel employer and employee contributions to build houses for workers. Throughout the PNP rule, the government managed to increase dramatically the number of houses, but failed to build as many as it had expected because of severe budget constraints. Notably, the government introduced a lottery for distribution of housing. As a result, this programme was the PNP initiative least tainted by political partisanship and patronage.

In addition to the establishment of various state corporations, the government passed a series of laws aimed at improving the standard of living. In 1973, the government instituted subsidies on basic food items and two years later, the government passed the National Minimum Wage and the Equal Pay Law. The government also established comprehensive price and rent controls. Other areas of social legislation included maternity leave for women, a removal of the legal stigma of bastardy, and protection of workers against unfair dismissal—all in an effort to reduce the economic burden on the disadvantaged members of society.

Despite the few programmes that achieved relative degrees of success, such as the literacy and housing programmes, most of the government programmes failed to make a successful transition from conceptualisation to implementation. As Manley himself would later reflect, "[our programmes] were theoretically good ideas and they were decent objectives, but the problem was they were...a disaster in implementation."[29] Stone identifies the major reasons for failure as "thin layers of leadership, limited technocratic skills and intellectual resources, lack of discipline among party cadres [and] rampant corruption and patronage excesses."[30] The government recognised these limitations during the late 1970's but continued to purchase enterprises, especially those that had been abandoned by private sector officials who had fled the country in fear of socialism.

An Increase in Political Awareness and Participation
The democratic socialist ideology rested upon a fundamental

principle of "inculcating new values and attitudes" among the populace.[31] As such, the party emphasised ideological education. In particular, the party stressed mass information campaigns as an essential means to explain the tenets of democratic socialism and to disseminate ideas such as community service, cooperation, patriotism, and self-reliance. This agenda arose directly out of Manley's own "conviction and fear that if you don't keep alive at the center of a political party some sort of ideal commitment towards social equitable means, what is there to stop a political party from becoming a totally miserable purveyor of benefits...with no central set of ideas which guide you strategically?"[32]

To facilitate this educational objective, the party established an organisational and propaganda machine largely under control of the more left-leaning members in the party soon after the election. The party established mandatory training sessions on democratic socialism for party members at all levels after the 1974 announcement. The vagueness of the programme led to a cancellation of political education classes. These classes did not recommence on a regular and sustained basis until 1978 when the power of the ideological left peaked. In the intervening period, political education fell largely in the hands of the active left-wingers who used the opportunity to push a hard-line socialist stance. PNP-affiliated organisations such as the PNP Youth Organisation (PNPYO) and later the PNP Women's Movement also served as vehicles of popular mobilisation.

The most important aspect of the educational programme was the creation of community councils and Community Enterprise Organisations (CEO's). Community councils were designed to coordinate activities of local groups, mobilise community members, advise the central administration on plans for community development, monitor the central government projects like rent assessment and price control, and organise self-help projects. To complement the socially-oriented community councils, the government also created Community Enterprise Organisations (CEO's), community-owned economic cooperatives designed to produce for the local community. The CEO's adopted two forms: pioneer farms in the rural area to produce food for local consumption and urban CEO's to manufacture goods and provide services in depressed areas.

Although both community councils and CEO's became

widespread throughout the island, their success varied depending on the region and on the commitment of community members. In urban areas, most councils and CEO's fell along party lines and served as nothing more than another source of party patronage. Political tribalism occurred less frequently in rural areas where community councils served a more functional and practical role. The government's decision to divide various functions of the councils and CEO's under differing ministries created severe bureaucratic hindrances. Moreover, many local government officials and Members of Parliament (MPs) opposed the councils and CEO's because these programmes posed a threat to established patronage and distribution systems. Stone concludes that "except for isolated areas the entire proposal [was] a grand bureaucratic programme without sufficient mass support to give it a significant impact on national politics."[33]

The mobilisation drive reached its peak in 1977 with the creation of a new Ministry of National Mobilisation and Human Resource Development, under the supervision of leading leftist D.K. Duncan. This ministry assumed responsibility for coordinating and monitoring the governments people-based programmes. More specifically, the ministry was responsible for supervising the democratisation process in education, the newly created Community councils, and worker participation programmes. With the decline of the left in the party and Duncan's resignation, the ministry atrophied and never succeeded in implementing any significant or long-lasting changes in the political process.

A Third World Alliance and the Pursuit of International Economic Reform

Michael Manley's political thinking occurs within an historical and global context heavily influenced by dependency theory. His ideological writings are replete with references to the imperialist world economic system where Northern countries regularly exploit countries in the South. To remedy years-of imperialist exploitation by the North, Manley argued that Third World countries needed to adopt "collective self-reliance" on the "long, hard road to economic independence."[34]

These ideological impulses fueled Manley's drive to bring Jamaica into the fore of the Third World struggle for international economic reform. Manley argued that Jamaica had two primary foreign policy objectives: "to construct economic alliances that give us the greatest chance to underwrite our economic independence...[a]nd...to make common cause with all developing nations of the world who share our fate."[35] This required an organised force determined to bring about change. Manley asserted that "[i]n the name of equality of nations we are seeking to organise the poor of the world to form a striking force that shakes up economic imperialism and creates a new world order."[36]

The success of the OPEC oil cartel and the blow to United States supremacy dealt by the Vietnam conflict emboldened Manley in his conviction that a united Third World could play a significant role in international affairs. Although Manley sought to preserve friendly relations with the United States, he also hoped to expand Jamaica's international relations with countries to which the United States was hostile. In the international arena, the government participated in the New International Economic Order (NIEO) and the Non-Aligned Movement which both sought to increase Third World cooperation. Under Manley, Jamaica moved from virtual isolation, obscurity and subservience to the West to a position of leadership in the Third World.[37]

Manley himself became a renowned international spokesman for the Third World. He repeatedly denounced apartheid and other oppressive practices while he praised liberation movements which fought against first-world imperialism. He became the leading Third World advocate in the Socialist International, an organisation to which he was elected Vice-President. Manley received international recognition when the United Nations General Assembly awarded him a prize for his work in securing a settlement in the Zimbabwe conflict. Manley's visible international role also led to Jamaica's election to the UN Security Council, a position it had never held before. In addition, Manley's international participation led to the election of P.J. Patterson, a leading government minister (and current Prime Minister), to head the African, Caribbean, and Pacific Countries (ACP) in the negotiations for the Lomé Convention.

Jamaica's close relationship with Cuba elicited sharp criticism both locally and from the United States. Early in his first term of office, Manley opened full diplomatic relations with Cuba (along with various other communist countries). In 1973, Manley attended the Non-Aligned Heads of State Conference with Fidel Castro and the Guyanese socialist Forbes Burnham. In subsequent years, Manley developed a close personal friendship with Castro. As this relationship grew, so too did the number of economic and political exchange programmes between the two countries.

Manley's extreme fascination with Cuba came from his many visits to the country. Although he opposed the totalitarian element of the Castro regime, he praised Castro for his impressive advances in health and education. Manley dreamed of implementing similar structures in Jamaica—although he recognized that "the Cuban system cannot work in Jamaica."[38] Jamaica became so close to Cuba that in a 1979 poll, a majority of Jamaicans felt that Cubans exerted too much influence on Jamaican politics.

Jamaica benefited from its increased role in international affairs. Its prominence in the Third World led to loans from OPEC, Libya, and Algeria and concessionary oil prices from Mexico and Venezuela. Manley's role in the Socialist International brought Norwegian and Dutch aid while closer relations with communist countries resulted in a line of credit from Hungary and a new market for products.[39] Manley's excessive rhetoric in this regard served to offset many of these gains. For example, his declaration that he would "climb to the mountaintop with Castro" only served to exacerbate hostility from the United States. Manley's militant posturing simply fed into the false perception that he intended to turn communist. This opposition from the United States, coupled with the economic crisis, contributed to Manley's defeat in the 1980 election.

CLASS SUPPORT AND THE STRUGGLE FOR IDEOLOGICAL CONTROL

The Pursuit of Class Consensus and the Fallout with the Private Sector

Historically, the PNP had enjoyed stronger support than the JLP among the middle classes, consisting of both blue- and white-collar workers. Conversely, the JLP had traditionally received greater support than the PNP from the lower classes and wealthy businessmen.[40] Although the PNP did not enjoy widespread support among businessmen prior to the 1972 election, it did depend upon a core group of wealthy families for most of its financial support (the party also had other sources of income primarily from union activites, but this income remained small). In the 1972 elections, Manley's populist appeal succeeded in winning him majority support among all class groups (see table 3.1). Manley hoped to channel his broad-based class support into a widespread consensus for change with significant overtures to all class segments and hostility toward none.

While most of the government's rhetoric and programmes targeted the poorer classes, the appointments of individuals to operate these organisations frequently fell to wealthy capitalist supporters. For a single example, K. Hendrickson, the chairman and largest shareholder in the National Continental Conglomerate and Caribbean Communications, was appointed chairman of the islands's electricity utility, Jamaica Public Service, majority owned by the state. The increasingly antagonistic legislation and economic stagnation toward this class led to a rapid decline in business support for the Manley regime by the time of the 1976 election. In addition, members of the upper class migrated from the island in fear of a total economic collapse or a communist takeover.

Unlike the situation during the Cuban revolution, the apparent PNP antagonism toward the business class was not intended or even desired. In an interview conducted one year before his election defeat, Manley confessed that "the extent of [the negative reaction by the private sector] is more than I had anticipated, and it has been more stubborn than I had anticipated."[41] Strong socialist elements within the PNP clearly approved of the capitalist exodus and Manley personally delivered a speech where he reminded the business class that there were "five flights a day to Miami" and the businessmen could leave the island anytime that they wished. Manley always felt, however, that capitalists had a vibrant and active role to play in the economy. For instance, Manley appointed some of the wealthiest men in the island (Mayer Matalon, Eli Matalon, Moses Matalon, Leslie Ashenheim, Peter Rousseau, and Patrick Rousseau) to major positions within the government hierarchy. He also appointed a leading private sector figure (R. Danny Williams) as Minister of Commerce and Industry in response to growing tension between the private sector and government. See table 3.1 for a breakdown of class support in the 1972, 1976, and 1980 elections.

As evidenced by the rapid drop in support among businessmen and high income professionals, the policies of the PNP inevitably created dissension and opposition from these groups. It was obvious that the strategy of change by national consensus was destined to fail. Manley's desire not to alienate any class or ideological group led to a fundamental contradiction that undermined the effectiveness of his agenda. Manley rejected capitalism but supported and made efforts to appease capitalists. He rejected communism but he warmly embraced communists such as Trevor Munroe, head of the communist Worker's Party of Jamaica (WPJ), which lent "critical support" to the Manley regime during the 1970's. Moreover, this contradiction led to substantial vacillation in PNP policy direction. Manley allowed the ideological factions within his party to gain ascendancy at differing times. This led to confusing and often contradictory policy directions which only served to fuel charges of mismanagement.

Table 3.1 Class Support for the PNP 1972, 1976, and 1980   (%)

Class	1972	1976	1980
Unemployed and unskilled	52	60	40
Manual wage labour	61	72	48
White collar wage labour	75	57	37
Business and management, and high income professionals	60	20	14
Farm labour	52	56	42
Small peasants	47	45	35

Source: Hoffman, *Politics of the Manley Regime,* 64, 111.

Ideological Factionalism and Contradictory Policy Direction
The two ideological factions within the PNP during the 1970's were the "left" and the "moderates". There also existed a right-wing within the party that espoused certain pro-United States policies and resisted significant changes in the role of the state, but this group never assumed control of the party. In fact, certain members were expelled from the party for these views.
The left consisted of political activists in the party hierarchy and members of the "radical intelligentsia." PNP leftists included D.K. Duncan (General Secretary of the PNP), Hugh Small (a former President of the Young Socialist League [YSL] and member of the PNP National Executive), and Anthony Spaulding (who held the relatively innocuous Housing ministry in the cabinet). Prominent members of the PNP-supporting radical intelligentsia included Norman Girvan, Louis Lindsay, and George Beckford, who were all professors in the social sciences at the University of the West Indies

(UWI). This group received significant support from leftist organisations such as the communist WPJ, the PNP Youth organisation, and the PNP Women's Movement.

Prominent members of the moderate faction included most cabinet members and financial technocrats. Major moderate cabinet members included P.J. Patterson, David Coore, and Eric Bell. Financial technocrats included G. Arthur Brown (Governor of the Bank of Jamaica), Horace Barber (Permanent Secretary in the Ministry of Finance), and Gladstone Bonnick (Director of the National Planning Agency). Although they had a smaller membership in absolute numbers, the moderates nevertheless exercised substantial power since they controlled most of the policy and economic decisions.

Until the formal declaration of democratic socialism in 1974, neither group exerted overwhelming influence over policy. Between 1974 and 1976, the left faction became increasingly dominant with the redeclaration of democratic socialism. In the 1976 election, two leftists (Duncan and Small) assumed relatively important ministries (National Mobilisation and Youth/Community Development), while two members of the dormant right wing left the ministerial ranks. In addition, a left-wing intellectual (Girvan) replaced a moderate (Bonnick) as head of the National Planning Agency, which gave the left significant economic control over policy decisions.

With this structure firmly in place, the left began to organise an Emergency Production Plan as an alternative to an agreement with the IMF—over the opposition of moderates. As Manley was moving increasingly leftward, the left received his support in their efforts. In a fiery 1976 speech condemning the IMF, for example, Manley announced that the government would "not accept anybody anywhere in the world telling us what to do in our own country. We are the masters in our house and in our house there shall by no other masters but ourselves. Above all, we are not for sale."[42]

Despite the leftist rhetoric and the efforts of the left to build an Emergency Production Plan, the "brutal realities" of Jamaica's situation and severe foreign exchange constraints convinced Manley that the Production Plan would not work. Manley argues that the prospect of a major collapse in the manufacturing sector of the economy, which would have resulted in 30,000 layoffs, played the crucial role in the decision.[43] Evidence suggests that Manley had held misgivings about the plan from its inception and had kept his options open by sending a member of the moderate group to secretly negotiate with the IMF.[44] Manley kept this information confidential and did not inform certain key members of the left. At any rate, a lukewarm response from alternate sources of capital and the possibility for improved relations with a new Carter regime in the United States clinched Manley's mind in his decision to accept the IMF route.

A receptive Carter Administration and Manley's close personal friendship with Prime Ministers James Callaghan of Britain and Pierre Trudeau of Canada, initially led to the adoption of a relatively painless IMF agreement. The government's unexpected failure of the December 1977 performance test changed this, however, and after renewed negotiation's with the fund, the government agreed to "one of the most savage packages ever imposed on any client government by the IMF" implemented a year later.[45]

The move to the IMF signified the decline of the left and the rise of the moderates to the fore of the party. In 1977, Duncan resigned as party General-Secretary and as Minister of National Mobilisation, joined by other notable leftists in the ministry. For the next two years, the economy stagnated further as the IMF recipe failed to generate economic reform. With the deepening economic crisis, the left made a resurgence. The unstoppable exodus of the business class convinced Manley that his development strategy could not succeed without the alienation of certain class groups. He thus capitulated to the left-wing forces.

In 1978, the communist Worker's Party of Jamaica (WPJ) announced its plan to ally with the PNP and not offer candidates in the next general election. In the same year, Manley delivered probably his most biting anti-capitalist speech to the Non-Aligned Nations Summit in Havana. In September 1979, Duncan won an uncontested position for General-Secretary and thus resumed his active role within the party. Two months later, the government failed another IMF test which signaled even greater austerity for the future. In response, the national executive of the party voted by a significant majority to break with the IMF, a decision which was later accepted by the cabinet.

To prepare for this new path, Manley replaced the conservative Finance Minister Eric Bell with prominent leftist Hugh Small. Although the anti-IMF plan was extremely vague, the party took it to the Jamaican electorate, where it was rejected.

AN ECONOMIC EVALUATION OF DEMOCRATIC SOCIALISM

In many ways, the PNP continued in principle most of the economic policies started by the JLP during the preceding decade. Stone demonstrates that of the seven major economic programmes adopted by the JLP between 1962 and 1972, all were continued by the PNP with the exception of the industrialisation incentive scheme.[46] As demonstrated in chapter I, the economy experienced significant growth prior to the PNP's election in 1972. Between 1966 and 1972, real GDP in Jamaica grew at an average annual rate of 6.5%, the bauxite/alumina sector grew at 6%, and net international reserves of the Central Bank doubled.[47]

Despite this impressive performance, the economy demonstrated certain signs of weakness. The economy was characterised by declining real output, an increasing current account deficit, unemployment of 23% (an increase from 13% in 1960), balance-of-payment surpluses dependent on capital inflows rather than export earnings, and an increasing share of banking sector credit going to the public sector. Between 1966 and 1971, the savings ratio to GDP declined from 14.7% to 11.7% and the current account deficit rose from 4% of GDP to 14%. Large capital inflows and a high investment rate were sufficient, however, to offset these problems. Despite clear signs of impending danger, the economy was not in crisis when the PNP assumed office in 1972.

The PNP intensified the import substitution programme started in the 1950's and, inspired by Keynesian fiscal expansionism, introduced numerous initiatives designed to increase state intervention in the economy. With the revenues from the bauxite production levy, the government created a capital development fund which it used to finance various state activities such as social service projects, employment programmes, and public ownership schemes. During the 1972-80 period, the ratio of central government expenditure to GDP averaged 36% per annum, which represented a 15 point increase over the 1966-70 period. The ratio of central government revenue to GDP averaged 24 percent per annum (a 6 point increase over the 1966-1970 period). As the economy worsened during the early 1970's, the government sought to alleviate the social effects of the crisis by increased expenditure rather than tackling the underlying structural problems.

In addition to an increase in taxes and the introduction of the bauxite levy, the government relied on a variety of sources to finance state expansion. First, the government depleted foreign exchange reserves. Between 1971 and 1980, foreign exchange reserves declined from J$132.2 million to J$-821.2 million, despite an increase in 1974 resulting from bauxite production levy inflows. Second, the government increased the printing of money. In 1972, the PNP started to print new money, accelerated the process in 1975 and 1976, temporarily halted it in 1977, but resumed printing in 1978. At its peak, the use of the printing press reached 63% in the financing of all government consumption expenditure and represented 13% of GDP financing.[48]

Third, the government extended its reliance on domestic and international sources of credit. The Banking Law of 1977 expanded the capacity of the Central Bank to lend to the government and placed responsibility for that capacity under the Ministry of Finance. As such, between 1972 and 1980, domestic credit to the public sector increased by an average annual rate of 44.6% compared to an increase of only 18.5% to the private sector. During the 1970's, the government displaced the private sector as the primary recipient of domestic credit. In addition, the government increased external borrowing. Aid from commercial bank loans initially formed the bulk of the borrowing and peaked at 68% of total foreign debt in 1975. As the economy grew worse, loans became more difficult to obtain and subsequently, the government became more and more dependent on friendly governments for capital inflows. By 1980, intergovernment loans made up 41% of Jamaica's external debt, commercial bank loans formed 31%, and international institutions constituted 20%. Between 1972 and 1980, Jamaica's net external debt increased from J$96 million to J$1,545 million. In addition, Jamaica's foreign assets minus foreign liabilities as a percentage of GDP decreased from 8% in 1972 to -27% in 1980.

In addition to the growth of the public sector, the government also increased controls on the economy, including price and exchange rate controls as well as quantitative restrictions on imports. The PNP government used the Prices Commission and an Economic Stabilisation Commission to determine price policy and to guide wage tribunals. The government imposed an absolute import ceiling and placed restrictions on the importation of capital, intermediate, and consumer goods.[49] As a result of these restrictions, the volume of imports was 35% less in 1980 than its peak of 1972. The value of merchandise imports increased significantly between 1972 and 1980 but the overall volume of imports declined during the same period. The government's ability to maintain a fairly strict control on imports (which the IMF included in its conditionality requirements) serves as one of the few examples of successful economic management by the PNP during the 1970's.

Table 3.2   Jamaica: Increases in GDP, Money Supply, and Domestic Credit 1972-80.

	GDP constant prices	GDP current prices	Domestic Credit		
			Total	Public Sector	Private Sector
1970	12.1	18.0			
1971	2.9	9.3	21.2	53.1	17.1
1972	9.6	12.4	39.9	100.0	27.9
1973	0.9	20.6	36.3	-4.6	46.9
1974	-4.1	25.0	28.5	61.0	22.9
1975	-0.7	20.3	33.7	76.3	24.2
1976	-6.6	4.0	23.4	81.3	5.0
1977	-1.6	10.0	9.8	37.5	-5.5
1978	-0.3	25.6	27.3	37.3	19.4
1979	-2.0	12.8	19.3	22.3	16.6
1980	-5.4	10.3	30.0	43.2	18.1

Source: Sharpley, *Jamaica 1972-80*, 134.

The government's exchange rate policy was based on the objective of reserving scarce foreign exchange for high-priority imports and for the servicing of the public sector's external debt. After its election victory in 1972, the PNP continued to peg the currency to the pound sterling, but in early 1973, the government tied the Jamaican dollar to the U.S. dollar at the rate of J$1.00=US$1.10. The government maintained a constant exchange rate—despite a devaluation in the US dollar in late 1973—until the government introduced a dual exchange rate in May 1977 as a part of the IMF agreement. Despite obvious disequlibria in the balance of payments, the government refused to devalue the dollar until 1977 largely because it feared the political repercussions associated with a rise in the cost of living, especially the increase in the domestic prices of imported food items.

A Critical Economic Evaluation of Democratic Socialism
       During the 1970's, Jamaica suffered from rapid and sustained

economic deterioration. Massive declines in real GDP, investment, real wages, and foreign reserves contributed to a precipitous fall in the overall standard of living (table 3.3). Payne concludes that, for ordinary Jamaicans, "the reforms of the Manley government...produced a severe decline in living standards, worse unemployment, acute shortages of basic goods in the shops, and a mood of depression that pervaded the government's few achievements. Against this dismal background the government's few achievements in the social field and in foreign affairs cannot be said to count for much."[50]

Economists and political analysts posit divergent theories to explain the economic crisis which Jamaica experienced during the 1970's. The explanations are not mutually exclusive and include (1) poor economic policies and mismanagement by the Manley government, (2) adverse world economic conditions and a hostile international environment, and (3) a structural argument that the nature of the Jamaican economy would have led to economic decline regardless of government policies.

This section will argue that negative international conditions did indeed affect the Jamaican economy, but that the policies of the Manley regime, particularly the government's failure to adjust to these external shocks, served as the major cause of the decline in the Jamaican economy. Although Jamaica suffered from structural dependence and an exceedingly open economy, policy measures could have been taken that would have mitigated these circumstances and contributed to economic growth.

International Circumstances and their Effect on the Jamaican Economy

External shocks negatively affected the economy during the 1970's. First, Jamaica suffered from a massive increase in prices associated with the international oil crisis. The rise in oil prices led to an unexpected 167% increase in Jamaica's fuel import bill in 1974 and a 600% increase in 1980, which moved fuel from 11% to 38% percent as a total value of imports in just seven years. Jamaica's nearly complete dependence on oil for energy exacerbated Jamaica's severe foreign exchange crisis.

Initially, the profits made from the bauxite production levy offset the increase in oil prices, but a decline in bauxite/alumina production reduced income from that source in the late 1970's. In 1972, bauxite and alumina provided the Jamaican economy with nearly J$194 million more in earnings than the total expenditure of energy and petroleum products. By 1979, this position had reversed, with the country spending approximately J$60 million more on petroleum than it received from bauxite and alumina.

Table 3.3   Jamaica: Economic Indicators (1970-80)

	Growth of GDP	Fixed Capital Formation/ GDP	Consumption/ GDP	Unemployment Rate	Consumer Price Increase	Net Foreign Reserves J$(million)	Net External Debt J$(million)
1970	10.3	31.4	72.7	n.a	7.7	94.4	80.3
1971	2.5	27.8	75.0	n.a	5.3	131.1	82.0
1972	0.70	25.5	81.0	23.2	5.4	87.2	96.0
1973	-0.1	25.8	78.3	21.9	17.7	34.3	150.4
1974	-5.5	22.0	86.0	21.2	27.2	79.5	243.3
1975	-1.9	23.3	84.7	20.7	17.4	-10.8	353.0
1976	-7.7	16.6	90.6	22.4	9.9	-216.9	421.5
1977	-3.4	11.7	89.3	24.2	11.5	-246.0	452.4
1978	-0.7	13.3	83.6	24.5	34.9	-625.5	1138.4
1979	-2.9	17.4	82.7	27.8	28.8	-861.2	1290.8
1980	-6.5	14.5	86.6	27.3	27.0	-969.8	1544.9

All figures represent percentages unless otherwise indicated.

Source: Looney, The Jamaican Economy in the 1980's, 9 and
Levitt, The Origins and Consequences of Jamaica's Debt Crisis, 12.

Second, a sharp rise in international real interest rates also impacted Jamaica negatively. During the 1960's and early 1970's, both the JLP and the PNP had borrowed from international financial institutions at low or negative interest rates and from commercial banks at relatively low interest rates. To finance its state expansion programme, the PNP government increased the level of short-term debt (under ten years) from 30% of all external debt in 1972 to 75% just four years later in 1976. Jamaica's extensive short-term debt requirement made the country particularly vulnerable to the rapid increase in interest rates which occurred in the international credit market during the mid-1970's. Real interest rates on Jamaica's external debt from international institutions averaged 3% annually between 1976-78, representing a substantial increase over the negative and low concessionary rates experienced in the previous decade. Commercial bank loan rates increased from 6-8% between 1969 and 1972 to rates of 12-18% during the late 1970's. This drastic increase in international interest rates multiplied the debt-service burden, which moved from 1.1% in 1972 to 7.0% in 1980 as a ratio of GDP.

Table 3.4   Gross External Debt by Type of Loan, 1971-80 (J$million)

	1971	1972	1973	1974	1975	1976	1977	1978	1979	1980
Market Loans	64.2	71.5	69.0	67.8	56.6	41.6	42.3	49.8	52.4	46.4
Commercial Banks	18.4	22.3	61.2	150.7	232.4	228.2	194.2	420.9	473.6	497.8
Multilateral										
Institutions	14.0	17.9	23.1	25.2	31.4	45.6	65.6	232.2	258.3	326.9
Bilateral	13.4	15.9	24.0	28.6	33.0	100.3	136.2	368.2	434.7	654.9
Other	-	-	-	-	28.3	29.3	46.4	109.1	123.3	68.6
Total	110.0	127.6	177.3	272.3	381.7	445.0	484.7	1180.2	1342.3	1594.6

Source: Manley, *Up the Down Escalator*, 289.

The economic recession in industrial countries hindered the growth of mining and tourism and, to a lesser extent, halted the penetration of Jamaican manufactures into these markets. The United States real per capita GNP grew at only 0.5% between 1975 and 1977, compared to an average annual growth rate of 5% in the ten years preceding this period. As such, American tourists spent less disposable income on travel, which partly explains the sudden and pronounced decrease in U.S. visitors to Jamaica. In mining, the recession in industrial countries contributed to a fall in the international demand for aluminum. Manley argues that "although the price of aluminum continued to rise, during [1974-75], the world market for alumina diminished. Thus, the aluminum industry contributed its share to the new economic phenomenon, stagflation."[51]   In addition, the growth rate of imports for industrial countries declined from 9% between 1963 and 1972 to 3.6% between 1973 and 1981. As businessmen left Jamaica, exports declined from 5.3% in the period 1963-72 to 1.4% in the years 1973-81.[52]

An Evaluation of External, Domestic, and Structural Factors
International factors dealt a devastating blow to the Jamaican economy during the 1970's. These external shocks do not adequately explain, however, the massive economic decline which the country experienced during this period. While the world recession hurt the aluminum industry, the policy of the Jamaican government toward the bauxite/alumina companies played the critical role in the decline of the production and revenues in bauxite mining. Jamaica's bauxite levy increased the cost of alumina from Jamaica by US$33 a ton. This increase led to a decrease in Jamaica's competitiveness, especially

since Jamaica's main competitors, Australia and Guinea, did not impose a bauxite levy, and later when Guinea did impose a levy, the rate was much lower. Mining firms thus had a strong economic incentive to shift their operations to other more hospitable nations, which most of them did.

In tourism, the actions of hotel owners and other entrepreneurs in the industry—to leave the country with large amounts of capital—played a significant role in the decline of visitors. Hoteliers left the nation in response to the increase in state activity, Manley's socialist rhetoric, and the resultant fall in visitors to the island. The negative image of the country portrayed in the United States media and the rapid increase in local violence also factored in reducing the number of visitors.

To examine the effects of the government's policies on the economy, we can compare Jamaica's performance to that of other nations with similar economic features. In comparison to five other Caribbean countries during this period, Jamaica performed significantly worse. Of six countries in the Caribbean—that all faced the same international circumstances in the 1970's—Jamaica fared the worse both in terms of real GDP per capita and in terms of per capita growth, even behind Haiti, the poorest country in the Western hemisphere (table 3.5).[53]

Table 3.5   Caribbean Real Income and Growth Rates (1972-1981)

	$\dfrac{\text{Real GDP per capita 1981}}{\text{Real GDP per capita 1972}}$	Per capita growth rate (percent per year)
Bahamas	1.00	0
Barbados	1.16	1.6
Dominican Republic	.80	-2.7
Haiti	1.13	1.5
Jamaica	.62	-5.4
Trinidad and Tobago	1.30	4.3

Source: Connolly, "Comments on 'Liberalization to Centralization, and Back?'" 294.

While Jamaica experienced an export decline of 1.4% between 1973 and 1981, all other non-oil developing countries actually increased their exports during the same period by an average 5.9%. The world recession contributed to the rise in exports in these countries because they increased their market share in wealthy oil exporting countries and (those that had a high share of manufactures in total exports) captured a larger share of the industrial countries' slow growing import value.[54]

Moreover, although oil prices did increase during the 1970's, the price of many Jamaican commodities also increased substantially, including bananas, cocoa, coffee, sugar, and, most importantly, bauxite. Significantly, while export agriculture declined, Rao documents the impressive growth in domestic agriculture which grew by nearly 4% between 1972 and 1980.[55] Domestic agriculture increased as food imports dwindled; local farmers quickly moved to fill the demand.

Domestic factors also serve to explain the massive capital flight, large fiscal deficit, and low investment rates in this period. The perceived hostility of the government to the private sector and a lack of investment incentives convinced nearly 40% of the island's businessmen, medical personnel, craftsmen, and other skilled workers to flee the country taking with them large amounts of capital. As a result, numerous factories and small businesses were forced to close which exacerbated the unemployment situation.

Table 3.6   Jamaica: Public and Private Sector Expenditure 1973-77 (%)

	1973	1974	1975	1976	1977
Consumption/GDP					
Total	77.4	80.6	82.8	88.9	88.4
Private	61.4	63.5	64.5	66.5	66.3
Public	15.9	17.1	18.3	21.9	22.1
Fixed capital formation/GDP					
Total	25.9	22.1	23.2	16.5	11.6
Private	23.2	17.8	18.6	12.1	7.6
Public	2.7	3.5	4.7	4.3	3.9

Source: Sharpley, *Jamaica: 1972-80,* 135.

Government expenditure to make up for the private sector capital flight had a negative impact on the fiscal deficit which increased from 5% of GDP in 1972 to 18% in 1980 (see appendix D). In addition, the social programmes of the government which consumed almost all government expenditure contributed little to long-term investment. Table 3.6 demonstrates that most of the increase in public sector expenditure took the form of higher consumption, not investment. Moreover, while public investment increased and private investment decreased, aggregate output declined. This meant that the government's economic strategy had the effect of replacing more productive private activities with less efficient public sector activities. This government emphasis on non-productive activity and the slowdown in exports also led to a significant change in the structure of incentives toward the production of nontradeable goods and services, which hindered long-term productive capacity.[56]

Other domestic policies also had negative effects on the economy. The extension of minimum wage legislation and the national minimum wage caused the export-oriented garment industry to move to Haiti and other locations—clearly making worse the problems of unemployment and foreign exchange scarcity. In addition, these wage increases, coupled with expansionist fiscal and monetary policy, fueled the rapid inflation growth during this period. The maintenance of the fixed exchange rate until 1977 and the increase in wages also contributed to the decline in export production. Quantitative controls led to an overprotection of the manufacturing sector and an underprotection of agriculture since cheap food imports were encouraged. Bonnick argues that the result was the relative impoverishment of the agricultural sector and continued dependence on imported food with attendant vulnerability to international food price shifts.[57]

On a positive note, Manley's social programmes resulted in significant gains including a decline in infant mortality and improved access to medical facilities (see social indicators in appendix E). In agriculture, domestic production increased during this period as local farmers filled the demand created by the reduction in imports. The reduction of imports created shortages that enticed many individuals to enter the informal economy. Between 1972 and 1980, self-employment and informal activity increased dramatically. Self-employment grew from 225,000 in 1972 to 300,000 in 1980—by far the largest increase among all occupational categories.

In sum, it is clear that much of Jamaica's economic crisis "was not so much the result of external factors (higher oil prices, declining terms of trade, world recession) as of domestic policies and structural factors affecting the demand for non-oil imports, the supply of exports, and net inflow of foreign finance."[58] Jamaica's structural dependence, high import content, and severe lack of foreign exchange contributed to the island's economic woes, while the fiscal and monetary expansionism of the Manley regime only made the situation worse.

MANLEY AND THE IMF (1977-80)

Between 1977 and 1980, the government signed three major agreements with the IMF: a 1977 Stand-by agreement, a 1978 Extended Fund Facility, and a 1979 Extended Fund Facility. As early as 1973, the government had signed a brief Stand-by agreement with the Fund, but the IMF's economic constraints came into conflict with the government's political objectives, so the government discontinued the relationship.

The economic crisis became so bad during the next three years that by March of 1976, international commercial banks had ceased making new loans to Jamaica. After the 1976 election and in spite of serious economic decline, the government still avoided the IMF path and instead it started to prepare a "democratic socialist alternative" to the Fund, an Emergency Production Plan. The Production Plan emphasised "tight controls over foreign exchange outflows and imports, expansion of bauxite and tourism earnings, development of local agricultural production and small-scale activity to substitute for imports, and expanded trade with and assistance from the socialist countries."[59] For various reasons discussed earlier, Manley rejected the Plan and instead he reluctantly accepted a two-year Stand-by agreement with the fund in April 1977.

Table 3.7 Major Jamaica/IMF Agreements 1977-80

Date approved	Type of Agreement	Amount (in millions)
August 1977	Stand-By (24 months)	SDR 64
May 1978	Extended Fund Facility (three years)	SDR 200
June 1979*	Extended Fund Facility (two years)	SDR 33
	Supplementary Finance Facility	SDR 227

*In March 1980 the Jamaican government decided to discontinue negotiations for an interim Stand-by agreement.

Source: Sharpley, *Jamaica, 1972-80,* compiled from various tables.

The 1977 Agreement: Necessity and Austerity

Consistent with IMF monetary doctrine, the Fund analysed Jamaica's situation and concluded that the major causes of Jamaica's economic crisis were excessive demand, wages, and monetary expansion and an overvalued exchange rate. As such, in the agreement, the Fund required a devaluation (with a dual exchange rate), a tax increase, and a wage guideline, in a package that was not as severe as the Fund normally required. The Fund acceded to many of the Jamaican demands largely because Manley used his political friendships with the leaders of Britain and Canada, and his relationship with senior U.S. government officials, to bring pressure on the Fund.

The most austere aspect of the agreement centered around the Fund's requirement that all outstanding arrears in foreign payments were to be eliminated in three months and that the net foreign assets of the Bank of Jamaica were to be stabilised, in spite of the substantial increase which occurred in 1976. These conditions were nearly impossible considering the small size of the IMF loan but the Fund expected that Jamaica would receive a high level of external flows to make up for the deficit. In 1977, Jamaica received only one-quarter of the funds the IMF had expected and in December, the government failed the first quarterly performance test by exceeding the ceilings set on the Bank of Jamaica's net foreign assets, foreign arrears, and net domestic assets.

The 1978 Agreement: Economic Crisis and IMF Failure

In response to the failure of the test, the Fund immediately suspended the agreement and required new negotiations. For the new agreement in 1978, the IMF required an extremely austere plan—described as "unnecessarily harsh and socially unacceptable" by the political directorate—but which the Fund felt was necessary to bring the economic crisis to a halt.[60] Essentially, the agreement called for a switch in resources from the public-sector towards the private sector, from consumption to investment, and from reliance on administered controls to the greater use of domestic market forces. Import controls were to retain a central role in balance of payments policy during the first year of the programme.

Because this agreement was an Extended Fund Facility and thus involved a larger loan than the Stand-by agreement, the Fund played a more active role in mobilising the additional external financing required for the agreement to succeed. Although the Fund succeeded in this objective, the package still failed to provide adequate financial support for the strict measures necessitated by the Fund. Although the government carried out every single aspect of the 1978 agreement in both letter and spirit, the economy never recovered. Jamaica's dependence on foreign resources and the failure to achieve high external financing contributed to the further decline in the economy and thus the IMF was forced to admit some error in its policies, assumptions, and projections.[61]

The 1979 Agreement: Political Constraints and Negotiation Breakdown

In 1979, the government and the Fund renegotiated the contract in response to the dismal performance of the 1978 agreement. In the new agreement, the Fund expanded the adjustment process period, suspended monthly currency depreciations, and revised targets to permit higher fiscal deficit and current account deficit targets. The Fund allowed the government to use a new Supplementary Financing Facility (SFF) to increase lending in an effort to substitute for commercial bank inflows normally expected by the government. The IMF did this because it wanted to improve foreign and local investor confidence and to finance the additional imports necessary for increased production.

In the next two years, the government suffered from a series of external shocks such as higher oil prices, a disastrous hurricane, and increased interest rates. These factors, as well as the government's inability to reduce spending, contributed to the failure of the test in December 1979. In the new negotiations, the government felt that the IMF requirements—a further wage squeeze, cutbacks in social programmes, and a massive reduction in government employees—were politically suicidal and thus it decided to break with the IMF. Although the government still remained a member of the Fund and continued to make repayments, it failed to sign a new agreement. After its electoral victory in 1980 over the PNP, the JLP quickly signed a new agreement with the Fund which provided for a massive influx of funds which totaled over three times that allowed in the 1979 agreement under Manley.

Manley and the IMF: An Evaluation

The PNP government's relationship with the Fund during 1977/80 highlights several important issues. First, the IMF's consistent application of pro-market measures constituted an ideology that was incompatible with the democratic socialist path of the Manley regime. The large sum and favourable conditions attached to Seaga's first IMF agreement support the contention that an ideological conviction consistent with the Fund's approach clearly facilitates positive agreement negotiations.

Second, the various agreements (especially the 1978 agreement) made clear Jamaica's essential economic dilemma. If economic reform had to take the form of structural adjustment and stabilisation as prescribed by the IMF, this could only succeed with massive capital inflows which increase external debt financing, drives up debt-service payments, and restricts funds necessary for structural adjustment to succeed—the very first objective. To resolve the vicious cycle, either debt constraints have to be reduced or capital inflows have to come from other sources, such as major private investment.

On the positive side, the IMF's relationship with Manley demonstrated elements of the Fund's flexibility in responding to political factors. The view of the IMF as imposing rigid blueprints regardless of political consequence has little validity in the Jamaican situation. The IMF initially accepted many of Manley's politically-based demands which resulted in a fairly innocuous 1977 agreement. On the other hand, the IMF's refusal to budge on certain items led to the break with the Fund in 1980.

Finally, the PNP/IMF relationship demonstrated that no matter how favourable agreements are with the Fund, this cannot compensate for the necessity of a committed government attitude toward the encouragement of foreign investment. In 1979, democratic socialist Jamaica was the largest recipient of IMF aid per capita in the world. Despite these inflows, the government was unable to increase investment or investor confidence in any substantial way. As we will see these issues became very important over the next nine years under Seaga and again later under Manley.

CHAPTER 4

THE POLITICS OF STRUCTURAL ADJUSTMENT (1980-1989)

And Joshua and all Israel were beaten before them and
they fled by the way of the wilderness.

—Joshua 8:15

Michael Manley lost the 1980 election to the JLP headed by Edward Seaga, who ruled for eight years. Over this period, Seaga returned the economy to a growth path, expanded tourism and non-traditional exports, and succeeded in holding down inflation and the public sector deficit. He did so, however, by increasing Jamaica's debt burden to crisis proportions. By 1988, the government had borrowed so much that it was paying more money to the IMF and the World Bank than it was receiving in new loans. This created extremely tight resource constraints which later had a major impact on Manley's transformation. Under Seaga, productivity remained at levels below those achieved in the 1970's, the trade deficit escalated with the sharp rise in imports, and income inequality increased substantially. Although Jamaica suffered from the sharp decline of the bauxite/alumina industry and the world recession between 1980 and 1983, these negative factors were largely offset by the oil windfall in the late 1980's.

Seaga implemented only parts of the structural adjustment agenda and he did so in a manner which seemed driven more by political rather than economic motives. Seaga's development strategy indicated the continuation of populist policies oriented more to short-term political objectives and less to economic development over the medium to long term. In order to mitigate the negative effects of the structural programme, Seaga convinced the IMF and World bank to postpone the major components of the strategy for over three years. Pressure from the international financial community increased, however, and between 1983 and 1986, Seaga implemented the bulk of the structural adjustment plan. If he had been more committed to the structural adjustment agenda and had not postponed the reforms, he would not have had to introduce the austere measures all at once. Had he acted earlier, Seaga might have prevented the massive riots and strikes which resulted from the sudden implementation of these measures.

As these programmes became more unpopular and as civil disobedience escalated, Seaga slowed down the economic reform and implemented measures designed to increase political support. Despite his rhetoric of economic liberalism and free enterprise, Seaga pursued a statist and centrist method of reform. He created new programmes and organisations that served as a drain on the budget. He set in place various initiatives (such as hotel privatisations) but never actually completed them. The centralisation of authority under Seaga's control led to numerous bureaucratic and administrative bottlenecks that prevented the successful implementation of various programmes. Moreover, through his distant and aloof personality, Seaga distanced the private sector and alienated the majority of Jamaicans.

One prominent journalist—a strident Manley critic and moderate Seaga supporter—accurately captured the mood of the country when he remarked in early 1988 that Seaga had "come to be identified with a deep, despairing feeling of oppression. He found a nation in chains, and instead of freeing it, added new ones of his own; and everyday devises new burdens and restrictions. That the country should now be turning to Mr. Manley is nothing but a measure of its despair."[1]

STRUCTURAL ADJUSTMENT: ECONOMIC AUSTERITY AND POLITICAL UNREST

After the 1980 election, Seaga immediately began negotiating with the IMF and embarked upon a programme of economic recovery. With Seaga's strident rejection of Manley's socialist path and his avowed commitment to private sector-led development, capital flowed into the country from a variety of Western nations and international lending agencies. In March 1981, at a meeting of the Caribbean Group for Cooperation in Economic Development, chaired by the World Bank, official lenders pledged to disburse at least US$350 million (excluding IMF resources), or 8.8% of GDP, in new resources during the next year to support Jamaica's adjustment efforts. In his first IMF agreement, Seaga used his free-market ideology to his advantage and received favourable terms. He secured J$681 million over three years and avoided devaluing the dollar or imposing wage and price controls. In 1981, the new economic path seemed destined for success as previously scarce goods poured into the country, tourism expanded rapidly, and violence decreased. In stark contrast to the previous year, the economy grew by 2%, inflation fell from 29% in 1980 to 6% in 1981, and unemployment leveled off slightly.

By 1982, however, Jamaica's spectacular growth came to a halt as the economy faced an international recession, the crash of the international bauxite/alumina market, and the increasing trade deficit (fueled by the deluge of imports). In just one year, bauxite exports decreased by almost 30%, the gross external debt increased by over 30%, and unemployment crept up to over 27%. As the economic crisis deepened, Seaga's popularity dipped in the polls and the JLP faced the prospect of becoming Jamaica's first one-term government.

Political events in the neighboring island of Grenada temporarily halted Seaga's decline in popularity. The violent overthrow of Grenada's Prime Minister by a group of leftists both shocked and offended the Jamaican people. Most Jamaicans felt that the scenario of events in Grenada might have occurred in Jamaica had the PNP won the 1980 elections. Seaga acted quickly to exploit the resurgence in anti-communist sentiment by accusing the Soviet embassy in Kingston of being involved in espionage and by firing a junior civil servant in the Jamaican foreign ministry for alleged dealings with a KGB agent.

Table 4.1   Public Opinion Polls on PNP/JLP Preferences (1980-82)

	PNP	JLP
October 1980	41	59
February 1981	38	62
1981 Local Gov. Elections (Actual)	37	63
July 1981	47	53
November 1981	46	54
May 1982	45	55
October 1982	53	47

Source: Stone, "Seaga in Trouble: Polling the Jamaican Polity in Midstream," 7.

With his party's temporary surge in popularity, Seaga called a snap election for December 1983. The election seemed politically wise because the government had failed both the March and September IMF performance tests, and further economic crisis seemed imminent. The PNP boycotted the election, however, on the basis that Seaga had reneged on his earlier promise to revise the electoral lists before calling new elections. As a result, in the 1983 election, Jamaica effectively became a one-party state when the JLP captured all sixty (60) seats in the House (although the PNP still had eight (8) opposition members in the much less important twenty-one (21) member Senate).

Seaga now had more time to implement his structural adjustment programme and thus he announced a new IMF agreement in 1984 which called for a sharp devaluation, large tax increases, and an immediate reduction in the public labour force. Political tensions burst into the open in January 1985 after Seaga announced a drastic price increase of oil and kerosene. In two days of nationwide demonstrations, lootings, and clashes with the police, seven people died and fifteen were wounded. Although the PNP played a role in the disturbances, most participants in the demonstrations were ordinary Jamaicans struggling under severe economic hardship.

Five months later, in June 1985, the government announced another IMF agreement which included a strict 10% wage guideline. In the face of declining real wages, workers participated in the first general strike in the island's post-independence history and essentially shut down the country for several days. Significantly, the six main trade unions—including the JLP-allied BITU—participated in the nationwide protest against the 10% wage offer to public employees (in the face of a 31% inflation rate), against redundancies (17,000 public sector jobs had been lost since 1981), and, more generally, against economic austerity policies.

In response to these mounting political pressures, Seaga sought an alternative path. In 1986, he invited the IMF, the World Bank, and US Agency for International Development (USAID) to evaluate the relative success of Jamaica's structural adjustment strategy and provide suggestions for the future. Much to Seaga's dismay, the tripartite review was highly critical of the government's efforts and suggested that the structural reform had to be broadened and intensified. In response, Seaga limited distribution of the report, delivered a scathing critique of the IMF at its annual meeting in Seoul, and even threatened to break with the Fund by creating a non-IMF contingency programme.

Recognising the limitations of Seaga's commitment to reform, the United States government cut Jamaica's aid substantially and reduced Jamaica's sugar import quota into the American market. Despite this setback, Seaga embarked upon a political campaign designed to increase popular support. In general opposition to IMF dictates, Seaga announced an expansionary budget which reduced interest rates, pledged to hold the exchange rate stable, introduced a variety of price controls, and expanded capital expenditure. This budget was announced just two months before the local government elections in 1986, which the JLP lost in an overwhelming defeat.

Seaga was able to pursue the new politically-motivated agenda because of the fall in international oil prices which provided the government with more room for economic maneuvering than anticipated. In the 1987 IMF agreement, Seaga exploited the oil windfall and demonstrated his savvy negotiation skills by announcing a socially-oriented package. The agreement called for large expenditures to support the economic infrastructure, greater investment in human capital, an improvement in social services, and a safety net for the poorer segments of society. On the harsher side, the agreement included a 10% wage guideline which was promptly rejected by nurses, doctors, teachers, and civil servants working for the government. By this time, Seaga had turned his sights to the next general election which he called for the latest possible date allowed by the constitution (1989).

As early as 1987, Seaga had started preparing for the next election when he announced that he had passed through the economic adjustment stage of his development strategy and that "the main thrust now is the second phase of adjustment, which is social adjustment aimed at a reduction in poverty."[2] Two years earlier, Seaga had announced a variety of social welfare services such as a massive Food Aid Programme. Under that programme, food stamps were provided free of cost to 200,000 indigent persons and 200,000 expectant mothers with pre-school children while 600,000 school children were promised free school lunches. Seaga shifted his emphasis from tight money orthodoxy when he announced a plan to spend over J$1 billion on a five-year Social Well-Being Programme to build new hospitals and schools. Seaga's shift from the structural adjustment agenda and his strained relations with the international financial community led one social critic to argue that Seaga had become a "traitor" to his benefactors.[3] Despite the party's many political overtures to the Jamaican people, the JLP lost the election in February 1989 gaining only fifteen (15) out of sixty (60) parliamentary seats.

STRUCTURAL ADJUSTMENT IN THEORY: THE SEAGA MODEL

Seaga's Ideological Background

Born in the United States of Jamaican parents with Syrian heritage, Seaga attended Harvard where he trained as a sociologist. On his return to Jamaica, he lived in the rural countryside for a short time studying Jamaican culture before he entered the family business. He was appointed to the Legislature at the young age of 29 where he developed a national reputation as a radical advocate for the poor based on a series of speeches he made criticising the government's failure to provide economic support to the masses. His most famous speech, delivered in 1961, condemned the severe inequality in Jamaican society between the "haves" and the "have-nots" and called for "basic structural changes" in Jamaican society.[4] This image was further reinforced by Seaga's transformation of his poverty-stricken West Kingston constituency into a modern progressive community.

In the JLP government of 1962-72, Seaga served first as Minister of Development and Welfare and then as Minister of Finance and Planning. As Finance Minister, Seaga advocated increased state intervention in the economy through ownership and control, increased taxation, and significant public welfare expenditure. Seaga's vigorous and successful efforts at increasing tax collections earned him the wrath of the private sector which began to shift its support to the opposition PNP. Seaga also presided over the government's "Jamaicanisation" campaign which managed to rescue his image with certain private sector officials.

In 1974, Seaga replaced Hugh Shearer as head of the JLP and thus became Jamaica's Leader of the Opposition. In that position, Seaga shifted his strategy, dropped many of his previous call for social programmes and, in response to the fiscal and monetary expansionism of the PNP regime, he stressed the need for greater fiscal conservatism. Based upon his elaborate and statistically detailed criticisms of PNP socialism, Seaga quickly acquired a reputation as an extremely capable technocrat with outstanding financial and management skills. In contrast to the flamboyant and outspoken Manley, Seaga projected an image of soberness and reality which appealed to the Jamaican people in a time of uncertainty, fear, and rapid economic decline. In a significant breach of protocol—which also indicated his impressive international connections—Seaga met with senior-level members in the IMF prior to the October 1980 election, which left little doubt as to the economic direction that Seaga intended to take when he assumed office.

The JLP and Structural Adjustment

Seaga recognised early on that a sharp change in government policies was required to arrest the decline in real income and foreign reserves left by Manley. His strategy was largely a reactive one designed to ensure stability and, in Seaga's words, "to restore sustained growth on a low inflation basis."[5] During the election campaign, he had condemned Manley as an ideologue who unwisely put political ideology above economic reality. Payne argues, however, that Seaga himself rigidly pursued an economic model—labeled "orthodox liberal development"—derived from theory.[6] Indeed, Seaga professed early on his commitment to the ideals of economic liberalism and free enterprise. In 1982, Seaga explained that his "underlying ideological framework" rested on the two precepts of "a parliamentary democractic system and a market system which rewards private enterprise."[7]

After the election, Seaga declared that his economic thinking was "in concurrence with the economic principles of the Reagan administration in terms of encouragement of private enterprise."[8] In 1991, Seaga argued that during the 1980's, the JLP "restored the free-market system. We moved away from the statism that had built-up in the 1970's. We tried to restore a system of reward for private initiative and enterprise as the guiding principle. Overall, we liberalised and deregulated the economy by divestment [and] by deregulation of bureaucratic systems that were in place such as import controls and price controls."[9]

Although Seaga expressed his belief in private initiative, he also supported regulation and government involvement to a certain degree. Seaga explained in 1982 that he did not "follow a system of unbridled or unregulated private enterprise but one which is regulated in the interest of the consumer and the worker—while not frustrating to the expansion of the various components of motivation which go into the investment process."[10] Many aspects of structural adjustment implemented during this period designed to help the private sector occurred in response to great pressures from the IMF and only with considerable reluctance on Seaga's part. Seaga recognised, based on his observations of various East Asian nations, that the state still had a critical role to play in the economy.

Seaga's structural adjustment agenda had several theoretical components. First, Seaga hoped to reduce Jamaica's structural dependence on bauxite/alumina production by expanding other sectors of the economy. The JLP sought to establish tourism, agriculture, and manufacturing as major economic contributors so that, combined with bauxite/alumina production, they would form the "four legs of the economic stool."[11]

Second, the government also planned to promote an open-economy export-led strategy and to deemphasise the traditional import-substitution which had dominated the Jamaican economy for the previous three decades. Seaga declared his intention to "convert [Jamaica] to [an] export-oriented rather than [an] import substitution econom[y]."[12] Seaga hoped to gear local production toward the export market while suppressing domestic demand and restricting domestic consumption. He identified certain subsectors which he expected to expand into export markets. In agriculture, the government focused on non-traditional crops to complement sugar and banana exports; in industry, it targeted garments and sewn materials, automotive products, furniture and electronics, and electrical products.

Third, Seaga placed liberalisation of the economy and the promotion of private sector-led growth as a priority. In a speech delivered at a White House luncheon in 1981, Seaga expressed his wish to dismantle Jamaica's interventionist policies and instead promote economic growth "powered by a dynamic private sector which would be the engine of economic recovery."[13] Toward that end, he announced his intention to divest state-owned enterprises and deregulate the government bureaucracy in order to eliminate obstacles to greater foreign and local investment. Although Seaga advocated increased private sector involvement, he also indicated his intention to develop a number of public sector projects as a component of his strategy for national reconstruction, as laid out in the JLP 1980 election manifesto, entitled "Change Without Chaos, A National Programme For Reconstruction."

Fourth, as a part of the deregulation strategy, Seaga envisioned the gradual elimination of exchange, price, and import controls, although he felt that wage controls would have to be maintained to contain inflation. To encourage export production in the private sector and to reduce the level of imports, he intended to devalue the currency so as to make it more competitive in the long-term. As a precondition to increased investment into the economy—and in line with IMF orthodoxy—Seaga emphasised his plans to stabilise financial imbalances in the economy by rectifying the balance-of-payments and current account deficits. In addition, he planned to limit monetary expansion in the public sector by reducing the budget deficit, decreasing real government expenditure, and implementing cutbacks in government employment In short, Seaga's economic strategy in theory mirrored the traditional IMF and World Bank approach. While Seaga shared the view of these external agencies that Jamaica needed more private and foreign investment, his strategy emphasised renewed confidence, access to imported inputs, and increased government efficiency more than structural changes.

Gradual Structural Adjustment and the United States Relationship

Several important aspects of Seaga's plan merit special attention. Seaga made it clear early on that his strategy was a gradual one intended to address structural concerns slowly with a primary emphasis on economic recovery. Seaga set a "three-year recovery period 1981-83" to restore confidence, ensure positive planning, and restore the credit-worthiness of the country.[14] During the first three years of his administration, he avoided the application of fundamental tools in the structural adjustment strategy. Between 1980-83, the public sector deficit, government expenditure and government revenue all remained constant, while direct controls on prices and foreign exchange did not undergo a profound change. For example, in his first agreement with the IMF, Seaga convinced the Fund that a devaluation was not necessary at the time because the devaluations that occurred between 1977 and 1979 had made Jamaican exports sufficiently competitive. Indeed, the stated objective of the agreement was simply to expand output and investment by relaxing foreign exchange constraints and not to implement any fundamental structural changes.

Seaga's strategy received tremendous support from the United States which sought to make Jamaica its free-market showcase in the Caribbean. To give the impression that Jamaica would not serve as a pawn for United States interests, Seaga announced early after his election victory that he intended to continue Manley's non-aligned foreign policy. He declared that "there is the expectation that every little country in the world is lined up behind two teams....We are neither a communist nor a capitalist country."[15]

Despite his rhetoric, Seaga broke diplomatic relations with Cuba and launched vigorous attacks on left-leaning states in the Caribbean such as the Nicaraguan Sandinista regime. Moreover, the Seaga government pursued an extremely close relationship with the United States. In 1981, Seaga was the first foreign head of state to visit the newly-elected U.S. President, Ronald Reagan, an act which symbolised the close ideological relationship the two men shared. Reagan responded to Seaga's new economic thrust by creating a special State Department office to coordinate overall U.S. government efforts toward the island.

Table 4.2   U.S. Economic Assistance to Jamaica 1980-81 (US$million)

	1980	1981
USAID	2.7	12.9
PL480	10.0	17.1
Economic Stability Fund	0	41.0
OPIC	0	51.0
EXIMBANK	0	21.4
Housing Guaranty	0	15.0
Totals	12.7	158.4

Source: Edie, *Democracy By Default*, 118.

In addition, Reagan played an instrumental role in the creation of the Caribbean Basin Initiative (CBI), a regional economic recovery plan that granted duty-free access to U.S. markets for Caribbean products. When bauxite production decreased during the early 1980's, Reagan instructed the General Services Administration to purchase US$67 million of Jamaican bauxite for the U.S. strategic stockpile even though bauxite ranks low on the organisation's list of needed materials. Reagan also asked his close friend and chairman of Chase Manhattan bank, David Rockefeller, to head a newly created U.S. Business Committee on Jamaica designed to increase American business investment in the island. Reagan found numerous ways to send aid to Jamaica (see table 4.2). Under Reagan, development assistance for Jamaica grew so much that during the early 1980's, Jamaica became the second highest recipient of U.S. aid per capita after Israel.

POLICY INITIATIVES AND THE REALITY OF STRUCTURAL ADJUSTMENT

During this period, the JLP made ten major agreements with the IMF and the World Bank which dominated the government's economic policy. With the IMF, the government pursued a stabilisation programme, while with the World Bank, the government developed a structural adjustment strategy. This section will examine the specific policy instruments of the Seaga regime by looking at the requirements laid down by both the IMF and the World Bank.

Table 4.3 Major Jamaica/IMF and World Bank Agreements 1980-88

Date approved	Type of IMF Agreement		Amount (in millions)
April 1980	Extended Fund Facility (three years)	SDR	477
	Compensatory Financing Facility	SDR	37
August 1982	Compensatory Financing Facility	SDR	19
June 1984	Stand-By (one year)	SDR	64
	Compensatory Financing Facility	SDR	72
July 1985	Stand-by (21 months)	SDR	115
March 1987	Stand-By (15 months)	SDR	85
	Compensatory Financing Facility	SDR	40
Sept. 1988	Stand-by (20 months)	SDR	82
Chronology of World Bank Adjustment Loans (1982-87)			
July 1982	Structural adjustment loan I		$76
June 1983	Structural adjustment loan II		$60
Nov. 1984	Structural adjustment loan III		$55
June 1987	Trade and Finance Sector adjustment loan		$40
	Public Enterprise Sector adjustment loan		$20

Source: Robinson and Schmitz, Jamaica: Navigating Through a Troubled Decade, 31.

IMF: Exchange Rate Policy and Controls Elimination

The IMF adopts a short-term economic perspective which requires a correction in the country's balance of payment through instruments such as devaluation of the dollar and the abolition of import and price controls.[16] Throughout the JLP regime, the government applied all these economic tools at differing times and to varying degrees. Seaga repeatedly demonstrated his reluctance to completely comply with IMF dictates and his intention to curtail his economic policy to bring about desired political objectives.

When the JLP assumed office in 1980, the official exchange rate was J$1.78 to the US dollar which the government maintained without a devaluation, despite pressures from the Fund (see table 4.5). As the black market exchange rate grew substantially higher than the official rate, the government still refused to devalue and instead de facto decriminalised the informal foreign exchange market. In March 1981, the government issued "no-funds" licenses which allowed local businessmen to use foreign exchange not legally obtained from the Bank of Jamaica for the importation of raw materials, spare parts, and capital goods. These licenses were automatically granted to legitimate exporters in an effort to promote export development and to reduce the use of foreign exchange for consumer imports. In January 1983, the government still opposed a devaluation and formalised the current system by openly declaring a two-tiered exchange rate. The higher exchange rate was expected to level out at around J$2.70.

Because this dual exchange rate formally violated the IMF's constitution, Seaga was finally forced to impose a unified rate and to devalue the dollar from J$1.78 to J$3.15 in November 1983. Seaga still argued the need for a fixed exchange rate but in the June 1984 IMF package, he agreed to a new flexible exchange rate system to be set by twice-weekly auctions conducted at the Bank of Jamaica. Under this "managed float" system, the exchange rate quickly devalued and reached as high as J$6.40 a few months later. To prevent the almost uncontrollable fall of the dollar, the government unilaterally intervened in the auction to revalue the dollar upward to $5.50, which it maintained (through regular interventions in the auction) from 1985 until its defeat in 1989. In IMF negotiations between 1985 and 1989, the government remained steadfast in its conviction that the economy needed a stable exchange rate to prevent speculation and hoarding which, Seaga argued, only fueled a precipitous fall in the currency.

A crucial aspect of the IMF strategy was the phased elimination of the 364 quantitative restrictions on imports left by the Manley regime. Seaga put off the bulk of these removals on import restrictions until February 1982 when 64 goods were removed and

February 1983 when a further 60 were removed. As IMF pressure increased, Seaga was forced to remove further goods and by April 1985, the bulk of restrictions were removed. Initially, removal of burdensome import restrictions led to a massive influx of consumer goods in the so-called era of the three V's—volvos, videos and venereal disease (the latter referring to the rapid growth in tourism).

Seaga never fulfilled the original IMF requirement of complete elimination and he maintained restrictions on basic food, vehicles, and goods needed for health and security reasons. Seaga also postponed a cut in subsidies or the removal of price controls until the June 1984 IMF agreement, and in the agreement, the government retained controls on basic food items, agricultural inputs, and medicines. Most of these removals were reversed just two years later when Seaga reintroduced price cuts, price subsidies, and price controls in the May 1986 budget.

In monetary management, Seaga pursued a policy of high interest rates which at times exceeded 30%. In addition, Seaga maintained all financial controls over credit allocation and the interest rate structure. In late 1985, he revised the banking legislation to facilitate greater dependence on market forces, but he still retained significant controls over credit policy such as cash reserve and liquid asset requirements through the Bank of Jamaica and Ministry of Finance.

Table 4.4 Balance of Payments (1980-88)

	1980	1981	1982	1983	1984	1985	1986	1987	1988
Trade Balance	-75	-323	-442	-439	-335	-436	-247	-356	-395
Exports (fob)	963	974	767	686	702	567	590	709	834
Imports (fob)	1038	1297	1209	1124	1037	1004	837	1065	1228
Service Balance	-182	-138	-97	-144	-77	-81	-74	36	224
Tourism	229	271	306	274	385	375	481	55	470
Investment Income	-252	-202	-184	-266	-259	-306	-314	-399	-407
Other Services	-159	-208	-219	252	-204	-151	-93	-116	161
Current Account Balance	-175	-338	-404	-488	-332	-364	-173	-202	-35

Source: Levitt, *The Origins and Consequences of Jamaica's Debt Crisis,* 64.

World Bank: Public Sector Reform and Reduction in State Participation

The World Bank focuses on long-term structural adjustment of the economy with particular emphasis on public sector reform, divestment of state enterprises, and the subjection of government functions to market forces. Although Seaga committed himself to these objectives, government expenditure remained fairly high and never fell below 25% of GDP between 1980 and 1985. In addition, Seaga kept the public sector deficit between 13.2% and 19.6% of GDP during the same period, well above the limits set by the IMF and the World Bank. Pressure from these institutions eventually peaked and the government reduced the public sector deficit dramatically to an average 5.5% of GDP between 1986 and 1988. Indeed, public administration as a percentage of GDP fell from 13.5% in 1980 to just 8.5% in 1988.

To facilitate this reduction, the government made significant cutbacks in social expenditure and government employment. Between 1980 and 1989, the government reduced the number of jobs by some 30%. Social expenditure on education and health fell from an average 26% of GDP during the 1970's to less than 20% in the 1980's. Indeed, Jamaica was one of the two countries in Latin America with the largest social expenditure cuts as part of adjustment in the 1980's.

The government divestment programme was similarly less extensive. Goverment rhetoric during the early 1980's actively supported privatisation and divestment. As early as 1983, however, Seaga's team admitted that outright sale of government properties "wasn't on the cards."[17] Although the government identified numerous hotels that it planned to sell, it instead leased the hotels to private hands, and never completed the sales. In agriculture, the government also leased large amounts of land to small farmers but expressed its intention not to transfer ownership to the farmers.

In 1985, as pressure from the IMF and World Bank intensified, the government sold its first major holding, SEPROD Limited, in a J$8 million public share offering, the first such since 1973. In 1986, the government accelerated its privatisation programme and sold shares in the National Commercial Bank (NCB) and in the Caribbean Cement Company (CCC). Importantly, the government retained shares in both companies which reflected Seaga's desire to maintain a controlling interest in these organisations (the government retained 49% ownership in NCB and 28% control in the CCC). Until the 1989 election, Seaga made only one other major divestment. In September 1988, a public offering was made for 15% of the government's 55% share holding in the Telecommunications of Jamaica.

These privatisations occurred largely in response to the 1986 IMF/World Bank/USAID tripartite committee report which had concluded that "[a]lthough the total number of public entities had declined somewhat since the PNP administration, there were still 534 in existence."[18] In response to these criticisms, Seaga privatised a number of service areas including Kingston's garbage collection and support services at three of the countries' major hospitals in the year preceding the election.

To finance the structural adjustment plan, the government relied on three primary sources. First, a substantial increase in taxation. In 1983, Seaga embarked on a comprehensive tax reform which increased taxes and greatly improved tax administration and collection. These efforts resulted in Jamaica's position as one of the highest taxed non-communist country in the region, second only to Guyana. As a result of the increase in taxes and the rationalisation of the tax machinery, government revenues grew substantially between 1982 and 1988 which contributed to a reduction in the overall public sector deficit.

Table 4.5 Jamaica: Financial Indicators as a percentage of GDP (1981-88)

	1981	1982	1983	1984	1985	1986	1987	1988
Current Revenue	28.1	26.9	23.6	27.2	25.2	31.0	29.4	30.3
Current Expenditures	32.1	30.3	31.6	28.6	26.0	26.0	25.7	27.8
Current Savings	-4.0	-3.5	-8.0	-1.4	-0.9	5.0	3.7	2.5
Fixed Investment	7.6	7.3	3.9	3.0	2.5	5.0	4.5	6.1
Public Sector Deficit	-15.9	-14.1	-14.6	-5.4	-3.6	0.7	1.5	-1.6
Domestic Financing	4.0	10.6	9.2	-5.0	0.2	2.5	-2.4	-0.6
External Current Account Deficit	-14.6	-15.7	-9.1	-10.6	-11.9	-3.3	-4.8	-1.3
Debt Service Ratio	29.2	29.3	27.9	28.6	39.8	43.8	47.5	40.2
Domestic Credit	65.1	71.7	80.6	64.1	54.4	56.1	49.5	41.5
Public Sector	44.9	46.4	53.6	41.2	34.2	36.2	27.5	15.9
Private Sector	20.2	25.3	27.0	22.9	20.2	19.9	22.0	25.5
Exchange Rate								
Official	1.8	1.8	1.9	3.9	5.6	5.5	5.5	5.5
Real Effective (1980=100)	94.0	90.7	96.3	137.7	157.0	146.6	148.1	146.5

Source: Economic and Social Progress in Latin America, 120.

Second, the government attempted to increase investment into the island by creating the Jamaica National Investment Promotion (JNIP) Limited designed to eliminate the bureaucratic and legal obstacles to investment. Moreover, Seaga expanded export-oriented free zones to target foreign firms involved in the production of manufactured goods for export to the international market. By providing numerous financial incentives such as 100 percent tax holidays, no import licenses, duty free raw material imports, and easy repatriation of profits, the free zones attracted numerous foreign firms that hoped to capitalise on the large supply of cheap labour. The government also created a Committee on Investment and Employment to work with the U.S. Business Committee on Jamaica in promoting foreign investment.

Between 1980 and 1988, the number of investments fell short of government targets, although total investment in the island increased from 15.9% of GDP to 24.9%. One commentator noted as early as 1982 that "Mr. Seaga's statistics of success look good in terms of proposals, less good in terms of implementation. By March 1982, 46 small US investment projects, worth US$134 million, were being talked about but only 18, worth US$6 million, had reached the production stage."[19] Private sector jobs did grow by 50% between 1980 and 1988, however, largely as a result of the increase in investment.

Table 4.6 Jamaica: External Debt and Debt Service (1975-1988)

	1975	1980	1985	1987	1988
Total External Long/ Medium Debt (US$M)	688	1,867	3,587	4,013	4,002
Debt Service (US$M)					
Accrued	83	341	734	1,037	895
Actual	83	263	503	774	816
Per Capita (US$M)					
Debt	-	875	1,562	1,760	1,699
GNP	-	1,166	759	1,077	1,183
Total Debt Service	-	123	219	330	327
Total Net Transfers (%)					
as % GNP	-	2.8	-7.7	-9.6	-14.5
as % Imports	-	6.8	13.4	-22.7	-33.1
as % Exports	-	4.8	-9.9	-14.3	-22.9

Source: Levitt, The Origins and Consequences of the Debt Crisis, 2.9.

Integral to the structural adjustment programme was a rapid increase in foreign borrowing coupled with extensive debt rescheduling. During the first three years of the Seaga administration, foreign inflows came in from a wide variety of bilateral, multilateral, and private sources, although the bulk of the aid came from the United States (USAID), the IMF, and the World Bank. As a result, Jamaica's total external medium- and long-term debt increased from US$1.8 billion in 1980 to US$4.0 billion in 1988, which placed Jamaica as the most indebted nation in the world per capita (table 4.6).

During the same period, the portion of debt owed to commercial banks fell from 22% to 9%, while debt owed to multilateral agencies grew from 30% to 40% (table 4.7). Because multilateral sources do not allow debt rescheduling, Jamaica's debt service ratio jumped from 29.2% of GDP in 1981-82 to 47.5% in 1987-88 and amounted to 50% of government revenue (table 4.6). This large increase occurred despite the fact that every IMF agreement with the government since 1980 was followed by debt rescheduling renegotiations with Paris Club creditors that eased Jamaica's debt service burden. Repayments became so large that by 1986, Jamaica began to pay more to creditors than it received in disbursements. Since 1986, negative net transfers to official creditors have averaged 12% of GNP (table 4.6).

The World Bank later recognised that Seaga had delayed the implementation of major structural adjustment measures. In a retrospective review of its relationship with the Seaga government published in 1989, the Bank concluded that the large amounts of the external capital flows during the first years of the regime delayed the pressure for structural adjustment.[20] Indeed, Jamaica received so much money from the bank that in 1981 it became the largest per capita recipient of World Bank loans. The report concluded that when adjustment became unavoidable, the pace of adjustment required by the Fund was too drastic and was incompatible with the economic objectives of encouraging the resumption of private investment.

Seaga did make some bold and politically dangerous moves to reform the Jamaican economy, although most of these came under extreme pressure from external agencies. Seaga removed most of the restrictive price controls set up under the previous PNP regime, abolished some of the quantitative restrictions on imports, and reduced public sector employment by over 20,000. In addition, Seaga established export processing in free zones and instituted rebates for exporters to compensate for trade taxes imposed on their inputs. Seaga's actions in this regard led to a modest upturn in output, although problems of low capacity utilisation, import intensity, and high costs remained.

On the other hand, liberalisation remained partial and

precarious. Indeed, "the import structure was riddled with concessions to special interests. Resistance to import liberalisation continued unabated [and] in 1986 some sixty items reverted to import licensing pending studies of comparative advantage. The Jamaica Commodities Trading Corporation (JCTC) continued to monopolise imports of certain staples and to subsidise their prices to consumers [and] management studies of public enterprises often were not followed by action."[21]

State Centralisation and Participation in the Economy
Under the Seaga regime, the state continued to play an integral and active role in the economy. A senior official who worked under the Seaga administration argues that Seaga's development strategy was "basically as state interventionist as the PNP but with less panache." Informally, Seaga centralised administrative control over the structural adjustment agenda by placing almost all decision-making authority in the Office of the Prime Minister. In addition to his Prime Ministerial duties, Seaga also held the positions of Minister of Finance, Minister of Defense, and Minister of Information and Culture. One prominent observer echoed the widespread view that Seaga possessed a "centrist type of management more appropriate to a socialist economy than a market-based one...his management style was that of centralising everything into one small office headed by himself." Carl Stone argues that this authoritarian leadership style served to emasculate the efficiency and discretion of other ministers of government and thus contributed to administrative bottlenecks which hindered economic reform.[22]

Table 4.7 *Total External Debt by Creditor Category (1975-88) (US$million)*

	1970	(%)	1975	(%)	1980	(%)	1988	(%)
Commercial Banks	-	-	409	(22)	393	(11)	392	(9)
Multilateral	81	(12)	545	(29)	1376	(38)	1562	(39)
IMF	16		309		693		464	
World Bank	44		176		435		490	
IDB	21		60		125		506	
Other	-		-		123		102	
Bilateral	137	(20)	467	(25)	1453	(41)	1841	(46)
USAID	25		57		482		464	
CIDA/EDC					52		111	
Total	688		1867		3587		4009	

Source: Levitt, *The Origins and Consequences of Jamaica's Debt Crisis*, 64.

Seaga also disbanded some of the programmes began under Manley. He scrapped the worker participation programme, discontinued community councils and community enterprise organisations, eliminated the Land Lease and other agricultural programmes, and turned over sugar cooperatives to multinational interests on a management contract basis. Despite these changes, the Seaga administration continued direct controls on prices, imports, credit, and rent, maintained numerous agencies and programmes started by Manley, and also expanded the role of the state in several areas of the economy. Seaga retained and renamed various Manley initiatives including the Special Employment Programme (which became the Relief Employment Programme), JAMAL (the literacy campaign), the State Commodity Corporation (the Jamaica Commodity Trading Company), and the National Investment Company Limited (the National Investment Bank of Jamaica).

In addition, the JLP government established a variety of new programmes to address employment, such as Human Employment and Resource Training (HEART) and Solidarity, both intended to increase training and to reduce employment. To promote exports, the government retained several external marketing organisations (EMOs) started by Manley, expanded the activities of two public sector organisations (the Jamaica National Export Corporation and the Jamaica Export Trading Company), and also created an Export Development Fund to provide financing for exporters. In agriculture, the government established the Jamaica Agriculture Development Foundation to finance agricultural projects, created an AGRO-21 program to promote agricultural investment, and started the Springs Plain project—a joint venture with an Israeli group designed to grow non-traditional crops for the export market.

The government also instituted a massive Public Sector Investment Programme designed to support economic infrastructure, invest in the social sectors, and provide direct aid to the productive sectors. Most importantly, the government increased its direct participation in the economy by buying the island's only oil refinery (Esso) and by purchasing the Clarendon Alumina Plant Ltd., a bauxite/alumina firm formerly owned by the Aluminum Company of America (Alcoa).

Seaga's centrism and the expansion of the state contributed to a negative relationship that he shared with the private sector. Stone argues that "both local and foreign capitalists [were] very disillusioned by the gaps between the pro-private sector rhetoric of Seaga and the actual policies and approaches to decision making and economic management."[23] Major private sector organisations became increasingly critical of the government's refusal to consult with them or involve them in significant policy formulation. Indeed, spokesmen in the island's leading business organisations became increasingly hostile to Mr. Seaga's economic policies and leadership style. These organizations included the Manufacturer's Association, the Private Sector organization of Jamaica, the insurance industry, the exporters association, and most other business lobbies except the Chamber of Commerce (which had close JLP affiliations).

In response to this hostility, Seaga became distrustful of the private sector and after 1987, stopped recognising the Private Sector Organisation of Jamaica (PSOJ). Economic controls and widespread bureaucratic obstacles also acted as a disincentive to investment and increased productive activity. While the private sector continued to support the government's stated ideological position, sharp disagreements over strategy, tactics, and power relations reduced initial enthusiasm for the JLP into growing distrust of the government's intentions.

International Circumstances and their Effect on the Jamaican Economy

External shocks adversely affected the Jamaican economy throughout the early 1980's. The first half of the decade witnessed the worst economic recession experienced in North America since the 1930's. This economic downturn caused a sharp drop in the demand for bauxite/alumina in export markets which resulted in a substantial fall in earnings from the industry. Government revenue from the industry fell from US$206 million in 1980 to US$137 million just two years later. The situation was made worse with the sudden departure of two large bauxite/alumina producers, Reynolds and Alpart, in 1984 and 1985, respectively. As a result, exports of bauxite/alumina fell from 54% of export earnings to 25% between 1980-88.

The government also experienced setbacks in traditional agricultural exports, largely as a result in the declining value of the British pound. Sugar production declined by 50,000 tonnes between 1980 and 1982, and banana production by 11,000 tonnes over the same period. Whereas GDP had grown by 1.1% in 1981, no growth was recorded for 1982 or 1983 (table 4.8). The recession in the United

States, combined with high interest rates, also hindered the government's attempt at securing foreign investment despite an aggressive promotional activity to attract investors.

The drop in oil prices provided unexpected economic recovery and an improvement in economic performance during the latter half of the decade (table 4.8). Seaga seized the opportunity created by the fall in oil prices to purchase three-years supply of oil at US$10 per barrel. The price drop created a 46% windfall gain in the cost of fuel imports, equal to 2.5% of GDP. Despite this good fortune, a major hurricane hit the island in September 1988 (Hurricane Gilbert), causing severe damage. The devastating effects of the Hurricane interrupted the economic programme, but the Fund and the Bank responded quickly to the crisis by providing additional emergency financing. This response allowed Jamaica to quickly craft a rehabilitation programme which restored much of the damaged economic infrastructure within a remarkably short period of time.

AN ECONOMIC EVALUATION OF STRUCTURAL ADJUSTMENT

Between 1980-88, Jamaica recovered from the economic decline of the 1970's and achieved an average 2.4% growth rate in GDP (3.1% real GDP) during the latter three years (table 4.8). Over that period, the economy witnessed a reduction in inflation, a decrease in the public sector and current account deficits, a modest increases in employment, and some structural adjustment in the economy—all achieved between 1986-88 under favourable international conditions.

Despite the economic growth, GDP output during the period actually averaged less than output during the 1970's. In the process of economic recovery, Jamaica also became the world's most indebted country per capita. In addition, the country suffered from a worsening trade deficit, a decline in social standards, and an erosion of the nation's productive capacity.

After an average decline of 3.5% in GNP growth between 1972 and 1980, the rapid increase in capital inflows and investment during the first year of Seaga's administration resulted in a 1.1% GDP growth rate for 1981. With the fall in bauxite/alumina production and Seaga's reluctance to implement significant structural adjustment measures, the GDP failed to grow between 1982 and 1983. In 1984, after a dangerous four-year delay of the structural adjustment programme, the government was forced to implement a wide range of serious deflationary measures that included devaluation, tax increases, expenditure cuts, large lay-offs, and monetary restraint, all in compliance with the IMF agreement. As a result, GDP contracted in 1984 by 2.5% and in 1985 by 5.9% (table 4.8). The favourable international environment coupled with Seaga's tight monetary policy contributed to an 0.8% growth in GNP in 1986 and an impressive 5.1% growth in 1987, although Hurricane Gilbert held the growth rate to 1.4% in 1988 (table 4.8).

Table 4.8 Jamaica: Economic Indicators (1979-88)

	Growth of GDP	Fixed Capital Formation/ GDP	Consumption/ GDP	Unemployment Rate	Consumer Price Increase	Net Foreign Reserves US$(million)	Net External Debt US$(million)
1979	-2.9	17.4	82.7	27.8	19.8	-430.3	1451
1980	-6.5	14.5	86.6	27.3	28.2	-532.2	1867
1981	1.1	18.1	89.9	25.9	11.9	-679.1	2293
1982	0	19.9	90.8	27.4	6.5	-522.3	2740
1983	0	20.5	90.6	26.4	11.3	-808.7	3267
1984	-2.5	21.1	83.6	25.5	27.8	-583.8	3262
1985	-5.9	22.3	85.3	25.0	26.0	-664.8	3587
1986	0.8	17.5	79.2	23.7	14.8	-688.8	3576
1987	5.1	21.7	77.0	21.0	6.7	-488.6	4013
1988	1.4	24.9	81.1	18.5	8.3	-345.3	4009

All figures represent percentages unless otherwise indicated.

Source: Levitt, *The Origins and Consequences of Jamaica's Debt Crisis,* 12 and *Economic and Social Survey,* (various issues).

Seaga's tight monetary policy resulted in lower inflation and a decrease in the public sector and current account deficits. Tight controls on public spending (primarily social expenditure), an increase in taxes, and high interest rates helped Seaga to reduce inflation from 29% in 1980 to 8.8% in 1988 and to lower the public sector deficit from 15.9% to 5.4% of GDP over the same period. In addition, the external current account deficit fell from 14.6% of GDP in 1980 to 4.8% in 1988.

Seaga's policies had less of an impact on unemployment, which never fell below 25% between 1980 and 1985. Unemployment remained high because of public sector layoffs and the shutdowns of enterprises unable to cope in the restrictive economic environment. The unemployment rate fell to 18.5% in 1988, although this reduction occurred primarily because the migration rate out of the island escalated from 20% between 1980 and 1985 to 68% between 1986 and 1988 (see table 4.10). Indeed, a *Daily Gleaner* editorial concluded that "any decline in the labour force is attributable mainly to external migration. Coming against the background of shortages of critical skills in various sectors of the Jamaican economy it must be viewed as adverse to the local development effort."[24]

Some structural adjustment of the economy also occurred under Seaga which can be attributed mainly to the growth in tourism and non-traditional exports. Between 1980 and 1988, bauxite/alumina fell from 54% to 25% of total export and service earnings, while tourism increased from 17% to 32%. Non-traditional exports nearly doubled from 8% to 15% during the same period. Tourism's contribution to the total exports and services jumped from US$241 million in 1980 to US$527 million in 1988, representing a significant rise over the 1972-80 period. Non-traditional exports moved from US$115 million to US$246 million over the same period, with most of the increase coming from free zone garment exports, which rose dramatically from a negligible US$7 million in 1980 to a substantial US$103 million in 1987.

Seaga's Economic Miracle: A Re-evaluation

Most of the economic growth that occurred under Seaga is necessarily biased because the statistics center around comparisons with 1980 which was a year characterised by very low levels of output. Although the economy did grow between 1981-88, the country still produced less than it did in earlier years under the PNP. In comparing GDP output in 1987 as a percentage of 1976 output, we see that all sectors—with the exception of tourism, finance, and domestic agriculture—have significantly lower output levels in 1987 compared to 1976 (table 4.9).

Indeed, average national output in the JLP years (1980-88) is below that of the average output in the second PNP term (1976-80) when production was at its lowest in the 1970's. Production levels in 1987 were still below real output in the economy over all the years between 1970 and 1976. Investment levels under Seaga increased by 40% compared to the 1970's although production did not grow much over the same period which suggests inefficient use of capital.[25] Under Seaga, the economy grew but output and capital efficiency was mediocre.

Table 4.9   Gross Domestic Output as a % of 1976 output   (1980-87)

	1976	1980	1987
Total Production	100	91	98
Hotels and Restaurants	100	89	141
Export Agriculture	100	68 ·	63
Domestic Agriculture	100	112	120
Mining	100	131	84
Manufacturing	100	74	86
Construction	100	58	68
Distribution	100	81	93
Finance	100	130	173

Figures represent Gross Domestic Output at Constant Prices.

Source: Stone, *Politics versus Economics,* 79.

Jamaica's trade deficit also fared worse during the 1980's than during the 1970's. With the gradual liberalisation of import controls during the early 1980's, imports rose rapidly from US$883 million in 1979 to US$1124 million just four years later. Importantly, most of the rise in imports came from consumer goods and not manufacturing inputs, which led to a rapid increase in consumption and a worsening trade balance. The devaluation of the dollar in 1983 and again in 1984 reduced imports from US$1124 million in 1983 to US$1065 in 1987 with a low of US$837 million in 1986. Imports surged in 1988 to US$1228 million largely as a result of inputs needed for rebuilding after the Hurricane. Despite this reduction in imports between 1983 and 1987, the trade deficit increased from US$75 million in 1980 to US$395 million in 1988 which reflected the inability of exports to make up for the rapid increase in imports.

The import boom also had a negative impact on local distribution and agricultural production. As consumer and other imports increased during the early 1980's, the purchasing power of the population increased only marginally which created conditions of oversupply. For wholesalers and retailers, sales declined rapidly as consumers tried to consume a much larger basket of goods with the same level of purchasing power. In a country which is 50% dependent upon imports for food, the rapid influx of imported food during the 1980's hurt local agricultural producers. Between 1980 and 1989, Jamaica received over US$200 million in PL480 farm surpluses from the United States, providing food for almost half of Jamaica's population. For specific crops (such as rice), cheap food imports forced down the price of domestic substitutes, causing serious financial damage to local producers and resulting in a long-term decline in agricultural production.

In the social arena, real income and living standards declined significantly over the period under the weight of devaluation, increased taxation, price increases, and strict wage guidelines. As social services declined, income inequality increased. Indeed, the share of labour income accruing to the top 20% of the population jumped from 67% in 1980 to 75% one year later, a trend which continued throughout the 1980's. Between 1980 and 1988, the distributional share of labour (wages/income) in GDP fell from 63% to 57% with a low of 54% in 1985. These figures demonstrate the shift in the economy from labour (and hence productive work) to capital. The rapid expansion of the financial sector, real estate, and other capital-related industries during the 1980's further reflects this trend. In 1989, the World Bank estimated that the top 20% of the population accounted for more than 60% of income.[26]

Table 4.10 Select Social Indicators (1978-88)

	1978	1979	1980	1981	1982	1983	1984	1985	1986	1987	1988
GDP per capita (J$1974)	946	919	867	867	863	860	845	795	801	842	854
Net Migration (000's)	17.8	21.0	24.3	5.9	9.8	4.3	10.5	13.4	20.1	30.9	38.9
Migration Rate	39%	47%	53%	13%	20%	9%	24%	32%	49%	77%	88%
Wage/Salary as % of Private Consumption	82	80	77	74	78	73	69	63	66	68	70
Unemployment %	24.5	27.8	27.3	25.9	27.4	26.4	25.5	25.0	23.7	21.0	18.5
Wage/Salary as % GDP	62	62	61	63	67	62	57	54	54	55	57
% Public Exp. on Education/Health as % Total Government exp.	24	21	19	21	21	19	21	17	18	17	-

Source: Levitt, The Origins and Consequences of the Debt Crisis, 12.

Social expenditure also fell throughout this period although conflicting evidence exists on the effect on social services (table 4.10).

Boyd and Levitt both argue that health and expenditure cuts as part of structural adjustment resulted in a severe deterioration in the provision of quality public health and education services.[26] Behrman *et al.* dispute this claim and argue instead that structural adjustment did not, in and of itself, result in a fall in health and education quality.[28] They provide evidence which suggests that the quality of health and education in Jamaica actually improved during the 1980's in an "apparent paradox." Although the issue remains unresolved, it is clear that budget cuts in association with the falling real incomes made it increasingly more difficult for many Jamaicans to afford and obtain quality education and health care.

*Prime Minister Michael Manley on a visit to Cattaboo, St. Elizabeth
(November 1972)*

Budget Debate (1975)

The new Cabinet, Jamaica Labour Party (December 1983)

Prime Minister Edward Seaga on his way to a joint sitting of Parliament; Opposition Leader Michael Manley addressing joint sitting—Gordon House (October 1983)

Michael Manley with private sector members (March 1989)

Prime Minister Edward Seaga announcing election date in Half-Way-Tree Square (November 1983)

Michael Manley's farewell speech in Parliament (March 1992)

*Passing the baton: Michael Manley and
P.J. Patterson (March 1992)*

PART III

Joshua's Exile, Return and Legacy: Evolution and Change

CHAPTER 5

MANLEY IN OPPOSITION: THE POLITICS OF PERCEPTION

And Joshua made peace with them, and made a league with them,
and the princes of the congregation swore unto them.
—Joshua 9:15

As the PNP reorganised after the 1980 defeat, it attempted to rebuild support and reaffirm its commitment to socialist principles. The lack of party finances gave rise to the the power of business elements who requested that members of the PNP left-wing be removed. This signalled the decline of the ideological left in the party. Although Manley blamed external factors as the primary factor in his defeat, he recognised that he had overestimated the capacity of the Jamaican state to enact a socialist transformation.

In addition, Manley understood that the abandonment of the private sector and his estranged relationship with the United States had hurt him in the 1970's. He therefore made extensive efforts to rebuild these relations by conducting meetings with these groups. By 1986, Manley realised that the socialist label created unneccessary hostility and thus the PNP abandoned it in all public documents and statements. In response to private sector demands, Manley also dropped the PNP platform of nationalisation. In spite of these changes, Manley had not notably altered his belief in the need for significant state intervention up to 1986.

The PNP's victory in the 1986 local government election signalled that Manley was within close reach of regaining national leadership. The international spotlight had returned and Manley needed to prepare a strategy to ensure eventual victory without the negative images associated with his tenure during the 1970's. This pressure—especially from the private sector—forced Manley to move increasingly to the right. He therefore moderated his views on state intervention as the election neared. He recognised that the private sector would not accept his view that the state would play the preeminent role in economic development and prior to the election therefore, he announced his belief in the private sector as the main "engine of growth." In order to strengthen his electoral appeal, he also emphasised the need for a social component to economic austerity, and projected an image of ideological moderation.

Entering the 1989 election, Manley had clearly returned to the populist campaign strategy which he had used in the 1972 election—lacking any ideological substance. In fact the Jamaican people and the international media seemed more intent on learning not what Manley planned to do when he reassumed power, but what Manley did not plan to do (return to the left). This fear, coupled with the ideological vacuum of the election, fueled widespread speculation and uncertainty about what Jamaica's future would be under a new Manley administration. Manley, however, capitalised on the current economic crisis and widespread dissatisfaction of the Jamaican people by emphasising a commitment to social development and welfare. His previous tenure in office had provided him with solid credentials as one who truly cared for the social well-being of the Jamaican people. His impressive image campaign of ideological moderation and his extensive efforts at wooing the private sector absolved him of economic mismanagement charges in the eyes of most Jamaicans. Bolstered by this broad based support and the positive response to his call for greater people participation, Manley won the election in February 1989 in a landslide taking forty-five (45) of sixty (60) seats in the House.

THE AGONY OF DEFEAT (1980-89)

During the first three years of opposition, Manley underwent a brief period of passivity while the party analysed the reasons for defeat. Manley offered his resignation, but this was rejected by the party, and he continued as leader. Eventually the party started a programme of rehabilitation, rejuvenation, and education as it prepared for a possible return to power. During the same period, Manley embarked on a lecture tour of the United States where he codified his thinking on the fate of socialism and the role it would play in the future development of Jamaica.

In 1982, Manley published a book, *Jamaica: Struggle in the Periphery*, in which he examined the events of the 1970's and concluded that various international and local forces conspired to destabilise the government. In the 1983 election which caught the PNP by surprise, Manley's decision not to contest the election created difficulties with large segments of the population that opposed the effective one-party state that emerged as a result of the PNP boycott. This decision further alienated certain segments of the Jamaican populace.

Despite this dissatisfaction among many Jamaicans, public opinion polls began to reflect a significant shift in support away from the JLP and to the PNP. This shift occurred largely because of widespread economic discontentment and the popular belief that the PNP (and Manley in particular) cared more than the JLP for the working class, which formed the bulk of the Jamaican electorate. Bolstered by this show of popular support, the party became more active and, because PNP members were no longer in Parliament, they started People's Forums to facilitate an "extra-parliamentary" opposition.

The party slowly began to formulate a coherent economic policy to provide an alternative to Seaga's structural adjustment. Initially, the economic plan simply reiterated the democratic socialist dogma of the 1970's and condemned Seaga's austerity programme. Recognising the vastly different economic conditions of the 1980's, however, the party began to modify its economic agenda, while retaining social welfare principles.

Manley also initiated a series of meetings with private sector and U.S. officials to convince them of his intention not to alienate them if he were to return to power. In addition, Manley became increasingly internationally-oriented as his participation in the Socialist International increased. After the PNP's victory in the 1986 local government elections, the party intensified its efforts at meeting with strategic groups in society. In the 1989 election campaign, Manley's agenda lacked a substantive ideological basis. In spite of this, Manley's widespread popularity resulted in a PNP victory at the polls in February 1989 when the party won forty-five (45) seats compared to the JLP's fifteen (15).

ANALYSING THE 1980 ELECTION DEFEAT

Divergent theories have emerged to explain the reasons for the PNP's defeat in the 1980 general election. The theorists fall into four broad categories: revolutionary socialists, orthodox socialists, moderates/realists, and conservatives. Each category encompasses a wide range of thought but the underlying principles of each remain fairly constant.

Revolutionary socialists accuse Manley of not really being a socialist. They argue that Manley could not have succeeded because only fundamental changes in Jamaican society (i.e. totalitarianism) can lead to a true socialist revolution. Orthodox socialists accept Manley's socialist credentials but charge that he failed to seize various opportunities (e.g. the Emergency Production Plan) to break dependent ties with the imperialist world and place the state as the dominant force in the economy.

Destabilisation and external factor theorists generally accept the premise that Manley pursued the correct ideological and policy objectives, but argue that these plans were subject to intense and, at time, destabilising opposition from critical interest groups such as the United States, the JLP, and the *Daily Gleaner*. Conservatives posit that democratic socialism could not be implemented in Jamaica at all because it ran counter to the Jamaican psyche which cherishes individual freedom and also because the system was inherently inefficient.

Revolutionary Socialists: The Failure of the Democratic Model

Revolutionary socialists portray the 1972-80 period as a "belated experiment in bourgeois-nationalist populism."[1] They describe Manley as a member of the "nationalising bourgeoisie" who, while progressive, was "nonetheless part and parcel of the repressive oligarchy that has ruled his nation since the Second World War."[2] They argue that the PNP attempted to promote a working class consciousness that was incompatible with the its class composition and evolved ideology. The fundamental problem lies in the two-party parliamentary system which is "the Jamaican elite's primary method of maintaining power."[3] According to them, Manley failed to recognise that revolutions "can never be wrought from above...without the shedding of blood."[4]

In a comparison of socialist experiments in Cuba, Guyana, and Jamaica, Jameson concludes that "it is only when a regime is in almost total control, e.g. after total repression of any opposition as in Chile, that theoretically rational and consistent policy will be undertaken."[5] Even some socialists who don't advocate revolutionary overthrow contend that Manley needed to have been more firm with the opposition. Kaufman writes that although he does not "advocate that the PNP should have responded by imposing a dictatorship...when the opposition decides not to play by the rules of the game then there must be a strong response against that opposition."[6]

Orthodox Socialists: Failure to Capitalise on Opportunity
Orthodox socialists adopt a less repressive approach in explaining Manley's failure during the 1970's. They posit that Manley failed to capitalise on his broad-based class consensus and support by breaking from external capital ties that hindered Jamaica's economic progress. As Levitt argues, "[t]he political mandate and immense popularity of the first Manley government of 1972 could have been converted into a national project to secure the independence of the country through a partial closing of foreign transactions and a lessening of vulnerability to external creditors."[7] Beckford and Witter argue that Manley failed to seize the opportunity provided by the Emergency Production Plan to forge an independent path of development and instead he took the "critical decision to keep Jamaica handcuffed to Imperialism." They add that Manley lacked confidence in "the capacity of the masses of black Jamaican people to assert their productive creativity," a view that "derives from [Manley's] brown Jamaican petit-bourgeois perspective."[8]

Orthodox socialists also believe that Manley did not make the successful transition to socialism. Downie states that "[t]he PNP may have nationalised more of the public sector and provided jobs, but it did not transform the democratic capitalist system in Jamaica into a democratic socialist one."[9] Although orthodox socialists blame Manley for rejecting the Production Plan, they also cite the failure of the left to coalesce organisationally as another major reason why the socialist experiment failed to work.

Destabilisation and External Factor Theorists
External theorists argue that the private sector and various other opposition forces conspired to destabilise the government. Payne concludes that although "a 'smoking gun' was never found...the weight of the evidence makes it likely that the CIA was at work, in league with the JLP, the *Daily Gleaner*, and opposition businessmen and trade unionists to undermine the elected government in Jamaica."[10] In a portion of Manley's *Struggle in the Periphery*, entitled 'Destabilisation Triumphs', Manley theorises that an organised campaign similar to that conducted by the CIA and *El Mercurio* in

Chile occurred in Jamaica during the 1970's.

For Manley, this destabilisation created an environment of fear and security that left Jamaicans feeling helpless and desirous of stability. In the 1980 election, therefore, Manley hypothesises that Jamaicans did not vote *for* the JLP but *against* the PNP: "the 1980 vote sprang largely from a negative impulse. The majority of people were frightened, insecure, confused, unsure of the future, and reaching for safety."[11]

Conservatives: Socialist Incompatibility and Inefficiency

Conservatives argue that Manley failed because the ideology of democratic socialism contradicted certain fundamental and deeply-rooted values held by the Jamaican people. Van Horne suggests that Manley "was never able to dispel doubts of faith about democratic socialism. He drew conceptual distinctions between socialism and communism which most of the populace neither discerned nor grasped. For [poor] Jamaicans [who] went to Church on Saturday or Sunday, complex hypothetical constructs, theoretic arguments and empirical generalisations concerning the organisation of the social order were merely vapors."[12] Jamaica's strong aversion to communism derives largely from the widespread evangelical tradition which pervades Jamaican society and which opposes communism vigorously.

In the last year of the Manley regime, 60% of the Jamaican public strongly endorsed the sentiment that communism was something to be feared in Jamaica and as much as 74% of the electorate endorsed the view that the PNP should disassociate itself from the communist fringe party, the WPJ. One prominent Jamaican business leader stressed this view that Jamaicans "are not inclined to go completely left." In addition, conservatives also believe that socialism represented an inherently inefficient system of resource allocation. The state lacked an adequate profit motive, which only the private sector possessed. The current Prime Minister argues that the 1970's model ran "contrary to the psyche of the Jamaican people who are themselves at heart individual entrepreneurs."[13]

These explanations are all based on particular ideological biases. I will argue, however, that four major factors serve to explain Manley's defeat in 1980: (1) structural deficiencies in Jamaica's political and social structure, (2) rhetorical excesses of the Manley regime, (3) ideological extremism and inconsistency throughout the period, and (4) alienation of the private sector.

Various structural factors prevented the successful application of Manley's reform programmes. These structural features include the tradition of political patronage, the weakness of an ideological tradition, the scarcity of managerial and technical personnel, and the partisan political alignments of the unions. Despite Manley's efforts at ending political patronage, he could not overcome the tradition of resource distribution by political parties in return for rank-and-file support. As a result of this patron-client tradition, Jamaica never acquired an ideological tradition and thus many Jamaicans found it difficult to accept Manley's ideological postulations.

In addition, Jamaica's lack of managerial capacity serves to explain the failure of Manley's many initiatives. Downie argues that "the paucity of good administrative talent, the absence of managerial skills, experience and creativity, as well as the lack of motivation on the part of many bureaucrats, resulted in poor policy formation and program implementation."[14] In addition, Bonnick demonstrates that no major construction project in Jamaica has ever been completed without at least one prolonged strike, and in the 1970's, many projects were simply abandoned.[15] He argues that because the governments of the two political parties depend upon the affiliated unions for financial support, they have both failed to introduce legislation aimed at procuring adequate discipline in industrial relations allowing unions to hamper productivity.

Manley's rhetorical excesses in government served to "antagonize and polarize, rather than mobilize."[16] Indeed, Manley himself contends that his political rhetoric—with terms such as "rapacious capitalists" and the fact that the PNP executive was called the "politburo"—provided enemies of the government a "ready means of turning uncertainty into panic."[17] As the economy worsened, Manley often used his persuasive oratory to reassure the Jamaican people and convince them that things would improve. But Kaufman correctly argues that "there are limits to the power of words...[which] Manley did not seem to recognize...He kept looking for the right things to say to turn the nation around."[18]

Stone writes that the confidence which surrounded Manley during the early 1970's turned to "doubts, disillusionment, hostility and a sense of betrayal as the dream of social deliverance that he projected in his many speeches was matched against the reality of the nightmare of hardships being experienced by the workers and peasants."[19] Essentially, Manley created high expectations among the Jamaican people but failed to deliver on these aspirations. If he had promised less and been more realistic about Jamaica's economic situation, he may have generated more support near the end of his term.

Manley's ideological extremism and dogmatism alienated a large part of the Jamaican population. Payne argues that the 1974 democratic socialist declaration proved counterproductive because it "further perturbed the US government and effectively gave official approval to the activities of the relatively small left-wing element in Jamaican politics both inside the PNP and outside the WPJ."[20] Indeed, Manley recognised that the WPJ's close relationship with the PNP "did us real harm because it seemed to confirm the years of propaganda asserting that the PNP had 'gone communist'."[21]

Manley's excessive concern for ideology served to over-politicise his programme and made his policies appear more radical and threatening to established interests than they actually were. Indeed, Manley admits in retrospect that his programmes were not that radical, but that the extreme ideological statements that accompanied them were "enough to play a part in a process that brought Jamaica to the verge of civil war."[22]

Manley's ideological shifts and internal PNP factionalisation both projected an image of uncertainty and confusion within the government. In the 1980 elections, Manley appealed to all class groups, but failed to gain majority support from any. In the words of a senior PNP official, Manley tried to "be all things to all people." Manley supported a variety of contradictory political and ideological approaches during the 1970's and failed to enunciate a consistent and unambiguous development path. More specifically, he lacked a clear and realistic strategy for dealing with the economy or with the IMF. Payne concludes that Manley "got caught in that no-man's land between rhetoric and reality in which so many populist politicians all over the world have found themselves. His failure teaches the need for consistency of purpose in the politics of development."[23]

As a result of the ideological extremes, Manley alienated the private sector, which serves as a primary cause of the defeat. With an exodus of support from the capitalist class, Jamaica's productive and entrepreneurial capacity quickly declined, which caused further economic erosion. Kaufman contends that "in the end [Manley] was defeated because social democracy—particularly one that employed leftist rhetoric—did not adequately express the oligarchy's interests."[24]   Indeed, Manley agrees that "the real and abiding cause of the problem was to be found in what we were doing to...shift the centre of power away from the wealthy apex towards the democratic base."[25] Manley concluded from his experiences that an antagonistic relationship between the state and the private sector was inimical to economic growth within a pluralistic framework.

Manley's Analysis

In the years immediately following the defeat, it became increasingly clear that Manley fell squarely in the destablisation/external factors camp. Although Manley felt that the parliamentary system had numerous failings, he nonetheless remained deeply committed to it and therefore rejected the revolutionary socialist explanations of the 1970's. He also rejected the conservative explanation that the Jamaican people did not want socialism because of the countervailing fact that the PNP had won the 1976 election in a landslide victory with an overtly socialist platform (in spite of increasing economic crisis). The overwhelming rejection of the non-IMF path by the Jamaican people in the 1980 election convinced him that orthodox socialist explanations were inadequate.

In these early years, Manley resolved that the ideology of socialism had not failed, but that various structural, external, and methodological factors had hindered the effective implementation of the democratic socialist society. He concluded: "[t]hat we lost an election eventually under the banner of [socialism] is not a reflection upon the ideology but upon us who were its exponents, and upon the circumstances in which and the methods by which we tried to apply it. That it remains the best hope for a country like ours, even placed as we are geographically, remains our firm conviction."[26]

REHABILITATION, REORGANISATION, AND REBUILDING FOR THE FUTURE (1980-83)

Before the PNP defeat in 1980, there were various indications that Manley had recognised the idealism of his belief that moral suasion was sufficient to create a democratic socialist society. Manley seemed unclear, however, as to whether he understood or was prepared to accept the alternative. In an interview that he gave a year before his defeat, Manley reflected on his efforts at changing the international system through the NIEO and Non-Aligned Movement. He concluded:

> I am one of these people who for years have had a tremendous sort of idealistic optimism that somehow one would make it work by sheer sincerity and reasonable argument; that something would yield in the system; some perception of the common humanity and interdependence would begin to make some difference. But nothing seems to work. [A conference of various international leaders held at] Runaway Bay was my last shot. You are talking to me at a time when I am going through an enormous reappraisal in my own mind. I cannot say that I have thought through the alternatives. Where are we going to go? I don't know yet. This interview could not have come at a worse time. Six months ago you would have found me much clearer in my thinking.[27]

A year and a half later, Manley lost the election. Manley's defeat made him realise the full extent of the tremendous power wielded by the United States and the capitalist system. Initially, this realisation would lead to great hostility and resentment. But Manley would eventually come to realise that he could channel that power and energy and use it to his own advantage.

Internal Re-Analysis and Political Education

After the 1980 defeat, the PNP formed an "appraisal" committee to analyse the major causes of the loss. The appraisal committee engaged in intense debate as the various ideological factions attempted to interpret the reasons for defeat. The PNP Youth Organization and the PNP Women's Movement also conducted in-depth analyses on the reasons behind the electoral defeat. The appraisal committee eventually listed six major reasons to explain the defeat—the economic situation; crime, violence and the role of the security forces; the communist scare; public perception of the PNP and its leadership; disunity within the PNP; and party leadership, MP's, workers and canvassers out of touch with the people—and added that it was meaningless to try and rank them in importance.

Although another party committee formally recognised three tendencies in the party—left, right, and moderate—the party did not fault the basic socialist path in anyway. Instead, the party concentrated on externalities such as crime and violence, or negative perceptions of the party. In mid-1982, Manley remarked that "[t]he most important thing that has happened in our movement is that it has reconfirmed the conviction that what we were trying to do is basically right. The party spent the whole of the first year in intensive introspection at all the levels of our democratic process and came up with that unanimous view."[28]

To address the demoralisation and lack of unity within the party, the PNP embarked on a major education campaign, despite protests from the party right which opposed further ideological indoctrination in democratic socialism. The education programme required all PNP officers, candidates for office, and over 1000 constituency level leaders to attend political education sessions aimed at providing a thorough education in party principles, ideology, development policy, and political strategy. Manley delivered the educational sessions to the National Executive Council (NEC) which were then continued down the party hierarchy until they reached the rank-and-file of the party in the constituencies. Over the next two years, the party established two party schools to facilitate and expand the education programme. The PNP union-affiliate (the NWU) also participated in the educational programme, started its own trade union education programmë, and resurrected the paper, *Rising Sun*, which it co-published with the party.

The Decline of the Left and the Political Reawakening
Although the party left had traditionally taken responsibility for the political education programme, this group began to decline within the party during this period. In early 1981, Manley announced an end to all formal and informal ties with the WPJ because he felt that the relationship had contributed to his defeat in the election. Significantly, 71% of the electorate supported the PNP move while only 47% thought the decision to break with the WPJ was genuine compared to 37% who did not agree. In addition, a major figure of the left, D.K. Duncan, resigned from his post as general secretary in January 1983. According to Duncan, Manley asked him to resign because business interests made it clear that they would not support the party financially with Duncan as General Secretary—a view substantiated by other senior PNP officials.

This incident signified a crucial fact which would affect many later decisions of the party: the dismal state of party finances. Up until 1972 the PNP had relied on its allies among the business class for finances; between 1972 and 1980, it was able to utilise resources of the state; but after 1980 it depended almost entirely on the small amount of money which could be provided by the NWU affiliate. Thus business interests began to play a greater role in the affairs of the party which they would continue to do throughout the 1980's.

In opposition, Manley and the other PNP members of parliament initially played a dormant role in the House where they only had nine (9) members (in addition to the eight (8) members of the senate). In an interview conducted in 1982, Manley explained that "we as an opposition have deliberately done everything as quietly as possible, giving the country every chance to try to catch its breath and recover."[29] One month after his defeat, Manley offered his resignation as head of the party, an offer which was soundly rejected by the National Executive Council in a vote of 129 to zero with 3 abstentions. According to his close associates, Manley took his defeat in the election very personally as if the Jamaican people had rejected him and not the party. He used writing as a catharsis, and after finishing his book *Jamaica: Struggle in the Periphery* in late 1981, Manley became more active both inside and outside of the Parliament.

In February 1982, Manley led a NWU bargaining team in a bauxite dispute and continued to participate actively in various labour negotiations. In June, Manley resurrected his old "Root of the Matter" column in *Rising Sun* in which he launched a series of attacks against the JLP government. Manley also began to turn his attentions to the international arena where he started a lecture tour at universities in the United States and elsewhere. Importantly, in April 1983, Manley was chosen as chairman of the Socialist International (SI) Permanent Economic Planning and Review Committee which had a mandate for formulating policies for relations between the North and South. These activities—of writing a newspaper column, lecturing to academics, representing workers against employers, and working on the SI economic planning committee—provided Manley with the valuable opportunity to reflect on the 1970's period and to examine errors that he had made.

Recommitment to Socialism and the 1983 election
The effect of Manley's reflections quickly became apparent. In his address to the 1981 PNP party conference, Manley reaffirmed his

faith in the democratic socialist path but announced that in the future his priority would be economic, not social, policy. In this speech, he tacitly admitted the mistakes of his previous government with regard to the economy and made clear his intention to rectify that fault in the future. Over the next few years, he repeatedly declared that the PNP would not try to fool people that things would be easy; sacrifices would be necessary, and those who were not willing to work hard and sacrifice for Jamaica's development should not support the PNP. Other incidences reflected moderation in Manley's views. When Reagan and Seaga announced the Caribbean Basin Initiative (CBI), for example, Manley expressed his "strong approv[al]" of the one-way free trade idea, but expressed his opposition to the military component of the plan and CBI's low regional impact.[30]

While Manley reflected on the past, he failed to develop a coherent and clear agenda for the future and still remained committed to the failed socialist model. In 1983, the PNP declared its belief that the "state will own and control the commanding heights of the economy."[31] Manley clearly had no cohesive alternative to Seaga's economic strategy. In a 1983 broadcast to the nation, Manley outlined the faults of the Seaga administration, concluding that the "dependent capitalist model cannot work" and announced that the PNP alternative consisted of "self-reliance, sacrifice, discipline, and cooperation among Third World Countries."[32] The party's capture of the lead in the opinion polls in October 1982 took the party by surprise and, recognising his lack of an effective election manifesto, Manley decided to reconstitute the economic commission (first established after the break with the IMF in 1980) and charge it with the task of developing a comprehensive economic development plan.

In November 1983, Seaga announced a general election for December, which caught the PNP by surprise even though the party had held its first mass meetings since 1980 only a few months earlier in May and June. Manley felt that Seaga had broken his earlier promise not to hold elections before a revision of the voters' list. Although Manley felt somewhat prepared to contest the election, he decided that he could not do so in principle, and thus two days after Seaga's announcement, The PNP National Executive Council voted 128-14 not to participate in the so-called "bogus election."

This decision not to contest the election served to alienate certain members of society who felt that the PNP had failed to live up to its responsibility in the established two-party parliamentary tradition. Manley received a particularly harsh response from the popular Governor-General which strained the relationship between the two men. The negative response to the PNP decision paled in comparison, however, to the response of the Jamaican public to the JLP. For example, just a few months after the election, 70% of people polled wanted new elections. Numerous polls conducted in the period following the election showed a rapid decline in JLP support.

REACTION, MODERATION, AND CONSOLIDATION (1983-86)

In a broadcast to the nation delivered a month before the 1983 election, Manley described the PNP as a "model opposition of restraint, moderation and good sense during the last three years."[33] In the same speech, however, he issued a "solemn warning" to the JLP not to mistake the PNP's restraint for weakness. Up to the time of the election, Payne decribes the PNP as "a rather sluggish opposition party until galvanised by Seaga's deceitfulness" and he adds that the party entered 1984 with substantially more vigour and indeed in an angry mood.[34]

Between the general election of 1983 and the local government election of 1986, the PNP formulated an economic development strategy, increased its efforts at meeting with the private sector and U.S. officials, and became more vigilant in its opposition to Seaga. Manley became more involved on the international scene and intensified his efforts in promoting the NIEO. Throughout all this, the party still remained committed to its principles of democratic socialism although it moderated its principles based on economic reality.

Criticising Seaga and Recommitting to Socialist Strategy
In a 1984 broadcast to the nation, Manley outlined what he viewed as the several major weaknesses of the Seaga administration.[35] First, he attacked the policies of divestment and deregulation, arguing that they had "a gravely adverse effect on the Jamaican economy." In addition, he charged that the Seaga regime failed to have discussions with the interested sectors of the society and Manley promised to provide leadership that would "consult and involve the various sectors." Moreover, Manley accused the JLP of lacking a cohesive ideology or a sense of priorities. He charged that

the JLP implemented "hodge-podge, piece-meal, half-baked measures which are enunciated from day to day [that] surely make the Seaga regime the greatest bunglers of all time." If his party were returned to power, Manley announced its intention to "maintain a consistent course that people can understand."

In another broadcast, Manley expanded upon his earlier generalities of self-reliance and discipline by presenting specific economic recommendations.[36] These recommendations reflected his basic commitment to state intervention and included the subsidisation of the transport sector, an establishment of a monitoring system for high prices, and increased restrictions on imports.

In the same year, the PNP economic commission finally published a development strategy.[37] The document claimed that the JLP policies of devaluation, deregulation, divestment, and debt were the prescription for "economic suicide and economic dependence." Citing the failure of the Seaga government to communicate with key sectors in society, the document called for the establishment of a National Planning Council to consist of political directorate representatives, the official technocrats, the business sector (large and small), farmers, and trade unions. In economic policy, the PNP announced its intention to stop the foreign exchange auction and implement a fixed exchange rate. The decision whether or not to continue an IMF agreement would depend on the IMF's conditions and the availability of foreign exchange.

The document also reiterated the philosophy of democratic socialism based on three fundamental premises: democracy, development, and social justice. It emphasised that if the PNP returned to power, the state might find it necessary to own certain sectors where the national interest demanded it. It also indicated the need for regulation on foreign investors, and announced plans to re-implement co-operatives and community enterprise organisations. Despite this basic commitment to a democratic socialist path, the document also reported that PNP efforts at dialogue with the US government had resulted in a "clear understanding and mutual respect" between the two parties which made the PNP confident of continued U.S. financial support on resuming office.

Rethinking the Democratic Socialist Model
Increasingly, Manley's speeches began to reflect the necessity for

certain changes within the democratic model to reflect economic reality. In a speech to one of the PNP party schools, Manley emphasised the need for "realism and dedication" to maintain a true course of democratic socialism "no matter what tactical adjustments we need to make."[38] He admitted that understanding the pace of political change was essential, noting that "as a political leader one has to try to learn to understand the environment [and to] learn to understand what may be the pace at which things are possible."

A few months before that speech, the PNP shadow minister for finance (Seymour Mullings) had announced the party programme in an update of the PNP development strategy.[39] In the announcement, Mullings warned against magical solutions to deeply-rooted socio-economic problems and stated that the PNP had no intention of buying cheap popularity by offering to fund expensive and wasteful programmes: "anyone who is looking to us for instant relief and prosperity, please look elsewhere." He highlighted several areas of economic management where the PNP intended to make major changes if it regained power.

The PNP intended to protect local industries through import restrictions, impose a credit policy with lower interest rates, establish a fixed exchange rate, prioritise the allocation of foreign exchange, increase food subsidisation, implement a national nutrition programme, and revitalise the National Housing Trust to provide more houses. Although the programme did not mention nationalisation of the commanding heights, the PNP demonstrated that it had not lost faith in the interventionist capacity of the state.

Five months after Mullings' announcement, the party issued its official *Strategy for Development to lead Jamaica into the 21st Century* in a 16-page supplement in the *Daily Gleaner*. The supplement emphasised many of the same things in earlier documents, but also included statements about foreign policy and trade.

It outlined five priorities: (1) stimulation of production, especially for export; (2) increased earnings and conservation of foreign exchange; (3) reduction of unemployment, particularly among the youth; (4) establishment of a national nutritional programme to provide minimum levels of nutrition for the entire population; (5) restoration of education and health services. The supplement restated the party's opposition to deregulation and outlined the controls it planned to implement—fixed foreign exchange, import licensing, and a pricing commission to protect consumers. Although it did not declare that it would reverse divestment, it reserved the right to "review" divestment agreements made by the JLP.

Significantly, the new strategy dropped the democratic socialist label although it emphasised that economic restoration had to be linked to social transformation toward a more equitable and cooperative society. It also highlighted the commitment to community enterprise organisations and community councils at the local level to mobilise local skills and resources. Importantly, unlike previous documents and speeches, the PNP announced its attention to abide by an IMF agreement but only so far as the agreement coincided with the government's development objectives.

As these documents reflected, the PNP hoped to build a broad consensus among social groups. Toward that end, the party intensified its efforts at meeting with various target groups, especially those with whom the PNP had shared a poor relationship in the past, especially the private sector. As early as 1982, Manley explained that "the most important thing we are concerned about is how to get our private sector to understand that the propaganda that we want to destroy them just isn't true. We [are saying] to our private sector: 'the fact that we are working for social justice, trying to set up a mixed economy and dealing with the whole problem of an egalitarian economy does not mean that you won't have a completely honorable and dynamic place in it. We want you to grow and expand and play your part and pull everything along.'"[40] In addition to a series of meetings with the Private Sector Organisation of Jamaica (PSOJ), a leading business organisation, the PNP also established good relations with U.S. policy-making circles at the US embassy in Kingston, the State Department, members of Congress and both the Democratic and Republican parties.

These meetings had a major effect on the PNP. For instance, one PSOJ official relates that when the meetings began with the PSOJ, the PNP expressed its opposition to the PSOJ slogan "Free Enterprise...and watch Jamaica grow," although within a few years, the PNP had dropped its objections. Manley played a major role in these initiatives aimed at reassuring the private sector and other groups that while the party had a social-oriented agenda, it had no intentions of alienating key sectors.

Moderation in Opposition and the Rise of Private Sector Influence

As an opposition party, the PNP became increasingly active during this period. In order to portray an image of moderation, Manley urged the members of his party in 1983 to "refrain from inciting the populace to stage street demonstrations."[41] Despite Manley's admonitions, the PNP and Manley himself adopted a restrained yet highly critical posture as the economy worsened under the Seaga regime. In the January 1985 riots, the PNP was careful not to issue any specific instructions to its members and activists, but it nevertheless gave approval for the organisation of "spontaneous" demonstrations, in which many PNP members took part. During the protests, Manley made calls for Seaga to resign, but reminded "the people of Jamaica to ensure that any demonstration of its anger is conducted in accordance with the laws and that there is due respect for the lives and property of all citizens."[42] Throughout the demonstrations, the PNP leadership maintained a low profile and none of its major figures appeared at any of the demonstrations. Indeed, the head of the communist Worker's Party of Jamaica later argued that Manley failed to "capitalize on these opportunities" provided by the popular uprisings against the government.[43]

In October, Manley addressed a meeting of eighty-thousand demonstrators and called for an end to the foreign exchange auction. The next day, he led a march on the Bank of Jamaica to protest the auction system. To reassure the private sector, much of which was hurt by Seaga's policies, he later held an informal meeting at the luxurious Pegasus hotel. In early 1986, Manley addressed a "Save the People" Rally and all-night vigil where he decried government policies toward students, teachers, doctors, and nurses. The next day, he led a march on Jamaica House, the Prime Minister's Office, to present a petition bearing ninety-two thousand signatures on how the J$450 million oil windfall should be spent. Manley left the rally, but his supporters stayed behind and were involved in a violent incident later described as a "reign of terror" by noted newspaper columnist and author Carl Stone.

Manley's aversion for militant action in opposition reflected the general downturn in extreme radicalism among working class Jamaicans. The Jamaican people have a historical proclivity for social unrest in times of economic hardship. During the 1980's, this mood began to wane. All previous disturbances had occurred because Jamaican's felt disenfranchised—that they lacked the opportunity to participate actively in political discussion. Manley's election in 1972 heralded a new era in which previously neglected social groups became the primary focus of political attention. With this access to political leadership and power, the Jamaican people had finally achieved the ultimate goal for which they had protested for centuries. Under Seaga, the private sector reasserted its dominance but the working class could not generate enough support among themselves to rise up against the austere economic conditions. Indeed, between 1980 and 1986, labour strikes and other reactive actions against business dominance began to decline (table 5.1).

Table 5.1   Indicators of Decline in Working Class Militancy (1982-86)

	1982	1983	1984	1985	1986
Work Stoppages	142	91	63	83	40
Industrial Polls	80	70	47	36	22

Source: Munroe, *Jamaican Politics*, 1990.

Manley also ensured that his party engaged in rigorous and regular internal debate and discussion. After the 1983 election, the party had established a monthly "People's Forum" in which senior members of the party would present papers on ideological issues relating to specific subjects they had previously been designated to work on. Executive members of the PNP participated in these and numerous other internal party meetings, in addition to the regular briefings with various private sector groups, which most PNP spokesmen were required to attend. The private sector meetings up to 1986 led to one major modification in the PNP political agenda relating to the policy on nationalisation.

Business leaders required from Manley that he abandon his belief in nationalisation of the commanding heights and instead adopt an agenda where businessmen would not feel threatened with extensive government interference. Manley made clear in a June 1986 People's Forum that the PNP had "no programmes of nationalisation" although he announced that in cases where "privatisation has failed, we may be obliged to organise activity under our new form of ownership" maintaining "full respect for the law and constitution as it relates to private rights and property."[44]

The Call for Reform: Manley Internationally and Domestically

During this period, Manley intensified his activities in the international arena where he became increasingly critical of inequalities between nations and became more vocal in his support for the NIEO. In 1985, the Socialist International (SI) Permanent Economic and Planning Review Committee, of which Manley served as chairman, published its findings in a book entitled *Global Challenge: From Crisis to Cooperation: Breaking the North-South Stalemate.* In addition, between 1984 and 1985, Manley delivered a lecture series at Columbia University later published as a book, *The Poverty of Nations: Reflections on Underdevelopment and the World Economy.* In the book, Manley provides a historical overview of capitalist development, calls for increased "South/South cooperation" and a "reform of multilateral institutions." He concludes that "the 'magic' of a pure free market system led to disastrous results" in Jamaica during the 1980's.[45]

In 1986, Manley wrote another book, *Up the Down Escalator: Development and the International Economy: The Case of Jamaica,* which was published a year later. The book's chapters, with titles such as "Confronting the Transnationals," "World in Crisis," "Structural Dependence," and "South/South Cooperation" reflect his NIEO agenda. Manley also traveled to Pakistan in 1986 where he delivered the second Manzur Qadir Lecture in which he renewed his call for a North-South alliance based in equity to replace past and present patterns of dominance.

Despite his retention of a democratic socialist platform, increased militancy in opposition, and strident calls for international economic reform, Manley continued to portray an image of moderation. In a speech before a local Chamber of Commerce and Industry, Manley abandoned the fiery rhetoric of the 1970's as he announced that there existed no magic solution to the country's problems and admitted the mistakes he had made earlier in government. Noted columnist Carl Stone described Manley's new posture as "statesmanlike" for its "rare display of political honesty."

In 1985, D.K. Duncan gave an interview to the *Daily Gleaner* in which he labeled the PNP as the mirror image of the JLP because certain elements in the party had pressured Manley to change.[46] Duncan described the party as a "Social Democratic Party capable of mild reforms which definitely cannot meet the aspirations of the people." Although Duncan was later censured by the party for his comments, incidences such as this interview combined with Manley's less radical posture came together to give the impression that the PNP had abandoned its democratic socialist ways.

Yet, the perception that Manley had deserted democratic socialism reflected more on his image campaign and not any substantive ideological change. Indeed, Manley described his alleged drift to the right as a "cliché of analysis. Where the policies of the party are concerned, there is no change. If we are less strident, that's no bad thing: one hopes to God that we've learned something about diplomacy and methodology. Some of the left has become less active...but the difference in the party is more of style than substance."[47] In all the party conferences between 1980 and 1986, the party reaffirmed its firm commitment to democratic socialism. At the 1985 party conference, Manley spoke under a banner which declared: "We are against Capitalism but we are not Communist. We do not quarrel with any country which chooses to live under Capitalism or Communism. That is their business. We prefer to build Democratic Socialism here in Jamaica."

By the time of the local government election in 1986, little had changed in Manley's core beliefs apart from his view on nationalisation. The local government election provided the PNP and the people of Jamaica with a referendum on Seaga's policies. Indeed, the election was run largely on national issues. In a broadcast to the nation a week before the election, Manley described the JLP as the "most insensitive, the most callous and the most uncaring in our history" which had made serious "errors of judgement," such as deregulation of the economy "which has to be the craziest thing that anybody has ever done in the management of the Jamaican economy."[48] In the speech, he re-emphasised that "the philosophy of self-reliance is the basis upon which we shall construct our economic policies" and that he intended to promote export and tourism when in power.

Although the JLP spent over J$50 million on the election campaign—ten times that spent by the financially strapped PNP—and countless more in pre-election government spending, the PNP defeated the JLP and won majority divisions in a nearly all of the parishes.[49] The results were significant because they indicated that in the general election which had to be held in less than three years, the PNP was almost certain to emerge victorious. Headley writes of the 1986 local government election:

The JLP initially pitched [the 1986 local government] elections as nothing more than the usual run-of the mill petty contest. But Manley and his supporters quickly raised the stakes: in their view, the elections should be turned into a referendum on the JLP's leadership. When it became clear to the JLP that it stood to take a licking, it resorted to the old red-baiting tactic. The image of Manley and Castro embracing in slow-motion TV spots, plus 'the use of the word 'freedom' associated with the governing party were supposed to evoke resonances of 1980, when the JLP swept to power on a tidal wave of anti-Cuba, anti-communist sentiment.' The voters, however, disregarded the strong anti-Communist propaganda and voted overwhelmingly against Seaga.[50]

Preparing for Victory (1986-89)

The 1986 local government election victory sent the PNP into an active campaign plan to resume leadership. The primary motivation during this period was to pacify all those groups which had doubts about Manley's return. Manley recognised this fact and attempted to reassure the Jamaican people that his intentions were genuine and that he had learned from the mistakes of the past. In a broadcast to the nation a week after the election, Manley admitted that the "PNP victory is a signal for some people to start reaching for the panic button."[51] To reassure these people, he declared that "we have no hidden agenda in our foreign and domestic policies...Our policy is straightforward...It is based upon full respect for people, for their lives [and] for their property." In addition, he stressed his respect for the private sector and the amicable discussions that the party was having with the PSOJ, and he stated that he respected and welcomed foreign investment, although he expected foreign investors to show a similar respect for Jamaica.

Pandering to the Ideological Right

In a poll of the Jamaican people conducted after the local government election to determine what advice they would give Manley if he returned to power, most people supported an increase and extension of the private sector role in national policy-making and further reductions in taxes. The main message of the Jamaican people was that the PNP should pursue a "mix of pragmatic economic policies of the sort carried out by the JLP combined with a strong dose of populist social policies."[52] The PNP realised that if it maintained a low-key style, reassured key groups, and emphasised its social programme, it would inherit power without much difficulty.

Manley therefore expanded his meetings with the private sector to include numerous other groups in society. The PNP also continued its policy not to use the democratic socialist label in public. Between 1986 and 1989, the party dropped the use of the statement in its public statements and began to criticise the JLP mainly on policy failures and on policy results rather than on ideology. In the 1986 local government elections, D.K. Duncan's name appeared on a constituency list as a campaign organiser for the PNP. Manley requested that Duncan's name be removed from the list because he had promised the private sector that Duncan would not be an officer of record in the party.[53] In an interview a year later, Manley informed the Jamaican people that Duncan held no post in the party and would have none in any future PNP government.[54]

Indeed, all of the leading leftists (Duncan, Small, Spaulding, and Bertram) had left the hierarchy of the party (for a variety of reasons, not all political) while moderate and right wing party members (Coore, McNeil, Pringle) had returned. In 1988, when Hugh Small rejoined the party as a candidate, Manley went to great lengths to reassure members of the private sector that Small had shed his leftist spots and would not pose an obstacle to private sector development in a future PNP government. To demonstrate his commitment to the private sector, Manley appointed the former President of the Jamaica Exporters' Association (JEA), to the PNP shadow cabinet as spokesman for commerce and industry. Manley even met with the Governor-General to mend their relationship in preparation for the future.

Manley also concentrated on improving his image in the international arena so his return to power would be a smooth one. Manley continued to meet with the State Department and other US government officials. In early 1987, Manley met with the conservative Heritage Foundation in Washington D.C. to develop strategies for Jamaica's small-business development. In addition, Manley was portrayed favourably in both the *New York Times* and the *Washington Post* in articles entitled "From Fiery Man of Jamaica Politics, a Mea Culpa," and "Manley Revamps his Image in Jamaica," respectively.

Moreover, although he remained committed to South/South

cooperation, he began to moderate his view on the IMF and multilateral institutions. In an article for a regional newspaper, Manley commended the IMF for its "big steps forward" in the organisation's agreement with Mexico.[55] Manley slowly began to realise that Jamaica's fortunes were inextricably linked to the international system and that independence from that system seemed improbable: "it becomes more and more apparent that any strategy of economic development, social distribution and popular empowerment is bound up on the nature of the world economy and the location of developing countries within it...the extent and nature of internal change possible is increasingly determined by the evolution of the global economy toward interdependence."[56] In an interview in 1987, Manley announced that the PNP would negotiate with the IMF in the future.[57]

The impact of Manley's meeting with the private sector was reflected in a series of policy documents published in 1988 which replaced *Strategies for Development* and other previous policy statements. In the new policy series, the earlier claims that the primary philosophy of PNP was self-reliance had changed so that the new philosophies were threefold: growth, equity, and self-reliance. Contrary to earlier statements, the PNP indicated that there would be no return to full-scale licensing of imports, although it did announce its intention to restrict non-essential imports.

The 1988 document also outlined the importance of subjecting the exchange rate to review based on various factors including "competitiveness and general market conditions." Notably, the document outlined the need for exchange control liberalisation, a view which mirrored that of the PSOJ exactly. As in earlier statements, the document stated that the decision whether to have an IMF agreement depended on the circumstances and practical options. The PNP promised to enact a foreign exchange code to protect foreign investors and inspire confidence in the government.

In addition, the document stated that the PNP was not opposed to divestment but would only use the policy when efficiency would clearly result and only in the national interest. The PNP remained committed to the development of community councils and community enterprise organisations, and to an increased emphasis on health, education, nutrition, housing, and other social services. The party never wavered from its commitment to people participation with the establishment of a national planning council and various other advisory bodies which would incorporate diverse sectors of society.

Although the document expressed its commitment to private sector development, it made no precise declaration as to the exact role of the private sector in the economy. In essence, the 1988 series of documents indicated the party's overtures and compromises with the private sector but still retained the party's basic socialist principles and it's core belief in the power of state interventionist policies.

Formally Burying State Centrism and the Embrace of Populism

Within one year, much of this had changed. While the private sector felt that the PNP had come a long way and was committed to facilitating private sector development, it also recognised that the party had failed to make this clear in its documents. In the 1989 election manifesto, which was essentially a condensed version of the earlier series, a few small but significant changes had been made. The previous document had cited "growth, equity, and self-reliance" as the main objectives, while the election manifesto outlined its basic objectives as (1) to achieve real growth of the economy on a self-sustaining basis; (2) to shift the main source of capital accumulation from borrowing to investment; (3) to provide opportunities for Jamaican migrant communities abroad to invest in Jamaica; (4) to restore education, health, housing, and public transport to the fore of society; (5) to develop more trading and economic relations with CARICOM and other Latin American countries and (6) to promote people participation in the economy through community councils.

In addition, the party made clear the "central role of the private sector in economic activities." The traditional proviso of whether or not to negotiate with the IMF based on circumstances had been removed—the PNP would definitely work with the Fund. Although community councils were emphasised, no mention was made of community enterprise organisations, which posed a threat to certain economic and business interests. This document reflected the formalisation of the PNP shift to the right which had occurred in the previous year.

Yet, the new document still retained a populist and socially-oriented nature although no mention was made of socialism in any form. The manifesto aimed to provide "leadership that will unite the people in a common effort, inspire them with some larger vision, and prepare them for shared responsibility for their own future well-being." In addition, it stressed the central theme of "people participation at all levels in the planning and implementation process."

In the 1989 election, the PNP offered a purely populist agenda aimed at pleasing all class groups: "our vision of the future is a crusade in which we invite all to participate, with the full knowledge that all can reap their just reward." Business leaders knew that the PNP would listen to them and allow them to lead the development of the country, while the rest of the nation understood that the PNP would implement policies with the "over-riding need to relieve the suffering through which the majority had passed over the last eight years." The PNP agenda differed from that of the JLP primarily in its emphasis and methodology and not in its substance, despite the PNP protestations to the contrary.

The 1989 Election: The PNP Pursuit of Power without a Plan

The election campaign was marked by a lack of ideological debate. In large part, the dearth of issues was as result of the short election period which consisted of only seventeen days between nomination day and election day. In addition, the PNP refused to participate in Seaga's numerous calls for a debate. The PNP, which had been out of parliament for nearly six years, refused to participate in a debate unless Seaga furnished certain information about governmental activities, which Seaga refused to do. On a smaller scale, the Governor-General attempted to mediate a meeting between the two leaders to discuss the issues, which Seaga refused to attend.[58]

The election was also foreshadowed by two issues: electoral violence and Manley's health. In the 1980 election, nearly 800 people had died in election-related violence, reflecting a pattern for political tribalism. Both Manley and Seaga recognised the need to prevent violence and thus, although they refused to meet for a debate, the two leaders met to sign a peace accord in 1988.[59] Manley's health also dominated the campaign. In 1985 and 1987, Manley had been extremely ill with diverticulitis and a severe viral infection which nearly cost him his life. On both occasions, Manley left the political scene for a time in which speculation about the extent and seriousness of his condition spread rapidly.

In the election campaign, the public seemed interested most in Manley's medical condition and his ability to complete a full five-year term. Most of Manley's billboards and full-page newspaper advertisements prior to the election depicted him with a small child and proclaimed simply "we put the PEOPLE first." In sharp contrast, JLP advertisements outlined in detail Manley's failures during the 1970's and threatened of a return to socialism and even a move to communism if Manley were to return to power.

In a major interview one month before the election, the interviewer focused on issues such as Manley's health, the role of women in the party, and how many seats Manley expected to win.[60] On economic concerns, Manley indicated his intention to continue the foreign exchange auction, to regulate imports—but not the "physical regulation system of the seventies," to lift taxes and other bureaucratic regulation on local producers, and to break out of the dependence of debt, although he did not specify how this latter objective would be achieved.

Manley's change on the issue of the foreign exchange auction—which he had always opposed—reflected the influence of the private sector on his thinking, as did his decision on lifting taxes and easing regulation on local producers. The business leaders that Manley had spoken to had not convinced him to change his mind on import restrictions, although they did support his efforts to ease Jamaica's debt burden. Up to the time of the election, the private sector—particularly the PSOJ—had come to have a tremendous impact on Manley's thinking.

Evaluating Private Sector Influence on the PNP
Several factors help to explain the influence of the private sector on the PNP in the years immediately prior to the election. First, Manley recognised from the 1970's that alienation of the private sector had played a major part in his defeat and that many businessmen still harboured residual doubts about him which, if expressed, would have hindered his attempts at reform. He therefore found it necessary to go to an extreme in order to convince them of his genuine commitment to private sector-led growth.

Second, as he demonstrated during the 1970's, Manley sincerely believed in class consensus and the importance of unity in the implementation of his reform agenda. He hoped to develop a tripartite government structure similar to that found in Japan and Germany in which (theoretically) government, labour, and business work in concert toward national development oriented goals.

Third, while Manley had identified the goals he expected to achieve, such as equality, social justice, and political empowerment, the means that he had employed during the 1970's to achieve these objectives—state intervention—had resulted in economic failure. During the early 1980's, therefore, Manley found himself without a coherent means of achieving his goals, to which the private sector willingly provided an alternative.

Fourth, Seaga's poor relationship with businessmen contributed to the warmth with which the private sector embraced the Manley regime. Had Seaga adopted a more consultative approach to business leaders, they would have been less inclined to support Manley. Fifth, as noted, the financial constraints on the party forced the PNP to seek private sector support for funds. As a condition for this financing, private sector officials required that the left element in the party had to be removed, which contributed to the ideological centrism pursued by the party during this period.

CHAPTER 6

MANLEY AND JAMAICA'S ECONOMIC TRANSFORMATION

So Joshua ascended and all the people of war with him, and all the mighty men of valour. And there was no day like that before it or after it: for the Lord fought for Israel. And Joshua returned, and all Israel with him.
—Joshua 10:7,14-5

On his return to office in 1989, Manley had moderated his socialist views and hoped to pursue private sector-led development. He attempted to place greater emphasis on social programmes such as land reform and increased worker participation in businesses. Tight economic constraints and a changing world environment led Manley to re-evaluate this strategy. In early 1990, therefore, Manley announced that he intended to "face the economic reality" by moving toward a limited policy of market reform.

Increasing social discontentment and the failure of the economy to respond to these reforms led Manley to the conclusion that a more fundamental transformation was necessary. Just as he had done in 1974 after two years of limited policy reforms, Manley embraced a "new" ideology—but this time around that ideology was market liberalisation and deregulation rather than state-centered democratic socialism.

In response to the economic crisis caused by the the short-term dislocation of liberalisation, Manley's political support began to wane and social unrest increased. Notably, no major social outbreaks occurred similar to the strikes and riots which took place under Seaga. Manley's personal popularity, relatively extensive communication with the Jamaican people, and his efforts at explaining the long-term benefits of liberalisation served to minimise social opposition. Although he shared an excellent relationship with the private sector, Manley's inconsistent policy shifts on the exchange rate hurt business confidence in the economy. This lack of business confidence and the rise in the black market led Manley to abolish all exchange rate controls in September 1991.

Following this announcement, the PNP suffered from a series of political misfortunes and "scandals" which led Manley to reshuffle his cabinet and reassert his authority at that level. The continued instability of the currency forced Manley to take some extreme steps which included a selective tax on banks, reneging on his promise to hold a public share offering for a bank, and the imposition of draconian economic policies (including the creation of the repressive Liberalisation Support Unit). Despite a decline in support, a rash of political scandals, and relatively poor economic management, the Jamaican economy had experienced a significant transformation by the time of Michael Manley's resignation in March 1992.

ECONOMIC CONSTRAINTS AND THE POLICY OF CONTINUITY (FEB. 1989—DEC. 1989)

Expectations of the Left and Reassurances to the Right

Manley's return to power was heralded by many as the rejection of the dependent capitalist path and a return to people-oriented government committed to the development of neglected social sectors. One Caribbean journal editorialised that Manley's victory represented the defeat of the "counterrevolution from right-wing and conservative groups and parties" with their "ideologies of 'privatisation' and 'restructuring' [which were] implemented in a manner in which the infrastructure, the health services, and the educational services in particular were severely neglected."[1]

Various commentators suggested that Manley needed to create new economic and political institutions in order to "shift the bases of power in Jamaican society even within a mixed economy."[2] To accomplish this, the PNP needed to build community councils, institute land reform, and establish community-owned enterprises and cooperatives—but this time with proper financing and training. A leading journalist echoed the view of many working class Jamaicans when he wrote that Manley needed to pursue a model of development "from the bottom up rather than via the trickle-down process."[3] These observers all agreed that Manley was uniquely poised to enact significant social change because of his immense popularity and his relationship with the Jamaican people.

Yet Manley seemed more concerned with reassuring the international community that he did not plan to "go back socialist" on his return to office. In a *Newsweek* interview, Manley explained his "rethinking of policy" against nationalisation and his support for divestment by arguing that the "country has evolved, the world has evolved, and...I have evolved."[4] In a series of other international interviews, he gave his assurances that he would honour Jamaica's debt burden, establish a "constructive" relationship with Washington as his top priority, and resume close ties with various multilateral lending agencies. Although he acknowledged that he would extend diplomatic ties to Cuba, he promised that these relations would be on a "moderate" basis and would create no tension with Washington. In response, the Secretary of State and other US government officials announced their intention to pursue close relations with Manley. One major newspaper editorialised that Manley deserved Washington's support "'as long as he sticks with sensible policies."[5]

A few days after Manley's victory, the U.S. government under newly-elected president George Bush delivered a US$30 million installment of post-hurricane aid to the Jamaican government. Based on this gesture, Manley acted quickly to cement his relationship with the United States. In March 1989, he met briefly with President George Bush and senior members of the Bush administration, including Secretary of State James Baker, Secretary of Commerce Robert Mosbacher, Jr. and William Bennett, Director of the Drug Enforcement Administration. Manley also met with the Senate Friends of the Caribbean Basin and Caribbean/Central American Action to lay a solid basis for future lobbying for Jamaica. In these meetings, the American officials seemed fairly impressed with the sincerity of Manley's change and expressed their commitment to provide further US aid.

Over the next six months, Manley embarked upon numerous travels around the world to meet with other international leaders. In addition to the United States, Manley also visited several other Caribbean Countries, Canada, Venezuela, Britain, Sweden, Norway, France, and Spain. Manley later came under harsh criticisms for the time he spent outside of Jamaica. In response to these criticisms, Manley explained to the Jamaican people that his extensive visits served a threefold purpose: to explain Jamaica's economic situation, to prepare for European integration in 1992, and to encourage trade, investment, and the maintenance of the best possible working bilateral relationships.

To reassure the local private sector and to encourage investment, Manley made various appointments of leading business people to government organisations and met with numerous private sector groups. For example, Manley appointed Barclay Ewart, a leading businessman and close friend, to head the government's major investment agency, Jamaica Promotions, Ltd. (JAMPRO). In addition, Manley formed a seven-member National Economic Council—called "The Wisemen"—which was comprised of four prominent private sector officials and three senior economists. The council was scheduled to meet four times a year and was designed to advise the Prime Minister on major economic decisions. To encourage foreign investment, Manley hosted a roundtable discussion with 20 senior US corporate leaders representing companies such as AT&T, American Express, and Texaco. He also gave a speech to over 200 US business leaders at a reception in New York in which he acknowledged that "the engine of growth and development must come from the private sector. Experience has taught me that government should not participate in business. We want and need foreign investment."[6] Manley's efforts paid off as the Jamaican Stock Exchange rose higher than it ever had previously and the number of investment missions to the island increased substantially.

In the weeks following Manley's election, critics began to question the close relationship between the government and the private sector. A former left-wing PNP minister declared that the "old guard" was running things in Jamaica despite the clear mandate given to the government to change that situation.[7] In an open letter to Michael Manley from "the working class," a local journalist warned the Prime Minister not to become too cozy with the "Big Man" and urged him to pursue greater economic justice for the middle and lower classes.[8] Another journalist forewarned that Manley would find it difficult to appease both the capitalist and the working classes: "[i]t is hard to see how Manley is going to keep his private sector promise...and his new pro-production image while remaining a populist Government."[9] One of Manley's most vocal critics argued against the close ties that Manley shared with the private sector and other groups. He described the partnership between the "old establishments of politics—including the trade unions—the bureaucracy, and business [as] a conspiracy against freedom and against change...It is a recipe for continuing poverty and frustration and political failure."[10]

Cooperation, Continuity, and Social Reform
Manley possessed a clear vision of a broad agenda in his own mind. Essentially, this vision had three components: a close working

relationship between government and the Jamaican people, the maximum utilisation of private sector initiative, and a loosely-defined commitment to social reform. In Manley's inaugural speech, he explained that he expected to preside over a government of honesty, openness, participation, and energy (which not coincidentally spells the acronym HOPE) dedicated to public integrity and in which the Jamaican people could place their highest confidence. He also clarified his priorities for the country. These goals included the pursuit of national unity, the reinforcement of patriotism, and co-operation with the opposition on various national issues. In addition to his numerous overtures to local and foreign businessmen, Manley also expressed his hope to release the "creative talents" of Jamaica's entrepreneurs in the "world of production, finance and trade." In the social arena, Manley stressed the need for community development with special emphasis on land reform and the broad-based democratisation of the workplace through employee share-ownership.[11]

To these ends, Manley set in process various initiatives. In government, he created a special "super ministry" of Development, Planning, and Production to "perform the role of catalyst and facilitator so as to stimulate production and economic development while ensuring the rational allocation of resources."[12] P.J. Patterson, Manley's Deputy Prime Minister, was appointed to head the ministry. Manley assumed a presidential role in his cabinet and decided to hold only the relatively unimportant titles of Defense Minister and Information Minister (from which he could communicate with the Jamaican people). Unlike Seaga, Manley distanced himself from the day-to-day running of the government which allowed him to "release a great deal of energy...that would otherwise have been consumed in the exercise of line responsibility."[13]

Manley also proceeded to secure a variety of loans from bilateral and international sources to rebuild the social sectors. Manley received significant assistance in this regard through the Social Well-Being Plan left behind by Seaga which had in the works numerous unsigned loans from the World Bank and the IDB to provide funding for various infrastructure repairs. These loans were targeted for social programmes such as the provision of low-income housing, the purchase of ambulances, and the repair of damaged roads. Manley had embarked on a cautious path of economic continuity with a social emphasis, particularly on limited land reform and worker participation.

Difficulties with Continuity: Criticisms from the Left and the Right

Despite his efforts at allaying the fears of his doubters, Manley faced criticisms from a small but vocal group who wondered openly whether he would eventually return to his "socialist adventurings."[14] One skeptic wrote a letter to the *Wall Street Journal* in which he attacked the "super ministry" of Development, Planning, and Production as a "bureaucratic danger" that hinted at "a tendency toward centralised government."[15] The publication of the article resulted in a negative rating assigned to Jamaica by the influential Political Risk Services (PRS) which advises multinationals and other corporations that invest in developing countries. PRS warned that the PNP had plans to "gradually increase restrictions on international investment and trade."[16]

Manley's critics also charged that while his rhetoric sounded persuasive, Manley had failed to demonstrate that he had "worked out the conditions precedent to production and efficiency."[17] They cited the relative inexperience of the ministers in Manley's cabinet and pointed specifically to the Minister of Finance—a former pianist and land surveyor—as being "incapable of managing" that important position. In numerous interviews with leading businessmen, former Minister of Finance Mullings was described as "out of his league" and not adequately equipped to handle the position. In explaining why Manley appointed him, some argued that Mullings had remained faithful as Opposition spokesman for finance for years and Manley felt that he had to reward that loyalty. Others argued that Manley simply wanted a scapegoat in the event that something negative happened to the economy.

Manley's problems were exacerbated by the strident criticisms of Opposition Leader Seaga who, in a "great disservice to the nation," issued repeated warnings of a devaluation in the Jamaican dollar.[18] This call caused worried businessmen to speculate and hoard foreign exchange and led the Minister of Finance to issue strong denials of any devaluation plans.

Most importantly, commentators wondered whether Manley had the political will to take the necessary but politically unpopular decisions to finally adjust the Jamaican economy. One financial analyst, a former JLP government official, expressed his hope that

Manley would not fall "into the same trap that Mr. Seaga fell into in 1981—postponing the inevitable. The time to adjust is now. If Mr. Manley has any plans of being a great Prime Minister, he had better bite the bullet now."[19]

Manley also faced criticism for his alleged lack of an agenda and his apparent continuation of Seaga's policies. To reassure foreign investors and local businessmen, Manley had stressed a policy of continuity in economic strategy, although he made clear his intention to shift his priorities to social matters. As his term progressed, critics became more vocal in accusing Manley of having "no plan of his own" and of being a "mere copyist, a man wearing someone else's clothes."[20] One critic wrote in June that "so far...there has been no sign of a new policy. What the party has to offer is 'continuity' which means the best the country can hope for is what it would have got had it persisted with the JLP."[21]

Economic Crisis: The Search for Solutions

Immediately after his election victory, Manley had warned that there was "trouble on our economic horizon."[22] In subsequent months, Manley began to fully understand the magnitude of the island's severe economic crisis. In a series of speeches, Manley stressed the theme that "this is going to be a tight year. We have no gravy train. We are going to have to maintain very, very tight financial discipline. If we don't control the Budget, we will never bring down interest rates [which is necessary] to facilitate productive development."[23] In a broadcast to the nation, Manley announced that Seaga had postponed certain "inescapable adjustments" because of the election and these could be put off no longer.[24]

The brutal economic situation left Manley with almost no room to maneuver. Debt service consumed 46 cents of every dollar earned and 42% of the national budget, and the trade deficit had escalated rapidly. The actual public sector deficit was 15% of GDP compared to the 9.4% targeted for the IMF agreement, and the national import company (JCTC) was spending J$200 million subsidising food—a major drain on the government. Jamaica owed so much medium and long term debt to the IMF and other multilateral institutions that even the former Governor of the Bank of Jamaica had to admit that for all intensive purposes, "Jamaica could borrow no more."[25]

Manley responded to the severe financial crisis with a series of desperate initiatives. To halt the drain on the government budget and meet the IMF public sector target, Manley lifted subsidies on various basic food items. This move also represented the pressures of the local private sector because continued subsidisation would have resulted in the bankruptcies of several local enterprises unable to compete with subsidised food imports. If these firms closed, unemployment would have increased—which Manley clearly did not want. Consistent with his social emphasis, Manley set up an inter-ministerial committee to work out how the poor could best be helped in the harsh economic climate when he announced the price hikes. To raise badly needed capital, the PNP began a programme to divest the thirteen government-hotels which Seaga had leased but had not sold. The PNP also began to divest its share ownership in various businesses and joint ventures.

In addition to rescheduling a large part of Jamaica's external debt, the government signed major presale agreements of its bauxite with a local bauxite company and international financier Marc Rich. The agreement with Rich was significant because when he was in opposition, Manley had repeatedly denounced Seaga's dealings with the known international tax fugitive. The government also approved a plan to introduce slot machines into the island. This policy angered the powerful Jamaica Council of Churches (JCC) and represented a reversal of Manley's earlier position against gambling. Increasingly, Manley began to sacrifice political principle on the alter of the "expedience of survival."[26]

In line with the need for a tight monetary policy, Manley announced a lean budget in June 1989. The budget called for minimal increases in education, health, security, and local government while most of the budget went to service debt. Manley commented that previously he had believed there "was a realistic possibility of substantial change [but] now [I am] literally fighting to see what in a budget can be squeezed to make a tiny incremental advance."[27] To finance the budget, the government increased taxes on travel, telephone services, education, and motor vehicle sales which prompted the Finance Minister to announce that there was "no need for a devaluation."[28] The government's tight monetary management paid off when it passed the June 30 IMF test and was rewarded with a new economic aid package.

International Focus and Domestic Neglect
Secure in the knowledge that he had passed the IMF test,

Manley focused his efforts on the international stage. Within the Caribbean community, Manley made a series of visits to other leaders in order to push for greater economic integration and the implementation of a regional Stock Exchange. He also delivered a number of speeches in which he called for an international multilateral paramilitary unit to attack the war on drugs, a United Nations Convention on drug trafficking, and an international convention to deal with the debt crisis. He also advocated the creation of an "international institution" to address the debt problem, and for Japanese action to assist the IMF launch a debt-reduction plan for the Caribbean.

As the number of his international engagements increased, Manley began to spend less time in Jamaica. He explained in an interview that "I've discovered that a high profile [locally] is counterproductive. Experience tells me to talk little and try and make what you say effective."[29] While Manley shifted his energies internationally and adopted a low profile in Jamaica, the domestic economic crisis began to worsen.

During the first months of the Manley regime, allocations of domestic credit to the private sector surged to unprecedented levels in response to growing demand. As a result, the exchange rate—which had been artificially held stable at J$5.50 for nearly five years—lost 23 cents in August, 20 more cents in September, and 24 cents in October. This slide in the dollar came against the background of a severe trade deficit which had grown by a massive US$548 million between January and August, a 50% increase over the same period in the previous year. Manley had used the proceeds from the divestments of the hotels and the presale of bauxite to maintain the stable J$5.50 rate in the foreign exchange auction. In late 1989, however, Jamaica had little bauxite to pre-sell and few short-term assets to divest. As a result, Jamaica failed the September 1989 IMF performance test.

In response to this setback, Manley's cabinet and his senior economic advisers held a retreat to discuss the slide of the dollar and then announced various measures to deal with the crisis. These measures included the scrapping of the foreign exchange auction, the implementation of a fixed rate, and the devaluation and stabilisation of the dollar at J$6.50. Restrictive monetary policy such as high interest rates and a tightening of credit were also implemented.

Business leaders had mixed feelings about the devaluation.

Some felt that the government had postponed the devaluation for too long. Others argued that the devaluation represented an "asinine" move destined to create even more economic hardship. Most businessmen agreed that the government lacked a consistent and coherent economic direction and was pursuing instead "stop and go" measures. One journalist concluded that the government "lacks aim. It lacks coordination. It lacks even energy. The impression it creates is one of drift. The ministers all seem bewildered [and] lost...The Prime Minister himself travels with a kind of desperation, as if wanting to be as much as possible, and as far as possible, away from it all."[30]

The Opposition Leader joined the critical chorus and blasted the government for sending contradictory signals to businessmen and for creating a climate of economic uncertainty inimical to productive activity.[31] One economist moaned that the government, "in a desperate move characteristic of a driver not heeding the road signs around a dangerously winding road, suddenly slammed on the brakes by hurriedly devaluing the currency and putting into place draconian credit measures which are likely to do irreparable harm to the domestic economy."[32]

Political Obstacles and Economic Change: An Evaluation

To further compound the government's problems, the Jamaican people became increasingly dissatisfied with the method by which the government was pursuing its divestment programme. While few complained about the hotel divestitures (since these went primarily to Jamaican-owned corporations), many Jamaican's expressed doubts about other government decisions such as a well-publicised incident in which the government sold 3000 acres of prime beach front property for development to a prominent American Businessman (John Rollins) at the generous price of J$36 million. The minister who conducted the transaction later explained that the move was a necessary one because Rollins was an extremely powerful businessman who would encourage other investors to come to Jamaica. Indeed, Rollins had earlier entered a dispute with the JLP government and had used his influence in the United States Congress to block a bilateral aid package to the island.[33]

In a December poll, 66% of Jamaicans expressed their dissatisfaction with the 11-month-old Manley government. Most complaints centered on the high cost of living and severe price increases which people blamed on poor management ability within the PNP. When asked whether their situation had changed for the better or worse since the PNP came to power, 41% of the people polled said their situations had worsened, 44% said it remained the same, while a mere 12% saw improvement.

Despite the economic hardship experienced by the Jamaican people, the economy actually grew by 4.3% during 1989. Most of this growth was fueled by impressive output levels in bauxite/alumina production, the record numbers of visitors in tourism, and the rapid expansion of the construction industry caused by post-hurricane reconstruction efforts. Private investment had expanded to 29% of GDP and increased taxation had led to a central government surplus of J$1.1 million. Increased construction activity also contributed to the relatively low unemployment rate throughout the year. In addition, development assistance from the United States increased after Vice-President Quayle's visit to the island in November, after which Jamaica received substantial inflows from the Economic Stability Fund (ESF), the least restrictive of US government aid sources.

Quayle's visit initially was not that positive because Manley had opposed the Panama Invasion which worried the Bush administration. Eventually, however, Manley reassured Quayle of his commitment to market reform and explained that he had no argument against the United States. Manley's credibility was also bolstered by the fact that although he said he would, he still had not re-established relations with Cuba (this was largely because of bureaucratic reasons, however, not because Manley had abandoned his earlier commitments). The Quayle visit was also significant because Opposition Leader Edward Seaga refused to meet with the Vice-President in response to what Seaga viewed as his desertion by the United States administration during his last few years in office. Seaga's move only made the relationship between Manley and the Bush administration that much closer, because Bush needed a strong ally in the Caribbean.

On the negative side, the worsening trade deficit, the slide in the Jamaican dollar, and a decline in the international reserves (compared to an improvement one year earlier) contributed to a general climate of economic instability. In addition, price increases and the devaluation contributed to a 14.3% inflation rate compared to 8.5% in 1988. While the Stock Exchange had experienced unprecedented levels of growth during the first half of 1989, the government's restrictive measures to stabilise the exchange rate led to a downturn in the market during the last four months of 1989.

FACING ECONOMIC REALITY (JAN. 1990-AUG. 1990)

Addressing the Crisis: A New Economic Agenda?
At the beginning of the new decade, Carl Stone reflected on the general mood in the country by observing that "optimism, faith in the future, hope, [and] confidence...are nowhere to be found."[34] He added that thirteen years of IMF prescriptions had provided painkillers rather than cures for the island's ailment. He echoed the sentiments of numerous businessmen who felt that the country needed a "whole new approach" to create a "climate of a dynamic and competitive market place, free of price controls, state over-regulation, crippling bureaucracy and excessive tax burdens." This widespread despondency and the need for a radical change clearly had an impact on Manley's thinking. After almost one year in office, he could clearly envision where he wanted Jamaica to go—toward greater production, efficiency, and economic growth—but he still could not adequately articulate or identify how to get the country there within existing economic constraints.

In a broadcast to the nation delivered just days before the announcement of the January 1990 IMF agreement, Manley provided an historical overview of the island's economic difficulties and outlined a new approach to the future.[35] He explained that Jamaica possessed a "bang-belly," which he defined as an economy that projected the image of prosperity but which was actually based on borrowed money, not on production and earnings. In the popular Jamaican dialect, a "bang-belly" refers to the medical phenonemon of distended stomachs caused by malnutrition or gastroenteritis rather than obesity. Manley's use of the Jamaican dialect and the simple imagery to explain Jamaica's complex economic problem reflected his ability to communicate with the public at large in a way that they would understand. Manley described the economy as "a bubble that sooner, or later, must burst." He acknowledged that Jamaica's problems were not really with the IMF, but with the structural features of the Jamaican economy, and that there existed no "quick fix to our problems." He admitted that he had held off devaluation as long as he could because he sympathised with the inordinate "level of hardship and suffering" which the Jamaican people had experienced. But Manley made clear that the decision to postpone the devaluation "was a mistake" and that the country had to address the structural problem of the "bang-belly" economy at once.

To accomplish this, Manley stated that the country needed a "liberalisation in the way we do business. Import licensing and quotas and other physical controls are simply not an option any more." He added that "demand management is the only effective tool for restraining the national appetite" and concluded that "there is no alternative to an IMF agreement." He hesitated, however, in his full support for liberalisation and expressed his opposition to "freeing up the foreign exchange market" because to do so would have required a foreign exchange cushion which he felt the Jamaican economy did not possess.

The IMF agreement announced soon after included a further devaluation of the dollar from J$6.50 to J$7.00 and various increases in electricity rates, motor vehicle sales taxes, basic food prices, and the wage guideline. The package also called for a massive hike in consumption duties to curb imports and the implementation of a General Consumption Tax (GCT) to shift the tax burden from producers to consumers. As usual, the IMF agreement required a reduction in the overall public sector deficit and external current account deficit as well as an increase in net international reserves. In return, the IMF granted a US$107 million stand-by loan to support the economic programme. Although most observers felt that the IMF terms were less harsh than expected, a JLP spokesman prophesied that the agreement would fail because it lacked major incentives to producers. Meanwhile, union leaders continued their protests against the restrictive wage guidelines, and business leaders admitted that the package would be a "bitter pill to swallow."

Clarifying and Intensifying the Economic Strategy

In a series of statements issued throughout this period, the government began to clarify its new economic agenda. In his budget presentation, the Deputy Prime Minister Patterson argued that the government had come to office "with a clear picture of the direction in which we felt the country should go," but that this direction was held up by the time it took to get acquainted with "reliable national data and privileged information" and by the complicated process of consulting "with all sectors of the society to receive the benefit of their experiences."[36]

In his presentation, Patterson officially presented the first five-year development plan since 1978, a document which reflected the work of the "entire government bureaucracy" over the previous fifteen months.[37] The plan was based on three philosophical principles: (1) the private sector should be the main vehicle for growth; (2) the public sector should provide the appropriate policy framework to support the private sector; and (3) an open, export-led approach to growth was critical for national development. Reflecting the severe economic constraints the country faced, the plan called for decreasing levels of expenditure in health and education although it laid out increased expenditure for housing and construction.

In line with the government's programme of speeding up the liberalisation process, the government initiated a series of market-oriented measures. In June, the Mining and Energy Minister announced that the government might allow the private sector to own power plants and sell electricity to the national system which was run by the state-owned Jamaica Public Service Co. Ltd. This overtly free-market move reflected a major shift in PNP policy which had always maintained that the state needed to retain control over certain natural monopolies such as electricity.

The government also implemented a system of foreign currency "A" accounts which allowed individual non-residents and residents to open foreign currency accounts in Jamaica, provided that the funds did not represent the proceeds of the exports of goods and services from Jamaica. Although the PNP had announced this plan prior to the election in 1989, the formalisation of the plan to remove this foreign exchange restriction reflected the government's commitment to the gradual liberalisation of the economy.

With the publication of the five-year plan and the firm commitment of the government to a clear and cohesive agenda, businessmen began to regain confidence in the economy. In early 1990, the trade deficit decreased significantly and the economy began to demonstrate fairly positive signs of recovery and growth. Despite polls that expressed dissatisfaction with the government's performance, the PNP won an overwhelming 136 of 187 divisions in the March local government elections. Commenting on these positive election results, the Deputy Prime Minister (P.J. Patterson) claimed that the Jamaican people "spoke loudly and clearly. They expressed resounding confidence in the government for the direction in which we have sought to lead this country."[38]

Prior to these elections, Manley had announced a variety of socially-oriented programmes within a market-driven context. For example, Manley announced that government-owned land would be sold or leased to private investors and farmers in a major land reform programme. He declared that "land reform and increased agricultural production are the key pillars on which we must build future development."[39] In addition, other efforts at building community councils and other local development programmes were underway.

Economic Reform and Social Discontentment

Despite these positive developments, the government was plagued with internal image problems and a worsening social situation. In February, Manley fired the Minister of Industry and Commerce (Claude Clarke) over an episode in which Clarke had denied earlier government statements about a price hike on food. This incident projected the image that the government lacked cohesiveness and coordination.

A few months later, Manley announced a massive pay increase for Members of Parliament and government ministers. Although the recommendation for the pay increases came from an independent and non-partisan committee, the public reacted negatively to members of the government voting themselves 200% pay increases while mandating a 12.5% wage guideline for the rest of the population.

The government's problems were further compounded when a large state-run hospital shut down part of its operations due to a shortage of nurses. Indeed, employees in a number of government-owned enterprises refused to accept the government's strict wage guideline which created the impression of internal bureaucratic difficulties.

Moreover, in August, a serious crime wave broke out in poorer sections of Kingston. To curb the rising crime, the government imposed an eight-hour curfew in those areas and reimposed the Suppression of Crime Act which gave police wide powers of seizure and arrest. While this crime wave was symptomatic of the austere economic conditions, most of the crime was confined to particularly depressed inner-city areas and involved gangs fighting for territorial control, drugs, and illegal guns.

International Economic Reality and the Need for Substantial Change

In March 1990, President Bush announced that he was diverting US$25 million of Jamaican aid funds to Poland. A shocked Manley questioned whether the decision was "wise and fair" and expressed the view that the "news from the United States is very sad indeed."[40] Bush's decision came as a blow especially since Manley's other attempts at debt reduction were producing impressive results. In the same month, the Canadian government canceled Jamaica's entire debt of C$93.4 million. In addition, Manley was working on a debt-equity swap with Mexico to reduce Jamaica's debt to Mexico by some US$30 million.

In May 1990, Manley organised a visit to Washington in order to meet with Bush, various multilateral agencies, bankers, and potential investors. In an unprecedented move, Manley included in his official entourage various private sector and trade union leaders in addition to his senior government officials. Manley made clear that one of his goals was to convince Bush that it was "amoral to support the development of Eastern Europe at the expense of places like the Caribbean, where many of us have long been in the trenches of democracy."[41]

More importantly, Manley used the opportunity to set out a "very clear agenda establishing the fact that the way we were heading now was very consistent with US traditions and ideology."[42] In the meeting which lasted over two hours, Bush praised Manley's efforts at economic progress. After the meeting, Bush established a State Department Task Force to examine the issue of debt reduction for the Caribbean, but he also explained that the United States faced severe budget limitations and could not afford to be too generous.[43] According to members on the mission, Bush seemed particularly impressed with Manley. The international agencies seemed more doubtful of Manley's commitment to market reform. Businessmen on the trip explained to Manley in one of the debriefing sessions that it seemed that these agencies did not completely trust him. In response, Manley approached the next series of meetings like, as one business leader put it, "Billy Graham on a crusade." The visit had a profound effect on Manley because he realised that if Jamaica was to successfully compete for United States support, it would have to do something radical to justify substantial debt reduction.

Between June and September, Manley fell ill and spent the three-month period in a hospital in the United States. During the interim period, it became increasingly clear to Manley, especially considering his meeting with Bush, that something more substantial had to be done with the Jamaican economy. Despite the introduction of numerous bold fiscal and monetary measures, the government had failed the first IMF performance test in March by a relatively small US$7 million on its net international reserves. Tight monetary policy had resulted in subsequent improvements in the trade deficit and the current account, but the economy still had not experienced the major structural adjustment which Manley envisaged.

Moreover, the country was having an increasingly difficult time maintaining a fixed exchange rate especially under adverse conditions. During the time of his illness, Manley kept in close contact with the Cabinet which met on numerous special occasions to discuss possible options for the future. On his return from New York in September 1990, Manley announced that Jamaica would be embarking on a new economic direction.

LIBERALISATION AND DEREGULATION—A NEW PATH? (SEPT. 1990-AUG. 1991)

Manley's Embrace of the Market

A few days before Manley's return, the Deputy Prime Minister P.J. Patterson addressed the nation on a new change in economic policy direction.[44] In his speech, he announced that the government planned to pursue "bold new initiatives involving further deregulation of the economy...to break out of the stop-go cycle which has characterised [the economy's] recent performance." The new strategy involved three phases: (1) the deregulation of the petroleum industry; (2) the liberalisation of banking regulations; and (3) the complete removal of government price controls and monopolies. Patterson explained that "we are now crossing the Rubicon from a sheltered economy into one driven by market forces."

On his return, Manley announced in a broadcast to the nation that "we are making a radical change in direction which will, among other things, involve the free play of market forces in the determination of prices. This is the only way that we will begin to ensure, in the long run, efficient use of our resources."[45] Manley also expressed his firm belief that the private sector "is the only means to dynamic increases in the production of goods and services." Jamaica was to embark on a radical economic transformation.

Under the new system, the exchange rate would be set by a

trading system among the commercial banks, with the banks able to buy and sell foreign exchange on their account without going through the Central Bank. Importantly, the liberalisation did not involve a complete removal of controls. Certain categories of foreign exchange revenue—exports of bauxite/alumina, sugar, and bananas, plus tourism inflows—were still required to be sold to the Bank of Jamaica. The inter-bank foreign exchange system made the exchange rate responsive to market forces but still left the government with ultimate control. Manley rationalised that "in the absence of any foreign exchange reserves in the Central Bank, it would be too great a risk, as some have advocated, to abolish all exchange controls."[46]

Multilateral agencies—which had become cautious about lending during the late 1980's—began to place their faith in Manley's desire to implement a meaningful structural adjustment of the economy. In early 1991, the Inter-American Development Bank (IDB) granted a US$50 million trade and finance structural adjustment loan for the liberalisation of trade and the removal of credit subsidies. Similarly, the World Bank finally approved the second installment of the 1987 structural adjustment loan (US$30 million) to reduce protection across all sectors and to increase competition and state enterprise efficiency.

Manley explained that the new strategy had four elements: liberalisation, privatisation, streamlining, and focusing.[47] He defined liberalisation as serving a two-fold purpose: to "reduce the mass of regulations and restrictions to encourage competition" and to "create an atmosphere in which people feel they can try new things in production." Privatisation involved the sale of "government-owned factories, commercial operations and services [including] hospital laundries, school canteens, aspects of the postal services, government repair shops, the government printeries, government lands and sugar factories, ports, airstrips, aspects of the public utilities"—an impressive and wide-ranging list. In this regard, Manley stressed the importance of protecting worker's rights and of opening the doors to all businessmen, not just the "big man." Streamlining referred to the reduction in the state apparatus to "cut out unnecessary areas, simplify procedure and open up decision making by decentralising the system where possible." Focusing applied to the development of human resources, infrastructure, and small business support.

Manley later clarified what made his strategy "new" and not merely the continuation of Seaga's agenda with new buzzwords.

Manley explained that during the 1980's, Seaga had pursed a model based upon "a partial experiment in a market economy."[48] Seaga's model erred, Manley continued, because it "failed to incorporate a dynamic social component...and a traditional private sector was encouraged but no attempts made to enlarge it." He issued a challenge that "we must—for the first time in Jamaica's history—create a market economy, but we must incorporate a social component in which we encourage both the existing private sector and enlarge it."

To facilitate these changes, Manley decided to "turn the full energies of the Office of the Prime Minister on to this task" of privatisation, administrative reform, and the streamlining of government operations. Manley disbanded the Ministry of Development, Planning, and Production and instead created a new Ministry of Industry, Production, and Commerce. Responding to the advice of business leaders, Manley replaced Mullings with Deputy Prime Minister Patterson in the renamed Ministry of Finance and Planning.

Manley recognised that his new programme would create severe social and economic dislocation, so he sought to put in place various guarantees to cushion the blow of his new measures. In this regard, Manley announced his intention to pursue anti-trust and anti-monopoly legislation to prevent collusion and price-gauging in the economy. Moreover, he stressed the important role of government agencies such as the Bureau of Standards, the Prices Commission, and the Consumer Affairs Department of the Ministry of Labour, Welfare, and Sports, in protecting consumers against unfair and illegal business practices.

In addition to these efforts, Manley also allocated J$100 million to a Social Support Programme intended to provide assistance through food stamps and other channels to shut-ins, households in poverty, and the elderly poor. The programme focused as well on creating direct employment and providing credit, training, and social programmes for a significant section of the population.

Business leaders responded to the new market-led strategy with enthusiasm and confidence for the future. The head of Citibank in Jamaica declared that "there is a feeling of excitement and challenge...Some people have been surprised by the willingness and aggressiveness with which the government has moved into this new system." Others remained less optimistic and argued that "what we have is not a 'freeing up' of the system but in fact re-regulation. All that has happened is that commercial banks have been given the task of setting a rate within a small band and we are not really going to see the market place determine the rate."[49] Doubters warned of a continued slide in the dollar as producers held out for the best rate and spiraling inflation as a result.

Some skeptics argued that the PNP moved to the market to shift blame from the government for escalating oil prices and the continued devaluation of the dollar: "'deregulation' has been conjured up once more from the void to saddle 'the market' with that unpleasant responsibility in the hope that the Government might then avoid the political fallout."[50] They still doubted Manley's commitment to or understanding of the market.

The Rise of Popular Cynicism

The government faced a series of internal setbacks throughout this period. Consistent with its new move toward liberalisation, the government began to identify targeted enterprises for privatisation and divestment of the 300 enterprises in which the government still held equity. The government's sale of its shares in the Telecommunication of Jamaica (TOJ) to a British firm and 50% of Petrojam to a Venezuelan company fueled charges that the government had reneged on its promise to offer broad-based share ownership since these shares were not publicly divested. The government explained that selling the assets to foreign ownership served two important purposes. First, foreign sales were made in US currency of which the government was extremely short. Second, public share offerings took a long time to complete and involved high costs (advertisements, legal fees, etc.), whereas foreign transactions were often much quicker. The government also came under fire in early 1991 for granting a J$1.5 billion housing contract to a firm whose owners were closely linked to the PNP—allegedly without offering the contract to open competitive bidding.

At the same time, a scandal surfaced in Parliament where ministers were found to have exceeded the allowances allocated for the purchase of furniture items. Although no minister was officially charged in the incident, the image of the PNP suffered another blow. Criminal charges were brought against the furniture company and the Parliamentary clerk, and at least one minister of state publicly apologized for his conduct. The rise in popular disenchantment had an adverse affect on the PNP. To make things worse, in a poll conducted two months after the deregulation announcement, 55% of Jamaicans questioned responded that their standard of living had fallen since the PNP had come to power in 1989, compared with 41% in the November 1989 poll.

While many Jamaican's complained about the PNP, this did not represent a massive shift in support to the JLP. Rather, it reflected the increased sense of cynicism with pervaded the country. One opinion poll showed that for the first time in the island's history over 40% of the electorate was politically uncommitted to either party.

A Major Breakthrough: The Enterprise for America's Initiative

In May 1991, Manley made another visit to see Bush and various multilateral agencies. On this meeting, earlier doubts about Manley's commitment to market-form had largely disappeared. Manley used the meeting to point out to Bush that "we were well on the road which we had discussed the year before and that it was now very important that some of the matters of that path be made to work effectively."[51]

The most significant development arising out of the Bush meeting was the debt reduction made available to Jamaica under Bush's new Enterprise for the America's Initiative (EAI) which was announced a month after the meeting. According to the terms of the agreement, the US government wrote off 80% (U.S.$217 million) of Jamaica's bilateral debt under the PL480 concessional commodity supply programme. The remainder of the debt was to be repaid over 10 years at an interest rate of 3% in local currency—which eased Jamaica's foreign exchange situation. In addition, the government entered into negotiations for a new debt relief agreement to reduce over US$500 million in additional bilateral debt.

In many ways, the EAI rewarded the efforts of the Jamaican government since September 1990 to liberalise the economy. In addition to debt reduction, Bush's EAI initiative had two other goals: the expansion of trade and investment within the hemisphere and the use of local currency resources for environmental programmes. The EAI called for the US government to work with the Inter-American Development Bank to provide funds for liberalisation programmes aimed at reducing the "structural impediments that hinder market allocation of resources and market decisions." Under the EAI, Jamaica was one of the primary beneficiaries among Latin

American countries.

Liberalisation Effects: Currency Slide and Black Market Growth
Within weeks after the new inter-bank exchange rate system had been implemented in September, the dollar began to slide from J$7.00 to J$8.00 and witnessed even faster depreciation in subsequent months. In the wake of these devaluations, prices began to soar which contributed to a sharp increase in the inflation rate. In response to these factors, the government continued to pursue a tight monetary policy to reduce the public sector deficit. The government passed on all increased costs in state-run enterprises to customers and once again increased taxes and implemented new taxes. The crisis in the Persian Gulf made the economic crisis worse as the price of oil nearly doubled in just two months. To protect Jamaica against the unforeseen rise in the price of oil, the government used the IMF's compensatory financing facility set up to help countries battered by higher oil prices.

In a series of moves over the first few months of 1991, the government began to intensify the liberalisation programme. These initiatives included the removal of credit ceilings on commercial banks, the removal of limits on cash deposits in foreign 'A' accounts, a reduction in interest rates on Bank of Jamaica Certificates of Deposits and Treasury Bills, a removal of the wage guideline, and the continued removal of subsidies on food and other items. In addition, the government instituted various foreign exchange incentives and tax write-offs to boost production for exporters. As a result of these efforts, the government passed the IMF performance test in December.

The government's efforts seemed to be working as the country experienced substantial improvements in the net international reserves, a further reduction in the trade and public sector deficits, and solid growth rates that averaged over 2.5% during late 1990 and early 1991. Indeed, Jamaica passed the March 1991 IMF performance test fairly comfortably. Despite these successful efforts, the economy suffered from the rapid devaluation of the dollar and the massive increase in inflation.

With the continued and rapid devaluation of the dollar under the inter-bank exchange rate system, the government felt that it needed to stabilise the rate. In June, the government announced a new exchange rate system in which commercial banks bought foreign exchange at a rate set by themselves and not at negotiated prices. Soon after the announcement of the new exchange rate system, many businessmen complained that the new system produced artificial rates and was "a major disincentive to investment."

The value of the dollar had fallen largely as a result of extensive trading in the black market which is estimated at over forty percent of the economy—one of the largest in the world. While the official market traded at rates of J$10.00 or J$11.00, the more realistic black market offered rates of J$16.00 and J$17.00. In reaction to this wide divergence between rates, the government reversed its policy and reintroduced the interbank system. These changes in government policy, coupled with the instability of the currency, led to a sharp fall of confidence in the economy. To exacerbate the situation, the inflation rate—fueled by devaluation—shot to over 50% in mid-1991, representing a whopping 300% increase over the same period in the previous year.

TOWARD A NEW ECONOMIC ORDER (SEPT.1991-MARCH 1992)

Abolition of Exchange Controls: Reaction to Crisis
    With the nation in an deepening economic crisis, the senior ministers in government held a retreat in July 1991 to evaluate options for the future. At the meeting, the ministers decided that the correct strategy was to move toward the complete liberalisation of the foreign exchange market. One month before the announcement of the official decision to liberalise the exchange rate, Manley delivered a speech to the nation in which he stressed that Jamaica needed to take the "hard decisions to establish an economy which is really productive, is efficient, and is adaptable. In order to do this, we have to do as our competitors do: we have to remove the obstacles in the way of an efficient, market-driven economy."[52] According to Manley, the government concluded that "we are never going to accomplish [the social] agenda unless we put first things first. I came to the conclusion that the only thing was to literally almost like a projectile, hurl Jamaica into the reality of a market economy."[53]

The actual decision to lift the exchange rate occurred prematurely in response to extensive speculation and black market trading which had driven the value of the dollar down and sent prices up. Two weeks before the announcement, the *Daily Gleaner* headline declared "Economy out of control" referring to remarks made by Opposition Leader Seaga who warned that the government "has lost control of the economy, and this has rendered it helpless to move along a precise path."[54]

Manley argued, however, that the government actually was on a clear path and had chosen the most opportune moment to liberalise the exchange rate. Manley demonstrated that the net foreign exchange position for the first part of the year was US$100 million better than that of the same period the year previously, and that the debt service had fallen from 48% of exports in 1987 to 28% in 1990.[55] Although the timing seemed opportune, Manley failed to take certain preliminary steps such as reducing the liquidity in the economy prior to the announcement. Indeed, one member of the important National Economic Council (Wisemen) confided that the council had not been informed of this momentous economic decision prior to the announcement.

In September, Manley formally announced the government decision to abolish exchange controls on the exchange rate—the "most important economic measure since independence that any government has undertaken."[56] Essentially, the system sought to attack the recent slide in the dollar by creating one market and cutting out the black market. Under the new system, foreign exchange earners could hold accounts either locally or internationally without restriction, current account payments would be free from exchange controls, and commercial banks were no longer required to surrender a fixed percentage of foreign exchange to the Bank of Jamaica. The Jamaican dollar remained the only legal tender in the country and this currency could only be obtained through authorised dealers. The Finance Minister explained that "our expectation is that with the new liberalised foreign exchange market, the exchange rate will stabilise, which in turn will result in significantly lower rates of inflation."[57]

To reduce inflation, the government announced its intention to pursue further stringent fiscal and monetary policies, such as high interest rates, which would restrict the liquidity on the market, reduce the surplus available for foreign exchange speculation, and eventually depress the exchange rate. In addition, Manley sought to provide a social cushion to counter the negative effects of liberalisation by announcing a 50% increase in the number of food stamps for the most vulnerable social groups: children, lactating mothers, and pregnant women.

In response to the liberalisation announcement, most businessmen expressed their support for the government measure. The PSOJ—which had long advocated exchange rate liberalisation—declared that "the move by the government is irreversible and provides the last chance for Jamaicans to take control of their economic destiny."[58] Most other bankers, exporters, and tourism sector representatives joined in the chorus of praise for the government's decision to move in "a direction which gives hope for an eventual solution to our declining exchange rate and shortage of foreign funds."

Other business leaders were more restrained in their prognosis for the future: "we are cautiously optimistic that the new system will work by facilitating some level of stability in the exchange rate."[59] Skeptics warned that the new system was not a panacea and would not necessarily work: "merely to lift Exchange Control does no more than legalise flows which heretofore were illegal. It will not, by itself, decisively influence the direction of these flows. This economy is not going to attract and hold capital because the Government has belatedly recognised its own inability to compel capital to do what capital will not want to do."[60] Naturally, the opposition expressed reservations about the timing of the move, but admitted the gravity of the decision—and the dire consequences which would occur if it would fail.

The Need for International Support and The Initial Effects of Liberalisation

Manley felt that international changes had to occur—primarily debt reduction—to make sure that the bold liberalisation move would succeed. Manley thus committed himself to securing new methods of debt reduction and international agreements. Manley explained that the NIEO—on which he had earlier written three passionate books—was "frankly a dead agenda."[61] Instead, Manley increasingly turned his attentions toward the free-trade integration movement occurring throughout the world.

He cited the US/Mexico Free Trade Agreement as an example that Jamaica should emulate and work towards. Manley felt that the "entire American hemisphere is on the verge of a major economic breakthrough" and that Jamaica was "poised to capitalise on the economic and political reforms that are transforming the region."[62] He described Jamaica's "economic revolution" over the past two years and stressed the need for increased economic integration to build on these efforts: "we have done all we can—at great sacrifice—to create an efficient market economy." His conclusion was that "obviously a plan for trade and investment for the region must be actively encouraged and considered...I wonder how we can associate Central America and the Caribbean with those discussions."[63]

In the wake of the liberalisation, the Jamaican dollar slowly began to devalue, although not at an alarming rate. The government had feared a rapid flight of capital following the liberalisation of the exchange rate, but initial signals demonstrated that no massive outflow had occurred. Indeed, Manley announced that the economy had actually experienced an increase in inflows following the announcement of liberalisation. He stated that in the 19 working days prior to the liberalisation, foreign exchange inflows amounted to J$38.7 million, but in the 19 working days after the liberalisation, inflows to commercial banks amounted to J$89.4 million.[64]

Despite these positive signs, confidence in the exchange rate still had not returned. Indeed, dollar speculation, panic buying, and a reluctance to bring back US dollars contributed to the creeping devaluation. In addition, the government experienced difficulties with meeting IMF targets and was forced to postpone a US$50 million loan expected for December. The political disintegration of the Soviet Union also hurt the Jamaican economy. Following the break-up, the price of Soviet-made cars in Jamaica jumped twenty fold and the number of bauxite shipments was reduced substantially.

Opposition Reawakening and the Rising tide of Political Misfortune

Between September and December 1991, the PNP suffered from a serious decline in popularity with the re-activation of the JLP, declining economic conditions, and internal PNP difficulties. In October, the JLP organised a peaceful march with over 5000 supporters throughout parts of Kingston in which Seaga called for the PNP to step aside. Seaga increased the frequency of his attacks on the government and predicted the failure of the liberalised system. Seaga also announced that 1992 would be the "action year" for the JLP and he started a series of monthly meetings across the island.

Seaga had reason to feel confident since a local poll showed that 53% of the population blamed the PNP government for the high cost of living while only 35% blamed "big capitalists" and 32% blamed the IMF. Moreover, the opposition received a boost from a local poll which showed that 61% of voters believed that Seaga and the JLP did a better job of managing the Jamaican economy than Manley and the PNP. Another poll showed that PNP support had eroded and 38% of voters supported the JLP, 26% supported the PNP, and 36% of voters were uncommitted. When asked which PNP ministers were not doing a good job, 35% of voters answered "all of them", 28% answered Manley, and 21% pointed to Deputy Prime Minister Patterson.

The populace became increasingly vocal in its disenchantment. In November, students at the University of the West Indies organised a shutdown of the university to protest the findings in a recent policy report which recommended an increase in student fees. As the discontentment with both the PNP and the JLP increased, opposition movements also began to increase. Two new political parties became extremely active, the Christian United Party and the Republican Party. Both of these small parties lacked a labour base but became increasingly vocal through speaking engagements and newspaper advertisements. More importantly, several prominent academic, political, and business individuals formed a group called the New Beginning Movement as an alternative to established institutional structures. The New Beginning Movement adopted a visible and critical posture but opposed the decision to become a political party.

A political scandal in December only added to the PNP's declining political fortunes. In the incident, the government granted a J$29.5 million duty waiver on an oil shipment to a large multinational (Shell) whose managing director was a member of the PNP National Executive Council. When details of the waiver came to light, the Minister of the Mining and Energy resigned. Social commentators also called for the resignation of the Minister of Finance (Patterson) who had approved of, but who had not been directly involved in, the decision to grant the waiver. This incident—of the "state granting largesse to a big rich multinational capitalist company"—served to reinforce the negative image of the PNP as having sold out to powerful private sector actors even at the expense of the national interest.[65]

Addressing the Crisis: Political Reform and Social Emphasis
Manley recognised that a change was necessary to halt the

erosion of his party's political support. To this end, Manley asked all his ministers, ministers of state, and permanent secretaries to resign in order to allow him to reshuffle the Cabinet. Manley then announced a major restructuring in the government which cut the number of ministries from 18 to 13 and the number of administrative bodies from 39 to 28. In the Cabinet reshuffle, the "older" cabinet members were set aside while a younger group of junior ministers were promoted to full ministerial rank. To pacify critics of the Minister of Finance (Patterson), Manley did not reappoint him (Patterson had requested not to be a member of the new Cabinet).

In addition, Manley abandoned his former presidential style of leadership and announced that he was going to take a more active role in government affairs. As one journalist described: "Manley....effected a return to his hands-on leadership-from-the-front posture, whipped his parliamentary majority, his Cabinet and the Party's National Executive Council into line behind him, and reshuffled and trimmed the Cabinet."[66] The general response to Manley's move was favourable. As Stone observed, "Manley's new-look Cabinet, his re-assertion of personal control of the party, his increase in the number of back-benchers in the House and his reduction in the number of ministers, his use of the waiver issue to challenge his fellow party leaders to go back to the grassroots and try to rebuild lost PNP support, and the show of party unity he has orchestrated over this divisive Shell issue reflected masterly political and information management and expert damage control at a high level."[67]

In addition to these political and bureaucratic reforms, Manley also announced the formation of a Committee on Government Structure to "direct the task of reshaping a government as enabler, co-ordinator, developer of our human resources and guardian of social justice and human welfare."[68] The "think tank" included a variety of prominent citizens from business, journalism, academia, and the government. The creation of the committee generated criticisms, however, from various circles as simply further bureaucracy. One commentator argued that the committee members were all former socialists who would have little in the way of new ideas for the government.[69]

In a broadcast to the nation, Manley outlined the social aspects of his programme and announced various initiatives for the future.[71] Manley stated that he would soon be implementing a Fair

Competition Act, something which he had promised when he first liberalised the exchange rate one year earlier. Manley also pointed to the government's achievement in the area of housing, in the creation of a Micro Investment Development Agency (MIDA), in the granting of land plots to over 500 farmers, and in the public divestiture of a major radio station. He promised that in the future there would be a major public divestiture of shares in the nation's largest bank and an expansion of the land reform programme. Despite the characteristic optimism which pervaded Manley's speech, the nation seemed largely unconvinced of a bright future. The *Daily Gleaner* editorialised that "the Prime Minister had said precious little...to generate sufficient public confidence in the Government's management of the economy."[71]

Economic Strife and Draconian Government Response

Economic crisis reclaimed Manley's attention, however, as the government faced severe resource constraints caused by the devaluation in the currency. Under these restrictive economic conditions, Manley reneged on his earlier promise to offer a public share offering for the government's National Commercial Bank (NCB) shares and instead sold the shares to a large bank. The Minister of Finance later explained that the government was desperately short of foreign exhange. In addition, a public offering would have created pressures on the demand situation which would have counteracted the government's efforts. This move generated significant opposition from various groups because it represented a violation of an early promise and a capitulation to special interests.

To meet fiscal targets for the March IMF performance targets, the Minister of Finance announced a special surtax on the assets of commercial banks—an act which created significant opposition and hurt the relationship between the government and the financial sector. Although there were numerous positive signs, such as the creation of a US$1.5 billion EAI Multilateral Investment Fund, the economy still faced numerous problems.

In addition, the economy was suffering from increased speculation and panic buying which created an unexpected slide in the Jamaican dollar. When the government had liberalised the economy in September, it had received an unofficial commitment from commercial banks to voluntary reduce their liquidity in the economy. In reality, the banks went in the opposite direction and the liquidity increased. This action by the commercial banks had created excess demand which contributed to the fall in the exchange rate.

In response to the economic situation, the government instituted a range of draconian measures which included a credit tightening to move some J$1.68 billion of commercial bank liabilities to the Bank of Jamaica, an increase in interest rates from 60% to 90% for commercial bank overlending, and an intensification of the Liberalisation Support Unit (LSU) designed to arrest illegal foreign exchange dealers. These drastic measure initially held back demand and led to some stability of the exchange rate. The government came under increasing fire, however, for the excessively prohibitive interest rates and the overzealous and arbitrary enforcement by the LSU which, in one well-publicised incident, had arrested a relatively innocuous domestic worker for trading a US$20 bill.

Manley's Resignation: The End of an Era

On March 15, 1992, Manley announced to the nation that he would be resigning as Prime Minister of the country because of ill-health.[72] In the broadcast to the nation in which he announced his resignation, Manley ensured that there would be "absolutely no compromise or equivocation about the existing policies of the government" under the new leader, whoever he or she might be. In addition, he guaranteed that the leadership race would "not affect the market economy path."

In the succession contest, Manley declared his neutrality. The two contestants were Portia Simpson, the Minister of Labour, Welfare, and Sports; and P.J. Patterson, the former Deputy Prime Minister and Minister of Finance who had left the Cabinet in the wake of the of the Shell waiver incident. The vote for the succession was held among PNP delegates in what one JLP member called an "extraordinary display of democracy."

Patterson commanded the support of almost all of the Cabinet and campaigned on a platform of continuity and experience. Simpson, who was backed by D.K. Duncan and the Minister of Finance Hugh Small, promised to add a "human face" to the economic adjustment process by working from the "bottom up" as opposed to the "top down." In the election of the over 3000 PNP party delegates, P.J. Patterson emerged victorious by a two to one victory and thus became the sixth Prime Minister of Jamaica.

MARKET-LED SOCIALISM: ANALYSING MANLEY'S IDEOLOGICAL JUSTIFICATION

Synthesising Socialist Principles with the Market

While Manley had dropped all references to democratic socialism prior to his election victory in 1989, he had never discarded the ideology. Instead, he subject his socialist thoughts to a critical rethinking in order to apply it to the new economic reality. Manley identified those areas of socialism that were consistent with market-based principles. For example, during the 1970's, Manley had defined one aspect of socialism as the provision of "new opportunities...for private businessmen [and widening] the base of ownership by providing opportunities for people to enter the field of business."[73] In 1989, Manley decided to focus on this aspect of his socialist thought. To that end, he realised that the state should play a crucial role in facilitating access to social ownership rather than directly procuring the commanding heights of the economy for the people. In early 1989, he explained:

> I do not think that I have abandoned socialism at all. I think I am trying to learn from profound experience in a very dynamic phenomenon—trying to find another way to see that, in the end, every human being in this country can either be a shareholder if he's a worker or a businessperson, or a small farmer with his little thing—a firmament, a meaningful state of participation. Socialism is therefore undergoing tremendous changes, but [it is] still trying to maintain a central philosophy about access and equality—and that the state is a critical intermediary—the state has to find the way to use the political process to make people want it, persuade them to want it, and be the enabler that helps them to do it.[74]

Manley also recognised that he needed to generate economic growth before he could adequately finance his broader social objectives. He explained that he still retained his "commitment to social justice and equality of opportunity. However, at the same time recent experience shows me that these objectives can only be achieved and maintained through a dynamic and expanding economy."[75] This "recent experience" was his evaluation of the international situation which made Manley conclude that "this evermore efficient world economy waits for no one and will not pause for any country to catch up." The role of the government would be to "create the framework to unleash the entrepreneurial energies of the sector" and to act as "the monitor to ensure fair play in social and economic activity [and] the enabler, the catalyst, and the supporter of people with ideas for production."

Pacifying and Responding to Internal Dissent

During the first months of his regime when Manley pursued a policy of continuity, many rank-and-file PNP members expressed doubts about this strategy, interpreting it as a betrayal of their interests. The rank-and-file became increasingly wary of the government selling off Jamaica's "national patrimony." Vocal PNP members, particularly D.K. Duncan, argued that Manley had reneged on his promise of broad-based democratisation of ownership and instead had capitulated to the demands of "big business."

In a special delegates conference of the PNP held two months after the February 1989 election, Manley addressed the party members and explained that the world had changed and that Jamaica needed to adapt to the new market-driven economy. He added, however, that continuity did not mean that everything would remain the same. Indeed, Manley emphasised that he intended to provide social programmes including subsidies for small farmers, increased worker participation, and the establishment of community councils.

At the November 1990 PNP Annual Conference, party members expressed doubt about the role of the private sector as the main engine of growth and disappointment over the non-implementation of community councils and other promised social programmes. They sought clarification on the ideological path of the party in relation to social empowerment of the people and how this related to the new economic strategy. One commentator described the atmosphere at the public session of the Conference as "subdued and almost like that of a graveyard—perhaps not inappropriately, since Democratic Socialism was being formally buried."[76] This charge Manley vociferously denied. Instead, Manley explained to the PNP that socialism was indeed alive and well—but revitalised.

Explaining the Revitalisation of Socialism

Within the first months of his term, Manley had recognised that while he possessed a coherent conceptual framework for what he hoped to do, he needed to reassess his implementation strategy. To address this issue, Manley created a committee of the PNP National Executive Council in July to look at the policy imperatives facing the party in the light of changes in the world economy. At the 1990 Conference, the Policy Review Committee delivered its report.

The report outlined the limited range of development options available to the government and argued that the "competitive exigencies of the world economy suggest a change in the role of the state."[77] Granted that the Jamaican "state is not particularly efficient in its use of resources," the report stressed the need for the government to focus its efforts on "facilitating entrepreneurial activity among private interests in order to maximise the nation's competitiveness in the world economy." The report also reaffirmed that the state had to be "an instrument to be used to secure expanded economic opportunities for the disadvantaged and power for those who have little control over or access to decision-making."

In his address to the conference, Manley delivered a major speech in which he justified liberalisation within the context of socialist ideology.[78] He stressed that the PNP's policies differed from those of the JLP because there "was no coherent philosophy attached to Seaga's performance. He acted...under instructions from the World Bank." Manley explained that the new strategy was designed to "liberalise the system, letting loose market forces and enabling the private sector to grow larger by releasing its energy and growth potential."

The government would actively encourage "the private sector [to] work for the empowerment of people so that more, not less, people will own and control their future". Manley reasserted his faith in the aim of democratic socialism—"to build a participatory democracy on the foundation of social justice and the broad ownership of the means of production"—but insisted that only by using market forces would these ends be achieved.

Consistent with his desire for consensus, Manley put his new economic strategy up to a vote of the more than 3000 PNP delegates at the conference. Prior to the vote, Manley made it clear that in the absence of overwhelming support for the new policy, he knew what to do on Monday morning—the obvious implication being that he would resign. Manley made it clear that if the party could not unite behind an ideological path, then he would "feel that my own historical relevance had come to an end."[79]

The results of the vote—in which only two delegates voted

against—reaffirmed the overwhelming support Manley wielded as head of the party. Manley discounts the role that his popularity played by pointing to the fact that in the debate preceding the vote, "speaker after speaker got up and spoke at high levels of understanding, of commitment, of now getting the thing clear in their minds, and being willing to go out and make this work."[80] Manley described the annual conference as a "huge intellectual breakthrough" in which members of the party finally realised that "our socialist objectives are not going to be thrown through the window."[81]

Intensifying Liberalisation and the Theoretical Justification

In 1991, when the government embarked on the bold liberalisation move, Manley had to justify this radical action to his party. To that end, Manley actively worked on a revision of the document, "Principles and Objectives of the Peoples National Party" which was presented to the PNP Annual Conference in November. In the new document, the party reaffirmed that the "central and continuing objective of the People's National Party is the transformation of the Jamaican society through the pursuit of democratic socialism."[82] In terms reminiscent of Marxist dogma, the new document decried the capitalist economic system as a method of "economic exploitation based on minority ownership of the means of production."

It emphasised the three clear and fundamental objectives of the party: (1) empowerment of the people, (2) democratisation of ownership for the majority of people, and (3) a commitment to social justice and equality. It argued explicitly that the state could not achieve these goals and that market forces were necessary to "generate the internal process of capital accumulation [and] to develop a productive and efficient and competitive economy." The document concluded, somewhat paradoxically, that "the economic policy of Democratic Socialism relies on the laws of the market but on a larger economic playing field."

In addition to the revised document, Manley also wrote a short piece entitled "the Role of the State" for party members to use in their liberalisation education programmes. In the essay, Manley outlined three types of political theorists within the broad ideology of democracy: minimalists, liberal democrats, and democratic socialists.

For Manley, minimalists believe that "the general welfare is best secured if you leave the market economy of the capitalist system alone to work its 'magic'." The minimalist system is based on two precepts, "traditional political democracy" (e.g. the right to vote) and "consumer democracy" (e.g. the right to choose). The state is seen as a necessary evil whose role should be limited to internal order and external defense—the two preconditions to a successful market economy.

On the other hand, liberal democrats recognise from historical experience that the natural tendency within market economies is towards the concentration of power and liberal democratic theorists envision two additional roles for the state: welfare activity (e.g. social services, subsidies, etc.) and access to social mobility (e.g. fully subsidised educational system). They also rely on the market, but recognise a more active state role.

Democratic socialists (like Manley) are concerned with the need for capital formation, but also recognise a need for national planning and the distribution of power in society to achieve its wider diversity. Fundamentally, democratic socialists seek the transformation of society through "empowerment" defined as the widespread dispersion of power through "land reform, small business development, micro-enterprise opportunity, co-operatives in farming, community-based production and in distribution, and worker ownership." Manley concludes that "democratic socialists see the state as the repository of the hopes of the people for opportunity, justice and a place in the general scheme of power." For the people to gain access to that repository, they had to use market mechanisms.

CHAPTER 7

EVALUATING MANLEY'S IMPACT ON THE NATION

And Joshua called for all Israel, and for their elders, and for their heads, and
for their officers, and said unto them, I am old and stricken in age.
Be therefore very courageous and do all that is written in the book of the law
of Moses, that ye turn not aside to the right hand or to the left.
—Joshua 23:2,6

This chapter will analyse the reasons behind Manley's transformation, the way in which Manley effectively used his political capital to facilitate the implementation of the liberalisation process, and the political and managerial obstacles to liberalisation in Jamaica. It will argue that Manley made many political and economic mistakes in the liberalisation process, but that his efforts at utilising his political capital and his attempts at incorporating interest groups into the political process all contributed to a significant transformation of the Jamaican economy.

JOSHUA'S REBIRTH: ANALYSING MANLEY'S TRANSFORMATION

By understanding why Manley embraced economic liberalisation, we will be able to adequately evaluate the possibility for its successful application to the Jamaican economy in the long term. Various theorists have attempted to explain Manley's shift from state-led to market-led democratic socialism. These theorists fall into five categories: leftists, moderates, conservatives, skeptics, and psychological theorists.

Leftists: Class Suicide and a Return to Bourgeois Liberalism
Leftists argue that Manley's centrism can be understood within the context of his class background. They posit that, as the son of a wealthy barrister (Norman Manley) and famous sculptress (Edna Manley), Manley has always been a member of Jamaica's upper class. Indeed, Manley could be thought of as a part of Jamaican "royalty" since his father was a senior member of Jamaica's early political elite. As a result, the younger Manley grew up in a very privileged environment. They argue that Manley's "entry into

politics was promoted by the PNP right-wing to counter the left...his perspectives were closer to right-wing social democracy than to left populism."[1] During the 1970's, they continue, Manley committed "class suicide" by abandoning his aristocratic roots and embracing the political concerns and aspirations of the working class.

Although leftists admit that throughout this period, Manley expressed a genuine concern for improving the socio-economic conditions of the underprivileged, they add that this impulse "was conditioned first and foremost by the growth of black consciousness and popular militancy in the late 1960's."[2] Indeed, "the historical milieu Manley found himself in seemingly carried him like a tornado beyond his own wildest expectations."[3] In the 1990's, the "bourgeois" element of Manley's true persona resurfaced and manifest itself in Manley's extremely close relationship with leading capitalists. Leftists point to "the absence of a progressive social-labor policy" as a "crucial weak flank of the Manley government" and proof that he had abandoned much of his commitment to social justice and equality.[4]

Moderates and Conservatives: Recognising Economic Reality

Moderates argue that Manley genuinely moderated his views but sold out to the pressures of external agencies and the United States. Most moderates are members of the JLP and argue that, unlike Seaga, Manley did not have the political will to face up to the IMF and the Bank. Instead, they argue that Manley "capitulated to external pressure" from these and other similar institutions. Moderates point to evidence such as Manley's sale of land to John Rollins at "give-away" prices—something which Seaga refused to do; and the PNP sale of government shares in NCB to a large conglomerate—especially when Manley had earlier promised to place the shares in a public offering.

For conservatives, Manley's ideological shift represents his understanding of economic reality and the way that Jamaica works. Although they decry his actions during the 1970's as a "painful memory," they accept that he had "good intentions" and was simply a "youthful missionary zealously pursuing his convictions."[5] In his later political career, conservatives continue, Manley shed his radical skin and instead clung to "prudent ways" consistent with prevailing international thinking.

After "dispassionate analysis", Manley eventually came to the "recognition that a market-based economy is the more rational basis for Jamaica." Indeed, conservatives argue that Manley finally realised that socialism was inherently inefficient and could not produce the economic growth necessary for Jamaica. They argue that Manley is an "extremely bright man" who was simply misguided during the 1970's, but who eventually "saw the light" that the private sector should lead in economic development.

Skeptics: Populism and Ideological Fantasy

Skeptics doubt Manley's commitment to the new economic path and argue that he remained a populist without any ideological convictions. They argue that all of Manley's actions could be understood within the context of his desire for popular approval. Although Manley changed his rhetoric, they posit that his inner political convictions "remain populist, and corporatist and welfare statist."[6] They deny that Manley learned anything from his past: "[t]he leopard has not changed his spots. Mr. Manley...learned less than he led us to suppose from the debacle of the seventies...Though his rhetorical flavouring [was] different, designed this time to please American rather than Russian and Cuban palates, he [had], in essence, nothing to offer but the same old rancid populism that sickened stomachs a decade ago."[7]

Indeed, skeptics predicted that Manley would resign before the end of his term because he did not have "the stomach for another 1980 [and he was] bankrupt both for cash and for ideas, not so much governing as playing messenger from the IMF and courtier to the Americans; denied his daily dose of popular acclaim, facing only failure and unable to arrest his once again slide into political disesteem."[8]

Psychological Theorists: Extremism, Failure, and Historical Greatness

Psychological theorists look to Manley's personality in explaining his shift. They argue that Manley represented a classical ideological extremist who, in embracing a particular development path, took it to the maximum limits. This extremism was responsive to ideological trends and reflective of underlying demagogic tendencies. During the 1970's—a period of popular militancy—Manley was a radical socialist; during the 1990's—a time of economic reform—he had become a rabid free-marketeer. Stone argues that Manley "had a passion and an inclination to fall in love with new ideas in times when those ideas enjoyed wide international currency as did socialism in the 1970's and the free market liberalism of the 1980's and 1990's...Manley was not an original thinker although he was fascinated with the world of ideas, intellectualism and intellectuals."[9]

To explain Manley's fervour, psychological theorists often point to Manley's difficulty living under the shadow of his father, Norman Manley, who is a National Hero. One close associate of Manley's described Michael and Norman Manley as "the same person." In 1969, Norman Manley delivered a famous speech in which he argued that his generation had accomplished the mission of independence; he then laid a charge for the next generation to tackle "the job of reconstructing the social and economic society and life of Jamaica."[10] Psychological theorists argue that this speech outlined the mission that the younger Manley saw for himself, "to be his father's critical counterpart as principal architect of the economic revolution [of] modern Jamaica."[11]

Psychological theorists posit two other factors that drove Manley in his fervour to implement both democratic socialism (during the 1970's) and economic liberalisation (during the 1990's). First, Manley desired to emerge from the powerful shadow of his father as a historical figure in his own right. He desired international greatness and recognition, as evidenced by his actions in the NIEO during the 1970's and in his international calls against drugs and debt during the 1990's.

Second, as he himself admitted, Manley failed during the 1970's to enact a successful economic revolution. To erase the devastating image of failure, Manley found it necessary to overcompensate by being an extremist in the opposite ideological direction. These theorists conclude that Manley possessed a deep desire to "expunge the ignominy of the 'seventies and to write his name in glowing letters in the Jamaican history book."[12]

While all the above factors probably have some validity in explaining Manley's transformation, they do not adequately address Manley's change. Indeed, I shall posit three primary factors that explain Manley's shift.

State Failure and Managerial Incapacity

First, Manley recognised that the Jamaican state did not have the managerial capacity to enact the economic transformation that he desired. During the 1970's, Manley always maintained a commitment to the broad distribution of power rather than simply amassing it in the state apparatus. In a speech he delivered to his party's National Executive Council in 1975—one year after he had re-declared his commitment to democratic socialism—he reminded the senior members of the party that "[w]e do not want more power for the state. What we want is more power for the people."[13]

During the 1970's, his actions demonstrated a desire to spread ownership among the population, evidenced by the establishment of sugar cooperatives and the distribution of shares in a radio company to employees, unions, and the public. Manley viewed the state as "an effective intermediary in production [that could] successfully be the short cut to incremental economic capacity and [the mobiliser of] management, capital and workers to produce something when the private sector was not ready to do it."[14] He always remained committed, however, to the need for private sector activity and investment.

In *The Politics of Change*, Manley hinted at a socialist model with extensive state participation in the short term to fulfill certain social objectives, but with a gradual shift to private sector dominance on the completion of the social goals. He wrote, "once certain priorities have been overtaken in the field of human resources, infrastructure and certain strategic areas of the economy, private enterprise is the method best suited to the production of all the other goods and services which are necessary to the functioning of an economy."[15] This view is entirely consistent with his position during the 1990's.

Manley recognised in the intervening period that "the state does not in itself create access to anyone [and instead is] a really inefficient way of trying to increase economic capacity."[16] For individuals to truly participate in the economy, they had to have ownership. To accomplish this, they needed access and opportunity which the state could provide—through privatisation, divestment, and the liberalisation of the economy.

International Circumstances: Free Trade and the Global Shift to the Right

Second, changes in the international economic environment reinforced Manley's new thinking and drove him to intensify his liberalisation efforts. The gradual intensification of the liberalisation process in Jamaica closely paralleled international changes such as the destruction of communism in Eastern Europe and the fall of communism in the Soviet Union soon after. As the trend of globalisation and integration increased, Manley's analysis of the situation indicated that Jamaica had to change in order to participate in the new international order.

The United States/Canada Free Trade agreement and the United States/Mexico Free Trade agreement were both predicated on an assumption of increased trade liberalisation. For Jamaica to participate in any such agreement in the future—or if Jamaica planned to receive any substantial benefits from the United States—it had to have the necessary preconditions of trade and economic liberalisation in place. Manley explained his shift this way:

> It came from a perfectly cold analysis of where the world economy was heading, what chance [we had] to work our way into...that world economy to earn...foreign exchange, in recognition of the fact that there were not increasing chances for a managed world economy...as was the dreams of the 1970's...[Look] at how easily the world's political powers had torpedoed the NIEO in the '70's, and now we are facing the fact that even they are having less and less influence over the economy. [T]he world economy is tone deaf—it doesn't listen to anybody. It only deals with [those] who can produce successfully for it...Then one day the coin began to drop in my mind: you know something, you just have reality reversed in your head. You cannot achieve these noble ideals in that way. And if you work back from the world economy and then get inside your economy in which...your capacity to become...competitive in production is not going to be assisted by a heavy state presence in the productive apparatus of the country. ..[T]he best you can do is just throw everybody into the sea and let them learn to be efficient and swim, with the government mobilising capital [and] helping [to] identify export markets—it's from all that that it began to develop in my mind the fact that one might just have the whole historical process—the historical possibility—reversed. And then we began the long anxious search for the ideas [of] how [to] serve the ideals of equality, mobility, empowerment, which are at the heart of socialist intention, in a context in which your country is going to survive and have some economic expansion to distribute.[17]

This thinking reflected simple pragmatism and realism on Manley's part—all in the best economic interest of Jamaica. As Manley described "I am not an ideologue, I do not have a frozen position in my head. I belong to a camp, but it is informed with a sort of pragmatic ability to try to interpret reality, which may be wrong—I am not being arrogant."[18]

The charge that Manley remained committed to a populist path seemed shaky considering the massive unpopularity of his economic reforms with which he persisted even as his negative ratings grew. Indeed, even Manley's most outspoken critic, Wilmot Perkins, recognised this fact as the liberalisation process intensified: "Mr. Manley is doing something heroically uncommon for him in thus swimming against the tide of popular approval. It would be marvelous to see his efforts crowned with success."[19] Despite his laudatory remarks, Perkins went on to explain that the liberalisation process would be "unnecessarily aggravated by the timidity, the uncertainty, the seeming lack of conviction and piecemeal fashion in which the Government itself seems to be approaching liberalization: the probable result of which is that Mr. Manley will find his 'historical relevance' put to severe and excruciating test before this present term is out." Although claims of Manley as lacking direct control over the direction of liberalisation have validity, charges of Manley as merely a populist have little substantiation.

Although Manley often embraced populism, a more accurate view of him would be that of someone who knew where he wanted his country to go but who struggled to allow the nation to catch up with him. In 1955, he described the West Indies Federation using words which capture what he hoped to do with liberalisation: "not [to tread] warily on tiptoe a generation behind the popular times, but [to stride] out to take history by the throat with the nation still asleep."[20] In short, Manley viewed himself as a visionary.

Economic Constraints and Limited Development Options

The third element of Manley's shift centers on his limited development options. When he inherited power in 1989, the room for economic maneuvering was extremely small because almost 50% of export earnings went to service debt and because he had inherited a backlog of over J$2.8 billion in Bank of Jamaica certificates of deposits which the government was obliged to honour. Three years before Manley's election victory, an international observer warned that Jamaica's financial dependence on the international capital market would prevent Manley from making any significant policy changes if he assumed power in the next election. In 1986, the Economist Intelligence Unit accurately foresaw Manley's success in the upcoming election, and then predicted that Jamaica would be "extremely dependent on foreign financing and the PNP will avoid clear policy reversals and confrontations, even though it has repeatedly warned that it will not recognise any agreement entered into by the JLP."[21] The tight economic situation was clear to most insightful observers who recognised early on Manley's limited room for economic or political maneuvering.

On his return to power, Manley could not have returned to a state-led socialist path because history had demonstrated that it had failed and the Jamaican people had passed judgment on it in the 1980 election. He also could not have continued Seaga's reforms since they had clearly not created significant structural changes in the economy. His initial decision—to continue Seaga's policies with a greater emphasis on social issues—also could not work because he lacked the resources. In addition, Seaga had pledged Jamaica's support to the restrictive methods of the IMF and World Bank. Seaga declared in 1991 that the liberalisation strategy was "worked out at the IMF and World Bank and it wouldn't be possible for [the PNP] to just break away."[22]

In a sense, the only option Manley had, if he hoped to make a significant impact on Jamaica's long term development, was to go beyond Seaga's reform and truly embrace the market. Once this decision had been made and Manley became convinced that liberalisation represented the way forward, he quickly began to intensify the process.

Throughout his three years of office, Manley never wavered from his commitment to liberalisation and never attempted to halt the process. Indeed, he often implemented liberalisation measures over the objections of various external agencies and the local private sector. Manley wavered, however, on the extent and methodology of liberalisation, but never the general economic framework. Clearly, Manley genuinely believed that liberalisation would successfully transform the Jamaican economy.

While Manley remained committed to the liberalisation process, he did not abandon his commitment to social principles and ideals. Even critics on the left who argued that Manley had become a "liberal democrat" still believed that Manley's "basic commitment to improve the lot of the masses and to raise the working people's social position remain[ed]."[23] In his public addresses, Manley repeatedly stressed his belief in the principles of social justice and equality.

In government, Manley created the Micro-Investment Development Agency (MIDA) to provide credit for small businesses, instituted a limited land reform programme that leased or sold land to small farmers, offered Radio Jamaica for a public offering, and created a small number of community councils throughout the island. His successful efforts to increase the number of low income houses even impressed members of the opposition. Seaga decried the declining levels of social expenditure in education and health as laid out in the PNP five-year plan, but recognised that Manley clearly was committed to increased housing, a view echoed by the Island Superviser of the JLP-affiliated BITU who also praised the Manley government for its efforts to increase housing. After the announcement of the "new economic strategy" in 1990, Manley announced a social support programme to mitigate its negative effects. Tight fiscal constraints often forced Manley to place economic objectives above desired social action—as in the sale of the government shares in NCB to a business group instead of to the public. Even in these cases, however, the government used the proceeds from the sale of government enterprises to fund other social programmes (such as the sale of shares in the West Indies Glass Company which went to support the MIDA programme).

Bureaucratic obstacles also hindered the implementation of various social programmes. For example, the government ran into "tremendous problems" with the land reform programme that included the lack of surveying capacity for land and difficulties with extension services. Budget problems also held up the costly community council and enterprise organisation programmes.

For Manley, the social dislocation and depression that resulted from his economic strategy had a significant impact on him. In an interview, Manley described his "greatest disappointment" in his three-year term in office during the 1990's as the "terrible pain from the so-called masses [during] the period of adjustment. It is a source of unending sadness to me...a terrible agony [because] the masses are very battered and sad and disillusioned...But what do you do? Where are the resources? How much money can we spend? We don't have the money to fix anything."[24]

POLITICAL CAPITAL AND ECONOMIC LIBERALISATION

Nelson identifies three crucial variables in the implementation of economic reform: (1) political leader's commitment to stabilisation measures (often called 'political will'); (2) governmental ability to implement stabilisation measures; and (3) the responses of key interest groups and the public at large to those measures.[25] Using these criteria, Manley clearly succeeded in the implementation of substantive preliminary aspects of the economic liberalisation process and in fact serves almost as a model of how the liberalisation process should be executed.

Political Capital and Stature

Manley's commitment to working class concerns and his overtly populist appeals during the 1970's contributed to his tremendous popularity among the Jamaican people. His socially-oriented actions in government during his term in office—passing minimum wage and maternity leave legislation, increasing access to education, attacking the problem of illiteracy, among many others—earned him the support of a wide cross-section of society. In the 1972 and 1976 elections, Manley received majority support from all major class groups and won resounding victories in both elections.

Ever since his election in 1972, Manley has indisputably been the most popular leader in the country—a position he held right up until the day he resigned (and beyond). In 1976, Jamaica's leading pollster found that 60% of the Jamaican people considered Manley to be the "most outstanding leader in the country" compared to a mere 17% for Seaga.[26] As the PNP's popularity declined with the worsening economic situation, Manley's "overwhelmingly dominant popularity" declined only marginally. Even when the PNP lost the 1980 election in the worst electoral defeat in Jamaica's history, Manley still remained the most popular leader in the country with 40% support compared to 36% for Seaga.

Throughout the 1980's, Manley's popularity returned to previous highs as Seaga's economic programme created increased hardship. Seaga's distant and technocratic style of leadership contrasted vividly with Manley's warm and personal leadership style—which further increased the support for Manley in opposition. In a 1986 poll which compared popularity levels for both Manley and Seaga, Manley was found to be "clearly the most popular of the two."[27]

Voters cited Manley's "concern for the poor, concern for the country, warmth and charm, Third World perspective, and eloquence" as the primary reasons for his popularity (in descending order—see table 7.1). More than 60% of PNP voters cited Manley's concern for the poor as Manley's best quality and nearly 40% of JLP voters agreed. In contrast, Seaga's most appealing qualities were his strong leadership, good managerial and economic skills, and sound foreign policy.

Table 7.1   Positive Qualities of Manley and Seaga as seen by Voters (1986)

Qualities liked about Mr. Seaga	JLP Voters	PNP Voters
Strong leader	41%	28%
Good manager	20%	5%
Good economic policies	30%	6%
Sound foreign policy	9%	4%
Total	100%	43%
Qualities liked about Mr. Manley	JLP Voters	PNP Voters
Concern for the poor	37%	61%
Concern for the country	9%	10%
Warmth and charm	20%	16%
Third World perspective	0%	7%
Eloquence	12%	6%
Total	78%	100%

Source: Stone, *Politics versus Economics*, 69.

When asked to identify Seaga's negative qualities, most voter's cited the following: "does not listen to anyone, dictatorial tendencies, not for the poor, does everything himself, and does not like black people." In contrast, Manley's negative qualities included "too close to communists, too weak and soft, bad policies, and poor manager." Some 26% of JLP supporters cited "too close to communists" as Manley's main negative feature, 28% felt he was "too weak and soft," 15% viewed him as having "bad policies," and 18% believed he was a "poor manager," For PNP supporters, only 14% felt that Manley was too close to communists, 24% viewed him as "too weak and soft," 10% felt that he was a "poor manager," and none viewed him as having "bad policies."

One year before the 1989 national election, polls showed that Manley still remained the most popular leader in the country with 38% support among the electorate compared to only 24% for the next highest political figure (Seaga). Two months before the election, Manley's popularity had shot up to nearly 60% while Seaga's had declined to 28%. Another poll conducted in the same year demonstrated that the PNP held a majority of all class groups (the largest majorities in the "working" and "lower" classes) except for the "upper class." The "upper class" comprised 5% of the electorate and four-fifths of that class supported the JLP. In the 1989 election, the PNP received 57% of the popular vote, compared to 43% for the JLP, and assumed forty-five (45) of the sixty (60) seats in Parliament.

Manley, therefore, assumed office with tremendous popular support. Most Jamaicans believed that Manley possessed a genuine concern for the poor and that his actions would reflect this concern. In all of Manley's broadcasts to the nation—right up until his resignation in March 1992—Manley always focused on social programmes and his commitment to social reform (regardless of the primary purpose of his message).

During the first year of Manley's term of office, his popularity rating remained high and the confidence of the people in PNP ministers was also high, with 42% of the public finding something impressive in at least one of the new government ministers. Public approval ratings slowly dropped as the economic crisis became worse, but even throughout 1990, overall ratings were high (in May 1990, the government got an overall favourable rating of 70%). It was only in late 1991—when the economy had been hit by a series of steep devaluations—that the PNP began to lose support to the JLP.

During the 1970's, Manley had set a precedent of communicating with the Jamaican people in broadcasts to the nation, an act which served to successfully mitigate the harsh effects of the IMF measures implemented between 1977 and 79. In July 1978, Manley announced an austere IMF package that had no social cushions and which reduced real wages by 25%. Nelson documents how the PNP addressed the measure:

[T]he announcement was promptly followed by a vigorous and extensive program of explanation in which the Prime Minister and members of his cabinet took the lead. The stabilization program was beset by broader economic and political pressures and collapsed inside of a year. But it is noteworthy that for seven or eight months labor unions confined their reactions to public grumblings, and restrained their members from more active protest...One is led to speculate that [Manley's] vigorous and clear campaign to explain stabilization measures [was extremely] helpful in avoiding initial outbursts.[28]

In 1979, Manley explained in an interview how he felt about the role of communication with the people of Jamaica: "One thing that I think is important too is that we have never run away from the people or tried to hold [our ideology] down oppressively. [We have] gone out constantly and ceaselessly just to talk, to explain, and in my case to apologize and say that I am sorry that it is so hard—because it is hard. But listen to the problem, and these are the facts. That may have helped in some way."[29]

In the 1990's, Manley continued this tradition of speaking with the nation on a regular basis to explain in simple language where the economy was headed. In addition, as the liberalisation process intensified, Manley himself traveled around the island to attend public education sessions to explain liberalisation and to allow citizens to ask questions about the process. Similarly, when Manley created the Committee of Government Structure, he instructed it to hold a series of public meetings across the island to gather public feedback and opinion, which it did.

Political Capital, Powerful Leadership, and Quelling Internal Dissent

Manley's overwhelming popularity within his own party helped to quell opposition and create consensus around the liberalisation strategy—which had created riots and a national strike under Seaga less than five years previously. As demonstrated, Manley sought to have the delegates of the PNP approve his new economic strategy because he felt that an official demonstration of unanimity would facilitate the implementation of the liberalisation strategy.

Prior to the 1990 party convention, Manley spent hours meeting with delegates and other party officials to explain the ramifications of the new liberalisation procedures. For Manley, it took "years of intensive and sometimes agonising political education work to carry the party with the changes in my own perception."[30] While Manley's efforts at education clearly had some effect, he still needed to use his immense popularity to generate widespread internal support. With the implied threat that he would resign if the PNP did not endorse his new economic agenda, the party voted overwhelmingly (only 2 of over 3000 dissenting) to support his plan.

Although many PNP leaders eventually came to understand and accept the new liberalisation process, it was clearly Manley who led the PNP onto the new economic path. As Manley himself admits,

> I am the one who ideologised the PNP...I was the one who said 'look here, you can't have a party without an ideology,' and I rammed it through and educated and taught. I took a lot of flak and made a lot of mistakes but...[the party members eventually understood] that I had not turned into an opportunist, but at the worst had embarked on a new round of mistakes, but thought-out and deliberate and sincere mistakes...They were accustomed by then to deal with ideas so they can talk about export orientation [and] economic formation preceding [social welfare], even if it took a reluctant difficult period to begin to come to a new understanding. And what they are now doing is largely reflecting my reaction to reality and their reaction to my reaction to reality. I don't mean that arrogantly. But that's what you have a bloody leader for.[31]

In addition, Manley's actions before and during his term in office demonstrated a serious commitment to preventing internal dissent. Prior to his election, Manley had either removed or ensured the removal of all major leftist members from the hierarchy of the party. His extensive political education campaign prior to his return to office ensured that the ministers all possessed a general agreement on basic principles such as the role of the private sector and the role of the state in Jamaica's future economic development. While Manley always strove for unity of purpose, this did not preclude extensive opportunity for internal debate. Indeed, in Cabinet meetings, numerous ministers confirmed that Manley actively encouraged debate and opposition, but always demanded consensus in the end—even if this required spending hours trying to convince someone of his position.

In this regard, Manley benefited from his obvious seniority in the party and the resultant respect which he commanded. PNP ministers fell into two categories with regard to their relationship with Manley. First, several ministers—especially the younger ones—were in "political hock" to Manley. Manley had actively encouraged and supported them when they first entered politics and they owed their political success to him. Second, many older ministers were Manley's close personal friends who had served under him during the 1970's and had tremendous respect for him. Without coercion, Manley assembled a team of ministers who professed absolute loyalty to him and who would not have publicly expressed their disagreement with him.

The Claude Clarke incident dissuaded ministers from insurrectionist tendencies. A few months after the 1989 election, Minister of Commerce Clarke had stated that basic food prices would not increase without his permission—although the Finance Minister had earlier announced that the prices would increase. Manley responded swiftly by firing Clarke in what was essentially a minor squabble. Notably, Clarke was a relatively young minister who had only recently joined the party hierarchy. Manley used him to set a precedent of intolerance for public dissension within the party because he felt that this would erode the government's credibility.

For the rank and file, Manley provided an ideological justification for his actions that helped to quell brewing internal dissent. This differed substantially from Seaga, who had projected an image of a healer trying to rebuild the economy by carefully following IMF and World Bank prescriptions. Seaga was a rebuilder, not a creator, moving toward intangible and inarticulated objectives.

Manley's "new" philosophy provided a guiding light that served to mitigate the harsh effects of deregulation. By constantly reminding his party of his long-term goals—social justice, equality, economic participation, and political empowerment—Manley was able to convince them to withhold their internal opposition and accept his new strategy even if they did not fully understand it. As demonstrated, party members were confused with the new methodology and many felt that the party had betrayed them. But Manley's reassurances that this was not the case prevented the spread of hostility within the party.

Manley dealt with his critics in a simple manner: he attempted to channel their criticisms to productive purposes. For example, both Trevor Munroe and D.K. Duncan condemned Manley for his sale of government enterprises without offering these businesses for public sale or without including worker representation on their boards. In response to these criticisms, Manley created ESOP—the Employee Share Ownership Plan. He then transferred the responsibilities of the privatisation agency (National Investment Bank of Jamaica) to the Office of the Prime Minister and appointed both Munroe and Duncan to the board of the NIBJ so that they would take an active role in ensuring the success of the ESOP programme. In this way, the criticisms were muted as Duncan and Munroe had a practical and useful outlet to vent their frustrations. Similarly, when Manley created his Committee on Government Structure, he appointed one of his most vocal critics and prominent journalist, Dawn Ritch, to serve on the think tank. Her attacks on the government were then channelled into productive use.

To the general public, Manley represented the elder statesman of Jamaican politics. In dozens of interviews and conversations with people from all ideological and political backgrounds—many of whom vehemently oppose Manley—less than a handful of those with whom this author spoke, expressed doubt about Manley's sincerity and commitment to improving the conditions of the Jamaican people. One such person is Wilmot Perkins. Despite their professional differences (for example, Manley sued Perkins for slander), the two men share a cordial relationship. Manley has a widespread reputation—that cuts across party lines—for fairness, justice, and the highest standards of personal integrity.

Manley put this popular image to good use, as demonstrated by the tremendous amount of time he spent communicating with the Jamaican people in broadcasts and in personal appearances at all-island 'liberalisation' education forums. It seems clear that no other Jamaican could have forged—and maintained—such a powerful national alliance and minimised opposition, while presiding over such a radical and admittedly economically painful ideological shift.

Relationship with Interest Groups, External Agencies, and the U.S.

Manley always professed his belief in participatory government. As early as 1973, Manley outlined a model of governance which he labeled the "politics of participation" that aimed "to make people feel that they have a part to play in the decision-making processes of government."[32] He argued that the government needed to "create institutions through which people feel continuously involved in the decision-making process as these unfold in response to the interplay between idealist commitment and realistic challenge." Central to this strategy was the creation of an "economic planning council...supported by advisory committees in which the politician, the government technician and the relevant institutional leadership meet regularly to discuss and plan."

During his time in opposition, Manley's call for a National Planning Council became a central plank of the PNP election platform. After his election in 1989, Manley established a National Planning Council under the direction of the Deputy Prime Minister. The Council included representatives from the private sector, the trade union movement, and the professional class; observers from the University of West Indies and the National Consumers League; and government representatives from seven economic ministries, the Planning Institute, and the Bank of Jamaica. In addition, Manley created the Economic and Production Council (a companion body to the National Planning Council) and several sectoral councils for tourism, education, and industry and commerce—all of which the private sector participated in actively.

In a significant move, Manley included private sector and trade union representatives on his negotiating teams with multilateral and bilateral agencies. This effort was warmly received by the private sector leadership. The unions also saw the trips to Washington as exceedingly helpful because they were able to state their case and petition for more favourable conditionalities in major agreements. Because Manley allowed explicit private sector and union support and participation in these negotiations, these groups had little basis to complain, because the more logical move was to intensify their advocacy position within the established channels that Manley had facilitated.   .

The decision to include these groups was particularly helpful for the Jamaican government in its relationship with external agencies. Trade union and private sector leadership projected an image of unity of purpose to the agencies and demonstrated that Manley had established close working relationship with these key interest groups. Manley's commitment to liberalisation reform and this support from the interest groups, so pleased the IMF that the organisation gave Jamaica a "clean bill of health" which helped to secure other sources of grants and loans.

On a more informal basis, Manley and all his minister's maintained a consistent record of being available to private sector representatives. Manley regularly sought private sector advice on many significant policy issues and even invited the President of the Private Sector Organisation of Jamaica (PSOJ) to chair an advisory task force on various aspects of the economy. Indeed, most businessmen argued that the relationship with the Manley government was the best that the private sector had ever shared with any government. While businessmen outside the official organisational networks still criticised the government, criticisms from powerful private sector organisations remained muted. Manley was also helped by the fact that his efforts at cooperation contrasted vividly with Seaga's highly imperialistic and distrustful style.

Manley also benefited from a close working relationship with the United States which he worked extremely hard to secure. Just one month after his election, Manley visited key officials in the United States government and met with senior Congressmen and Senators to persuade them of his commitment to market reform. During his term in office, he visited Bush on two occasions. Bush was impressed with Manley's reform efforts and pushed for Jamaica to become a major beneficiary of the Enterprise for America Initiative—which reduced the island's debt burden by a substantial amount. In this regard, Jamaica also benefited from the work of both the Jamaican Ambassador to the United States (Bernal) and the American Ambassador to the Jamaica (Holden). Bernal had conducted extensive research on EAI and lobbied hard for Jamaica to be a beneficiary. Holden is a personal friend of President Bush and had long suggested that Jamaica could be a 'model' for the EAI program. Bush repeatedly praised Manley for his efforts and provided Jamaica with access to various sources of financing, such as the highly prized Economic Stability Fund.

In addition to official relations, Manley also appealed to private investors in the United States by attending and speaking at several investment conventions. He made a particular plea to expatriate Jamaicans, and even set up special foreign currency accounts, among other measures, to increase investment from this group.

Favourable Conditions—A Neutralised Opposition and The Economic Environment

Manley also benefited from numerous exogenous factors that helped him in the reform process. Manley effectively swept the ideological rug from underneath the JLP which left the opposition party dormant during the first year-and-a-half of the Manley government. In 1991, Seaga did not criticise the government on any major policy issues, but argued instead that the PNP ministers were "not managers of this type of economic system. They are managers of a state model....They do not understand that the wrong signals can set things in motion which are counterproductive."[33] When Manley assumed office, he initially proclaimed a policy of continuity which left the JLP with little room for criticism. As such, during the first few months of the PNP term, the JLP did "not raise a dissenting murmur in criticism of the Government's position and policy" although Seaga did issue a few statements and published a small number of advertisements decrying the rise in prices. The JLP's dormancy was reflected in Seaga's refusal to grant interviews to the press as well as in the limited public activity of the JLP hierarchy.

In the next few months, the JLP suffered from a major internal crisis when five senior shadow spokesmen within the party (labeled the "Gang of Five" by the press) openly challenged Seaga as the leader of the party. Seaga quickly moved to strip these party members of their shadow responsibilities and attempted to prevent them from running in the next election for the JLP. Although the press and the public considered the "continuing crisis in the top leadership of the Jamaica Labour Party...the most serious matter facing the nation,"[34] Seaga dismissed that charge and argued instead that the departed shadow ministers were easily replaceable. The leadership issue occupied the attentions of the media for months and reflected just how autocratic the JLP had become under Seaga's leadership.

In addition to this incident, the party also suffered a setback when a former JLP Minister was convicted in the courts for corruption—which only increased charges that other members of the JLP had been similarly corrupt. Thus, even though voters were growing disenchanted with the PNP under the declining economic conditions, the JLP did not seem like a particularly appealing option since it was riddled with internal strife and tainted with signs of dubious practices.

In late 1991, the JLP began to awaken from its opposition slumber. In October, the party staged a peaceful march against the government. This march drew sharp criticisms from various private sector groups that felt such incidences hindered Jamaica's tourism and investment prospects. Journalists and political commentators also condemned the JLP for "political dishonesty and hypocrisy of the basest kind."[35]   In the wake of this disapproval, the JLP discontinued public marches and instead re-activated its party machinery to prepare for a future election. In addition, Seaga launched a series of vocal and biting attacks on the PNP government.

Manley benefited from a favourable external economic environment for most of his term in office. For the three years of Manley's tenure, the bauxite/alumina industry and the tourist industry both witnessed unprecedented levels of growth and expansion. Major bauxite companies (which had closed under Seaga) returned as the aluminum market experienced boom conditions—and the production levy had been reduced to 3.5%. Existing companies also began to establish plans for multi-million dollar expansion projects. The price of other traditional exports such as sugar and bananas also increased during this period, which gave a boost to both these agricultural industries. The construction boom in the post-rehabilitation period of Hurricane Gilbert also helped the economy and managed to keep down unemployment.

In the middle of Manley's term in office, the government was hit by the effects of the crisis in the Persian Gulf—an unexpected jump in the price of oil and a slowdown in the tourist industry as Americans became cautious about international travel.   Fortunately, the Gulf crisis did not persist for an extended period and Jamaica quickly recovered from the effects. In addition, near the end of his term of office, the recession in the United States also had a negative impact on the Jamaican economy. At the time of Manley's resignation, the United States remained mired in the recession which continued to hinder the expansion of certain sectors of the Jamaican economy.

THE MANAGEMENT AND APPLICATION OF ECONOMIC LIBERALISATION

Political Inexperience and Liberalisation Delay

On assuming power in 1989, the PNP faced numerous difficulties. All the senior members of the party (including Manley) had been out of parliament for six years. Even though the PNP had held a number of special education meetings in oppositon, had underwent significant ideological preparation, and had participated in a series of public sessions, it was very difficult for the party to readjust to leadership. This difficult period of readjustment was exacerbated by the fact that the PNP did not have access to privileged information about the JLP government strategy prior to the 1989 election.

The first few months in office are often known as the "honeymoon period" when a government has the best opportunity to implement unpopular measures without fear of much opposition. The PNP spent this time simply coming to grips with and fully understanding the state of the economy. The only economic measures—such as lifting food subsidies and divesting hotels—were done out of sheer necessity rather than as part of an overall economic plan, as Manley groped to find resources anywhere he could.

Several other factors also held up the application of the liberalisation process. In opposition, Manley did not possess a detailed election platform. Manley won the election largely because the people rejected Seaga and because they hoped Manley would provide a "human face" to the austere structural adjustment process. Manley had not jeopardised his chances by embarking on a complex economic plan for the future (which would have been subject to criticism). Rather, he had opted for populist platitudes such as "we put the people first" to woo the working class, and "the private sector should lead economic development" to win over the business class.

In office, Manley delayed the liberalisation process at first because he was not fully committed to it in the beginning. Recognising that he had no long term comprehensive plan, Manley met with the PNP National Executive Council two months after his election and charged it with developing an agenda for the future. While a special committee of the NEC worked on this task, numerous government committees and working groups prepared a five-year plan. Manley concentrated on finding scarce resources and establishing international relationships. Only in the beginning of 1990 did Manley finally embrace the harsh economic realities and embark on the liberalisation course.

Liberalisation in Implementation: Gradualism and Caution

When Manley fully adopted the liberalisation path, he did so gradually and cautiously at first. This caution turned out to be an extremely wise decision. To have moved any faster would have fueled charges of desperation and would have eroded business confidence. Manley kept a close pulse on the levels of business confidence through feedback from business groups and by watching the activity on the Stock Market. Manley was cautious to act only when Stock Market activity seemed particularly buoyant and only after he felt that private sector leaders would, on the whole, approve. Indeed, this extensive period of pre-consultation and negotiation before the announcement of major acts only slowed down the reform process even more. But again, this consultation and communication was essential for the measures to succeed.

For example, in the implementation of the General Consumption Tax (GCT), Manley delayed it by nearly one year (bureaucratic obstacles also held up the implementation of the tax). During that period, the government spent millions of dollars on an advertisement campaign—which included newspaper, radio, and television advertisements as well as public education sessions across the island—to explain how the tax would work and the make clear that the tax was not a new tax, but merely a shift in taxation from production to consumption. The months of deliberate education eventually paid off as, despite some initial confusion, there was limited opposition to the tax when it was introduced and the rates of return were higher than the government expected.

In spite of successful cases such as these (and others such as MIDA), Manley's government did not adequately address some significant concerns. For example, the government failed to implement necessary anti-trust legislation before deregulating certain industries. In a cartelised economy like Jamaica's where companies have a long history of protected markets and oligopolistic production, deregulation provided the opportunity for a small number of companies in specific markets to collude and fix prices. Although Manley promised anti-trust legislation from the very beginning, the Fair Competition Act to fulfill this purpose was not tabled until early 1992 (and still has not passed) because of the complexities associated with the subject matter.

While the PNP addressed economic liberalisation, it never seriously tackled the liberalisation of the political process—the enactment of major bureaucratic reform. During the 1980's, Seaga had established the Administrative Reform Programme (ARP) to address the massive state bureaucracy. The ARP had resulted in only marginal improvements and the bureaucratic apparatus still posed a major obstacle to economic development and investment. Manley recognised this fact and sought private sector leadership to help reform the civil service and other aspects of the government bureaucracy. These efforts were continued and intensified under P.J. Patterson. Indeed, Patterson took the politically dangerous (but necessary) decision to reduce the civil service by over 8000 members, something Manley failed to do.

Personal Leadership: Manley's Lack of Control and Strong Crisis Management

In his personal leadership, Manley failed to project the image of a leader who exerted control over the actions of his ministers. Manley made a poor decision to adopt a hands-off approach to leadership during his first few months in office—when a more direct and participatory role was needed the most. Manley's distance from the day-to-day affairs led to the numerous "scandals" that plagued the party during the three years. Interestingly, despite that fact that numerous ministers were charged with poor judgement and irresponsible behavior—including the current Prime Minister—Manley was never accused of any wrongdoing or inappropriate behavior. Despite this fact, these scandals dealt a particularly painful blow to Manley, who held ultimate responsibility and who had always called for the highest standards of integrity and honesty within government.

One of Manley's best demonstrations of leadership was his crisis management in response to these "scandals." After each incident, Manley called a major press conference to explain in full detail the events in the incident, commissioned a report or study to investigate for any misconduct, personally accepted responsibility for all wrongdoing, and, in the case of the Shell scandal, totally reworked his Cabinet. His assumption of a more direct role in the affairs of government reassured the Jamaican people that the PNP had not gone astray, and emphasised that Manley had not abandoned his task at hand—to transform the economy.

EXAMINING JAMAICA'S POLITICAL AND ECONOMIC FUTURE

Manley's Impact: A Political Evaluation

Several major political changes arose both in Manley's term of office and since his departure. First, Manley's departure marks the beginning of the end of the "cult of personality" in Jamaican politics. Manley's overwhelming popularity allowed him almost unlimited freedom to act within his own party and substantial room to implement economic reform in a generally receptive public arena. As demonstrated, however, the economic hardships—caused by uncontrollable devaluation and resultant bouts of price increases—began to erode Manley's political capital. Indeed, in the months preceding his resignation, the signs had become clear that Manley's power of political persuasion had diminished somewhat. As early as 1990, polls began to show a dip in Manley's popularity—even though he remained the country's most popular political leader.

More importantly, even within his own party, Manley's influence was waning. In a race for the new General Secretary of the PNP, Manley openly supported one candidate who won by only 20 votes out of over 3000 delegates. In the past, if Manley had supported someone, there would have been no doubt that the person would have won an overwhelming victory. Now that Manley has departed, his successor, P.J. Patterson, lacks the popular grassroots support within the PNP that Manley possessed. Patterson is forced to use his ability and competence rather than his personality and charm to generate internal support—and indeed the support of the public at large. Although populist tendencies may resurface later (Patterson beat a populist candidate in the race for party leader), it seems clear that economic results and managerial competence will be the critical factors in future elections and leadership races.

Manley's shift to the right and his ostensibly weak emphasis on social policy resulted in an increase in popular cynicism and a decline in the power of the traditional political party structure. This cynicism was reflected in a popular song by noted reggae artiste Mutabaruka called "The People's Court" in which Manley (who is mockingly called "Senator change-my-mind") is impersonated and is put on trial for his crimes against the Jamaican people. Seaga is also impersonated and put on trial; both leaders are then sentenced to 1000 years as punishment.

The shift from the JLP and PNP is also manifest in the rise of popular "third party" movements such as the New Beginning Movement, which generated significant national interest. As noted, however, the New Beginning Movement, although it supports third party candidates, is not itself and does not intend to be a third party. Although the group has come under attack for its seeming lack of an agenda, the publicity it has received indicates a shift away from the established party system. Moreover, polls demonstrate the highest levels of uncommitted voters in Jamaica's history, further illustrating the decline of both the PNP and JLP.

Most significantly, Manley succeeded in enacting a psychological transformation in how the Jamaican people view the role of the state. Manley took the extremely bold and unpopular move not to capitulate to the persuasive patron-client network which has pervaded Jamaica's political culture for the past fifty years. This is not to argue that the clientist state has been dismantled. Indeed, it persists. Manley made many efforts to heighten awareness about the patron-client structure and spent a great deal of time encouraging people to abandon it. Manley has been helped in this regard by the diminishing amounts of resources to distribute as a part of the patron-client network. In his many speeches, Manley repeatedly stressed that the state could no longer serve as the provider and that individuals had to use opportunities available to them in order to improve their standard of living.

In his actions, Manley did not employ cheap political tricks and overt partisan policies to secure political support. Indeed, he implemented various measures to avoid this. In the development of the MIDA programme, for example, Manley instituted a system where political affiliation would not play a role in the disbursement of credit. Manley appointed Ronald Thwaites to chair MIDA, which reflects Manley's commitment to incorporate his critics into the political process. As Convenor of the New Beginning Movement, Thwaites repeatedly attacked the Manley government—and continued to do so despite his political appointment within the government.

Manley's Impact: An Economic Evaluation

On the economic side, Manley's reforms clearly produced several negative results. One of Manley's most vocal economic critics—a former Governor of the Bank of Jamaica—evaluated Manley's contribution in his three-year term and concluded that the massive devaluation of the dollar and spiraling inflation had instigated a period of economic instability reminiscent of the 1970's.[36] He argued that Manley demonstrated "how costly in terms of missed opportunities and suffering, have been [Manley's] ideological adventures...and the inappropriate policies implemented by [him]."[37]

After Manley's resignation, noted pollster and academic Carl Stone compared the Manley regime of the 1970's, Seaga's term in office during the 1980's, and the recent Manley period of rule in the 1990's.[38] Stone rated the three periods out of a total 150 points based on fifteen criteria including economic growth, export and manufacturing levels, the cost of living, business confidence, and private sector profits. Stone awarded 91 points to Seaga (who "tops the scale"), 81 points to Manley during the 1990's, and 71 points to Manley during the 1970's. In addition, Stone stressed that Manley (in the 1990's) improved his score "by following what Eddie [Seaga] did in the 1980's."

When Manley resigned, Seaga also reviewed Manley's term in office, arguing that in the first seven months of his rule, Manley was lax in controlling liquidity which led to increased inflation; after imposing tight monetary policies and returning to stability, the government reduced interest rates and lifted the wage ceiling which resulted in excessive demand and caused devaluation of the currency; in a move of desperation, the government lifted exchange controls which put the economy on a "downhill course."[39]

One of the greatest weaknesses of the Manley government was its inability to control inflation which skyrocketed to unprecedented levels. To counter this inflation, Manley implemented draconian monetary policy to restrict demand. This led to a severe contraction of credit with the implementation of exceedingly high interest rates that ranged upwards of 60% (these remain today). This lack of credit led to a temporary halt in inflation, but in the process, it effectively crippled the productive capacity of the nation. With little credit, producers and exporters couldn't expand to meet the demands of the market.

Although the dollar devalued massively, this devaluation represents a necessary move if the currency hopes to find its realistic market rate. Despite his vigorous efforts, Manley failed to establish confidence among business leaders in the stability of the currency. These efforts were hindered by two factors. First, Manley's indecision in the early stages of liberalisation, such as vacillating between the auction, interbank, and fixed exchange rate systems, created the image of poor mismanagment and weak control over economic affairs. Second, Manley made some unwise moves such as targeting the banking sector for taxation. This selective taxation—clearly born out of necessity—only made commerical banks wary of future unilateral acts on the part of the government.

Despite obvious blotches on Manley's economic record, he did achieve limited success in certain areas. In central government management, Manley kept the public sector deficit at minimum levels—and even generated a small surplus. The current account deficit was also reduced, although consumer imports still need to be reduced further. Manley also managed to halt—and reverse—Bank of Jamaica arrears and net international reserves (although these still remain at critically low levels).

Economic expansion reached new highs under Manley as new corporations and small enterprises had vast opportunities and various incentives opened up to them. After a brief lull, the stock market climbed to new highs, setting record after record. Businesses began to expand and financial institutions established branches in the United States—which had never been done before. Private and foreign investment increased substantially, although bureaucratic obstacles remain that hinder greater levels of investment.

Most importantly, Jamaica made substantial headway into reducing its foreign debt. Manley's efforts at reducing and rescheduling debt resulted in a drop in Jamaica's debt from US$4.1 billion in 1990 to US$3.8 billion at the end of 1991—a major decrease. As a result, Jamaica's credit rating—which had plummeted in the past—improved substantially. The percentage of export earnings that went to debt servicing was also reduced, although the devaluation of the currency has offset many of these gains. Manley placed the economy on footing where it was poised for an economic take-off.

Patterson in Power: Implications for the Future

In March 1992, P.J. Patterson, the chairman of the PNP and long-time Manley associate, became Prime Minister of Jamaica. Patterson had served as an ideological moderate during the 1970's and had played a critical role in the PNP's move to the right during the 1980's. He possesses extensive political experience, but has been accused on many occasions of poor judgement. In addition, at the time of Manley's resignation, many commentators viewed Patterson as lacking Manley's personal popularity, and he was widely perceived as a technocrat. On his assumption of office, Patterson faced a difficult task. Patterson had to address (and continues to address) several critical areas to continue the liberalisation of the economy.

First, Patterson had to make his immediate priority the

stabilisation of the currency, which is the necessary prerequisite to production and expansion. This issue was made explicit in an open letter written to the Prime Minister published in the *Daily Gleaner* in which columnist Carl Stone outlined the various issues that he felt Patterson needed to address as Prime Minister. Interestingly, Patterson sent a personal response to Stone, which indicated Patterson's intentions not to alienate significant social actors, and instead to maintain an open and cordial relations with them.

If Manley failed in establishing business confidence in the currency, Patterson's chances at succeeding seemed very slim indeed when he came to power. Patterson has benefited, however, from the so-called "Butch Stewart Initiative" in which the Sandals hotel chain (of which Stewart is majority owner) offered to sell US$1 million at a fixed rate of J$25 to one to the productive sector in Jamaica. In his first few weeks of office, Patterson made some wise decisions, such as not reshuffling the Cabinet when he had the opportunity to do so. Instead he kept the same team—and most importantly kept the Minister of Finance (Hugh Small) who had opposed him in the race for Prime Minister—which led to a smooth succession and little economic turbulence.

Second, Patterson had to perform a careful balancing act of both reducing obstacles to production and maintaining tight monetary policy to contain inflation. Patterson faces a dilemma. On one hand, he must maintain high interest rates and tight monetary policy to hold liquidity; on the other hand, he needs to reduce interest rates so as to allow an increase in productive activity. To resolve this dilemma, Patterson must make an effort to target select industries and reduce interest rates in them to allow investment in these areas (necessary for growth) while still restricting inflationary tendencies in other spheres of the economy. In this way, he can adequately address both objectives.

Third, Patterson must continue and intensify incentives to businesses in order to increase export and production. Toward this end, Patterson has continued the implementation of tough and restrictive monetary policy to halt the slide of the dollar. Under Manley, the selective taxation of the banking sector and the repressive practices of the Liberalisation Support Unit (LSU) created an environment of insecurity within the business community. Patterson has met regularly with bankers, exporters, manufacturers, and other businessmen and assured them that the government will not implement arbitrary measures in the future.

Most importantly, Patterson must not fall victim to political pressures for fiscal expansionism that will reverse the crucial reforms in place so far. In the succession race, Patterson ran against a populist who promised the Jamaican people an increased focus on social policy if she became Prime Minister. In doing so, she raised the expectations of the people which intensified the political pressures that Patterson faces. While Patterson has expressed his firm commitment to the new path, whether he will succumb to powerful political temptation remains unknown. Only time will tell.

Summary and Conclusion

Manley and Liberalisation: An Evaluation

Unlike Seaga, Manley possessed a significant amount of political capital that allowed him to implement the socially and politically unpopular liberalisation process without significant opposition. In addition to sweeping the ideological rug from under the opposition (the JLP), Manley also made significant overtures to key actors—such as the private sector, trade unions, and the United States—that helped him to implement the free-market reform. Moreover, his fairly extensive communication with the Jamaican people and his explanation of the ideological justification and long-term objectives of the liberalisation strategy played a critical role in winning the support of the electorate and the rank and file of his party.

Despite his success in transforming the economy, Manley suffered from numerous difficulties that included his inconsistent and delayed application of the liberalisation programme, worsening image problem, and relatively poor economic management. External factors such as the Gulf War crisis also hindered the liberalisation efforts and exacerbated the short-term decline of the economy. On the other hand, the country benefited greatly from the government's efforts at reducing Jamaica's bilateral debt through the Enterprise for America's Initiative (EAI) and similar debt reduction plans.

The PNP's internal and external difficulties, coupled with a sharp decline in living standards, conspired to erode Manley's political capital and generated an increase in social opposition to the liberalisation strategy. By the time of Manley's resignation, the nation had already undergone the substantive aspects of the economic liberalisation. Although the gains will not be realised until the currency stabilises and investments reach fruition, the framework is in place to ensure positive economic gains in the future. Many economic problems, obstacles, and hardships remain, but Manley has successfully utilised his political capital to implement the difficult part of the liberalisation process. Provided that the liberalisation process is continued, Manley's efforts in transforming the Jamaican economy will result in significant long-term gains, to offset the extensive short term suffering that these efforts have produced.

Reassessing Manley's Ideological Transformation

Several similarities exist between Manley's actions during the 1970's and then during the 1990's. In both 1972 and 1989, Manley ran on purely populist platforms without ideological substance. On both occasions, Manley realised after a few years in power that he needed an ideological framework to clarify his long-term objectives and to revitalise the Jamaican people. In 1972, Manley embraced socialism because it had always been the ideology of the PNP—and thus would silence criticisms that he had embarked on a radical ideological experiment. The vague definition of democratic socialism allowed Manley to embark on just such an experiment, which resulted in internal PNP factionalism.

During the 1970's, Manley's ideological extremism alienated the private sector and the United States while his overestimation of the capacity of the state quickly led to economic crisis which resulted in his 1980 defeat. During the 1980's, Manley realised that he needed private sector support and thus he actively pursued improved relations. He also recognised that the state could not serve as the means of social transformation and thus he expressed his belief in the private sector as the engine of growth.

Manley still believed, however, in the principles of equality and social justice. At the same time, he recognised that the state could not provide the resources necessary to finance these social objectives. His initial policy of continuity with a social emphasis failed to produce the desired economic results and—bolstered by the rapidly changing international environment—Manley embraced the market. To make it compatible with his principles, Manley synthesised elements of his earlier socialist beliefs with the new market strategy. Whereas in the 1970's, Manley believed that the state could provide direct access to social ownership, in the 1990's, he had come to believe that he could facilitate greater opportunity to participation through the market.

Manley's ideological transformation has been profound. He effectively abandoned a central tenet of his earlier beliefs (state-led socialism) and adopted a strategy he had opposed vigorously (free-market liberalisation)—while still maintaining a general philosophical framework (democratic socialism). Throughout the process of his transformation, he was driven by a burning desire to improve the social and economic conditions of the Jamaican people.

In the Bible, the children of Israel experienced a period of stability and prosperity under Joshua's leadership. Upon Joshua's departure, however, the cry for a return to the ways of the past resurfaced and engulfed the nation of Israel in crisis. Eventually, the children of Israel forsake the Lord and returned to the worship of the pagan god, Baal. The people of Jamaica face such a critical juncture in their history. Michael Manley has forcefully and painfully brought the nation to the brink of economic viability by reducing the protectionist chains that have hindered its productivity for decades. Under Patterson, Jamaica can either surge forward into the economically competitive world of the future or it can gradually withdraw into the politically-biased cocoon of the past. Necessity dictates that it must choose the former path if it ever hopes to enter the promised land.

ENDNOTES

Chapter 1

[1] Owen Jefferson, *Post War Economic Development of Jamaica* (Jamaica: Institute of Social and Economic Research, 1972), 285.

[2] Gene Tidrick, "Wage Spillover and Unemployment in a Wage-Gap Economy: The Jamaican Case," (*Economic Development and Cultural Change*, vol. 23, no. 2, 1975), 306-24.

Chapter 2

[1] See M.G. Smith, "The Plural Framework of Jamaican Society," (*The British Journal of Sociology*, vol.13, no.3,1961), and M.G.Smith, *The Plural Society in the West Indies* (Los Angeles: University of California Press, 1965).

[2] Quoted in Jackie Ranston, *From We Were Boys: The Story of the Magnificent Cousins Manley and Bustamante* (Jamaica: Bustamante Institute of Public and International Affairs, 1989), 119.

[3] Winston Van Horne, "Jamaica: Why Manley Lost," (*The World Today*, vol. 37, no.11, 1981), 428.

[4] Norman Manley, *Manley and the New Jamaica: Selected Speeches and Writings (1938-68)*, Rex Nettleford, ed., (London: Longman Caribbean Ltd.1971), 61.

[5] Quoted in Trevor Munroe, *Jamaican Politics: A Marxist Perspective in Transition* (Jamaica: Heinemann Publishers (Caribbean) Ltd., 1990), 58.

[6] Michael Manley, *The Search for Solutions: Excerpts from the speeches and Writings of Michael Manley*, John Hearne, ed., (Canada: Maple House Publishing Co., 1976),173.

[7] Manley, *Manley and the New Jamaica*, 90.

[8] Anthony Payne, *Politics in Jamaica*, (London: C. Hurst & Co., 1988), 4-5.

[9] Payne, *Politics in Jamaica*, 3.

Chapter 3

[1] Michael Manley, "Jamaica's New Economic Growth," (Broadcast to the Nation: Office of the Prime Minister, September 16, 1990).

[2] Michael Manley, *The Search for Solutions: Excerpts from the Speeches and Writings of Michael Manley* (Canada: Maple House Publishing Company, 1976), 171.

[3] Quoted in Darrell Levi, *Michael Manley: The Making of a Leader* (Jamaica: Heinemann Publishers (Caribbean) Ltd.,1989), 64.

[4] Winsome Downie, *Democratic Socialism: The Jamaican Experiment* (Unpublished Ph.D. Dissertation: Columbia University, 1985), 135.

[5] Norman Manley, *Manley and the New Jamaica*, Rex Nettleford, ed., (London:

Longman Caribbean Ltd., 1971), 62.

⁶ Quoted in Levi, *Michael Manley*, 80.

⁷ Adam Kuper, *Changing Jamaica* (London: Routledge & Kegan Paul, 1976), 130-1.

⁸ Michael Manley,"Address to PNP Delegates, 36th Annual Conference of People's National Party," (Jamaica: PNP National Archives, 1974).

⁹ Manley, *The Search for Solutions*, 157.

¹⁰ Anthony Payne, "Jamaica: the 'democratic socialist' experiment," in Anthony Payne and Paul Sutton, eds., *Dependency under Challenge: The Political Economy of the Caribbean* (Manchester: Manchester University Press, 1983), 30.

¹¹ Michael Manley, *Jamaica: Struggle in the Periphery* (London: Third World Media,1982),122-3.

¹² PNP, "Principles and Objectives of the People's National Party," (Jamaica: PNP National Archives, 1978), 7.

¹³ PNP, "Principles and Objectives," 65-6.

¹⁴ Janis Johnson and Robert Rankin, "Interviewing Michael Manley: The Role of the Opposition in Jamaica,"(*Caribbean Review*, vol.13, no.3, 1982), 28.

¹⁵ Manley, *The Search of Solutions*, 71.

¹⁶ Johnson and Rankin, "Interviewing Michael Manley," 28-29.

¹⁷ Manley, *The Search for Solutions*, 136. Emphasis mine.

¹⁸ PNP, "Principles and Objectives," 14.

¹⁹ Quoted in Michael Kaufman, *Jamaican Under Manley: Dilemmas of Socialism and Democracy* (London: Zed Books, 1985), 72.

²⁰ PNP, *"Democratic Socialism: The Jamaican Model,"*(Jamaica: PNP National Archives, 1974), 157.

²¹ Michael Manley, *The Politics of Change: A Jamaican Testament* (London: Andre Deutsche, 1974), 130-1.

²² PNP, "Principles and Objectives," 24.

²³ Quoted in Linda Hoffman, *Politics of the Manley Regime in Jamaica, 1972-80* (Unpublished Ph.D. Dissertation: University of Wisconsin-Madison, 1983), 80.

²⁴ Quoted in Kaufman, *Jamaica Under Manley*, 79.

²⁵ Manley, *The Politics of Change*, 84.

²⁶ Personal Interview with Rt. Hon. Michael Manley (former Prime Minister of Jamaica, July 1989).

²⁷ Payne, "Jamaica: the 'democratic socialist' experiment'," 33.

²⁸ Evelyne Huber Stephens and John Stephens, *Democratic Socialism in Jamaica: The Political Movement and Social Transformation in Dependent Capitalism* (London: MacMillan Press, 1986), 174.

²⁹ Personal Interview with Michael Manley, July 1989.

³⁰ Carl Stone, "Democracy and Socialism in Jamaica, 1962-1979," (*Journal of Commonwealth and Comparative Politics*, vol.29, no.2, 1981), 123.

³¹ PNP, "Principles and Objectives," 42.

³² Personal Interview with Michael Manley, July 1989.

³³ Stone, "Democracy and Socialism in Jamaica," 126.

³⁴ Manley, *Struggle in the Periphery*, 220.

³⁵ Quoted in Kaufman, *Jamaica Under Manley*, 87.

³⁶ Quoted in Hoffman, *Politics of the Manley Regime*, 84.

³⁷ Stephens and Stephens, *Democratic Socialism*, 296.

³⁸ Manley, *The Search for Solutions*, 286.

³⁹ Stephens and Stephens, *Democratic Socialism*, 297.

⁴⁰ Carl Stone, *Class, Race and Political Behavior in Urban Jamaica* (Jamaica: Institute of Social and Economic Research,1973), 43.

⁴¹ "Is Michael Manley a saint or a sinner?" (*Euromoney*, August 1979), 90.

[42] Quoted in Anthony Payne, *Politics in Jamaica* (London: C. Hurst and Co.,1988), 73.

[43] Michael Manley, *Up the Down Escalator: Development and the International Economy: A Jamaican Case Study* (London:Andre Deutsch),156-7.

[44] Stephens and Stephens, *Democratic Socialism*, 131.

[45] Manley, *Struggle in the Periphery*, 160.

[46] Carl Stone, *Democracy and Clientelism in Jamaica* (New Jersey: Transaction Books, 1980), 250-2.

[47] Gladstone Bonnick, "Jamaica: Liberalization to Centralization, and Back?" in Arnold Harberger, ed., *World Economic Growth* (San Francisco: Institute for Contemporary Studies,1984), 266-70.

[48] Michael Connolly, "Comments on 'Jamaica: Liberalization to Centralization, and Back?'" in Arnold Harberger, ed., *World Economic Growth* (San Francisco: Institute for Contemprary Studies, 1984), 296.

[49] Mahmood Ayud, *Made in Jamaica* (Washington D.C.: John Hopkins University Press, 1981) documents the increase in quantitative restrictions on imports in detail.

[50] Payne, *Politics in Jamaica*, 80.

[51] Manley, *Up the Down Escalator*, 56.

[52] Robert Looney, *The Jamaican Economy in the 1980's: Economic Decline and Structural Adjustment* (Colorado: Westview Press, 1987), 24.

[53] Connolly, "Comments," 294.

[54] Morris Goldstein and Mohsin Khan, "Effects of Slowdown in Industrial Countries on Growth in Non-oil Developing Countries,"(Washington,D.C.: IMF Occasional Paper 12, 1982).

[55] See Mohan Rao, "Aspects of Jamaican Agriculture," (*Social and Economic Studies*, vol.39, no.1, 1990).

[56] Roger Robinson and Lelde Schmitz, "Jamaica Navigating Through a Troubled Decade," (*Finance and Development*, vol.26, no.4, 1989), 30.

[57] Bonnick, "Jamaica: Liberalization to Centralization, and Back?", 287.

[58] Jennifer Sharpley, "Jamaica,1972-80," in Tony Killick, ed., *Developing Country Experiences* (New York: St. Martin's Press, 1984), 129.

[59] Norman Girvan and Richard Bernal, "The IMF and Foreclosure of Development Options: The Case of Jamaica," (*Monthly Review*, February 1982), 42.

[60] Looney, *Jamaican Economy*, 47.

[61] Sharpley, "Jamaica" 147-9.

Chapter 4

[1] Wilmot Perkins, "Mutterings from Afar," (*Money Index*, 23 February, 1988), 28.

[2] Quoted in Joseph Treaster, "From Fiery Man of Jamaica Politics, a Mea Culpa," (*The New York Times*, 21 September 1987).

[3] Personal Interview with Hon. Rex Nettleford (Chairman, Committee on Government Structure, January 1992).

[4] Rex Nettleford, *Mirror, Mirror: Identity, Race and Protest in Jamaica* (Jamaica: Collins Sangster, 1970), 87.

[5] Personal Interview with Rt. Hon. Edward Seaga (Leader of the Opposition, August 1991).

[6] Anthony Payne, "Orthodox liberal development in Jamaica: theory and practice," (*Third World Quarterly*, vol.16, no.3, 1988).

[7] Edward Seaga,"Government Policy and the Economic Turnaround,"(*Atlantic Economic Journal*, vol.10, no.3, 1982), 6.

⁸ Warren Brown, "Jamaican Leader Cites Reagan's 'Opportunity',"(*The Washington Post*, 26 January, 1981).

⁹ Personal Interview with Edward Seaga, August 1991.

¹⁰ Edward Seaga, "Government Policy and the Economic Turnaround," 8.

¹¹ Personal Interview with Bruce Golding (Chairman, Jamaica Labour Party, August 1990).

¹² "Interview with the Prime Minister of Jamaica, Edward Seaga," (*Courier*, no.72, March/April 1982), 7.

¹³ William Fisher, *Experiment in Development: the U.S. Business Committee on Jamaica* (U.S. Business Committee on Jamaica, Inc., 1985), 6.

¹⁴ Seaga, "Government Policy and the Economic Turnaround," 2.

¹⁵ "Seaga Announces Nonaligned Policy," (*The Washington Post*, 3 November, 1980).

¹⁶ Kari Levitt, *The Origins and Consequences of Jamaica's Debt Crisis* (Jamaica: Consortium Graduate School of Social Sciences, 1991), 22.

¹⁷ James Goodsell, "Free Enterprise in Jamaica: Caribbean Lazarus," (*Journal for the Institute for Socioeconomic Studies*, vol.8, no.3, 1983), 52.

¹⁸ IMF, World Bank, USAID, *Jamaica: A Medium-Term Assessment. Report of the Tripartite Mission* (Washington D.C.: IMF, 1986), 40.

¹⁹ Basil Caplan, "Seaga's sea-change in Jamaica,"(*The Banker*, June 1982), 38.

²⁰ Quoted in Levitt, *The Origins and Consequences of Jamaica's Debt Crisis*, 27.

²¹ Joan Nelson, "The Politics of Adjustment in Small Democracies: Costa Rica, the Dominican Republic, Jamaica," in Joan Nelson, ed., *Economic Crisis and Policy Choice: The Politics of Adjustment in Developing Countries* (Princeton: Princeton University Press, 1990)," 195.

²² Carl Stone, *Politics and Economics in Jamaica: The 1989 Elections in Jamaica* (Jamaica: Heinemann Publishers (Caribbean) Ltd.,1989), 88.

²³ Carl Stone, "Running out of Options in Jamaica: Seaga and Manley Compared," (*Caribbean Review*, vol.15, no.3, 1987), 10.

²⁴ Quoted in Levitt, *The Origins and Consequences of Jamaica's Debt Crisis*, 36.

²⁵ Stone, *Politics and Economics*, 79-81.

²⁶ See *Jamaica: Adjustment Under Changing Economic Conditions* (Washington D.C.: World Bank, April 26, 1989).

²⁷ Levitt, *The Origins and Consequences of Jamaica's Debt Crisis*, and Derrick Boyd, "The Impact of Adjustment Policies on Vulnerable Groups: The Case of Jamaica, 1973-1985" in Giovanni Cornia, Richard Jolly, and Frances Steward, eds., *Adjustment with a Human Face - Vol.II* (Oxford: Clarendon Press, 1988).

²⁸ Jere Behrman and Anil Deolalikar, *Health, Nutrition and Macroeconomic Adjustment with a Human Face; the Analytical Basis for the UNICEF: Advocacy and Case Comparison* (Philadelphia: University of Pennsylvania, mimeographed, 1989).

Chapter 5

¹ Fitzroy Ambursley, "Jamaica: The Demise of 'Democratic Socialism'," (*New Left Review*, vol.128, 1981), 86.

² Arthur Lewin, "The Fall of Michael Manley: A Case Study of the Failure of Reform Socialism,"(*Monthly Review*, vol.33, no.9, 1982), 49, 57.

³ Lewin, "The Fall of Michael Manley," 59.

⁴ Lewin, "The Fall of Michael Manley," 57.

⁵ Kenneth Jameson,"Socialist Cuba and the Intermediate Regimes of Jamaica and Guyana," (*World Development*, vol. 9, no.9/10, 1981), 887.

⁶ Michael Kaufman, *Jamaica Under Manley: Dilemmas of Socialism and Democracy* (London: Zed Books, 1985), 219.

[7] Kari Levitt, "Jamaica: Manley's Defeat—Who's Responsible?" in Jill Torrie, ed., *Banking on Poverty* (Toronto: Between the Lines, 1983), 257.

[8] George Beckford and Michael Witter, *Small Garden...Bitter Weed: Struggle and Change in Jamaica* (Jamaica: Maroon Publishing House, 1982), 93, 151.

[9] Winsome Downie, *Democratic Socialism: The Jamaican Experiment* (Unpublished Ph.D. Dissertation: Columbia University, 1985), 230.

[10] Anthony Payne, *Politics in Jamaica* (London: C. Hurst & Co.), 59.

[11] Michael Manley, *Jamaica: Struggle in the Periphery* (London: Third World Media), 207.

[12] Winston Van Horne, "Jamaica: Problems of Michael Manley's Politics of Change, 1972-1980," (*Journal of Caribbean Studies*, vol. 2, no.2/3, 1981), 217.

[13] Personal Interview with Rt. Hon. P.J. Patterson (Prime Minister of Jamaica, March, 1992).

[14] Downie, *Democratic Socialism*, 234.

[15] Gladstone Bonnick, "Jamaica: Liberalization to Centralization, and Back?" in Arnold Harberger, ed., *World Economic Growth* (San Francisco: Institute for Contemporary Studies, 1984), 288.

[16] Downie, *Democratic Socialism*, 470.

[17] Manley, *Struggle in the Periphery*, 87.

[18] Kaufman, *Jamaica Under Manley*, 223.

[19] Carl Stone, *Politics and Economics in Jamaica: The 1989 Elections in Jamaica* (Jamaica: Heinemann Publishers (Caribbean) Ltd., 1989), 9.

[20] Payne, *Politics in Jamaica*, 81.

[21] Manley, *Struggle in the Periphery*, 210.

[22] Manley, *Struggle in the Periphery*, 95.

[23] Payne, *Politics in Jamaica*, 81.

[24] Kaufman, *Jamaica Under Manley*, 214.

[25] Manley, *Struggle in the Periphery*, 87.

[26] Manley, *Struggle in the Periphery*, 57.

[27] Michael Manley, in Altaf Gauhar, ed., *Talking about Development*, (London: Third World Foundation for Social and Economic Studies, 1983), 131-2.

[28] Janis Johnson and Robert Rankin, "Interviewing Michael Manley: The Role of the Opposition in Jamaica," (*Caribbean Review*, vol.11, no.3, 1982), 28.

[29] Johnson and Rankin, "Interviewing Michael Manley," 26.

[30] Johnson and Rankin, "Interviewing Michael Manley," 26.

[31] PNP, "Report to the 45th Annual Conference,"(Jamaica: PNP National Archives, 1983), 20-1.

[32] Michael Manley, *Broadcast by the Leader of the Opposition* (Jamaica: PNP National Archives, 26 June, 1983).

[33] Michael Manley, *Broadcast by the Leader of the Opposition* (Jamaica: PNP National Archives, 6 November, 1983).

[34] Payne, *Politics in Jamaica*, 101.

[35] Michael Manley, *Broadcast by the President of the People's National Party* (Jamaica: PNP National Archives, 8 April, 1984).

[36] Michael Manley, *Broadcast by the President of the People's National Party* (Jamaica: PNP National Archives, 10 July, 1984).

[37] PNP, "Our Achievements and Our Development Strategy," (Jamaica: PNP National Archives, 1984), 4.

[38] Michael Manley, "Speech Given at Vernon Arnett Party School Graduation: Kingston Campus," (Jamaica: August 1985).

[39] *Latin American Regional Report: Caribbean*, (WR-85-72, 16 Aug. 1985).

[40] Johnson and Rankin, "Interviewing Michael Manley," 28.

[41] Manley, *Broadcast by the Leader of the Opposition*, (Jamaica: PNP National Archives, 26 June, 1983).

[42] *Daily Gleaner* (17 January, 1985).

[43] See Trevor Munroe, *Jamaican Politics: A Marxist Perspective in Transition*, (Jamaica: Heinemann Publishers (Caribbean) Limited, 1990), 279-80 for a good analysis of Manley's moderate agenda during this period.

[44] Quoted in Munroe, *Jamaican Politics*, 277-8.

[45] Michael Manley, *The Poverty of Nations: Reflections on Underdevelopment and the World Economy* (London: Pluto Press, 1991).

[46] Franklin McKnight, "When Manley Lost his Nerve," [Interview with D.K.Duncan], *Daily Gleaner* (5 May, 1985).

[47] *Latin American Weekly Report* (WR-85-37, 20 September, 1985), 6.

[48] Michael Manley, *Broadcast by the President of the People's National Party* (Jamaica: PNP National Archives, 25 July, 1986).

[49] Carl Stone, *Politics versus Economics: The 1989 Elections in Jamaica* (Jamaica: Heinemann Publishers (Caribbean) Limited, 1989), 54, 57.

[50] Bernard Headley, "Behind a Manley Victory in Jamaica," (*Monthly Review*, February 1987), 29-30.

[51] Michael Manley, *Broadcast by the President of the People's National Party* (Jamaica: PNP National Archives, 10 August, 1986).

[52] Stone, *Politics versus Economics*, 71.

[53] Personal Interview with D.K. Duncan, November 1991.

[54] Dudley Stokes, "Interview with Michael Manley," (*Jamaica Weekly Gleaner*, 5 October 1987).

[55] *Trinidad Express* (12 October 1986).

[56] Manley, *The Poverty of Nations*, 111.

[57] Stokes, "Interview with Michael Manley", *Jamaica Weekly Gleaner*.

[58] Personal Interview with Sir Florizel Glasspole (former Governor-General of Jamaica), March 1992.

[59] Stone, *Politics versus Economics*, 97.

[60] Carl Wint, "Michael Manley: My Policies if Elected," *Daily Gleaner* (17,18,19 January, 1989).

Chapter 6

[1] "PNP's Victory: Implications" (*Caribbean Contact*, 3 March 1989), 3.

[2] Michael Kaufman, "Manley Returns," (*The Nation*, 6 March, 1989), 293.

[3] Rex Nettleford, "Ideas," (*Money Index*, 4 April 1989), 22.

[4] "A Comeback in Jamaica: Eight Years after losing, Manley wins again," (*Newsweek*, 20 February, 1989), 29.

[5] "Jamaica Goes Half-Left," (*The Washington Post*, 13 February, 1989), A22.

[6] "U.S. Business Leaders Turn Out for Prime Minister Manley," (*Money Index*, 11 April, 1989).

[7] Arnold Bertram, "Who is Running Jamaica?" (*Jamaica Record*, 26 February, 1989).

[8] Byron Buckley, "Welcome back, Mr. Manley but..." (*Daily Gleaner*, 19 February, 1989).

[9] Dawn Ritch, "Devaluation—first of tough decisions for new Government,"(*Daily Gleaner*, 19 February, 1989).

[10] Wilmot Perkins, "Mutterings from Afar,"(*Money Index*, 28 February, 1989), 36.

[11] Personal Interview with Rt. Hon. Michael Manley (former Prime Minister of Jamaica, June 1989).

[12] Michael Manley, "Throne Speech," (Jamaica: Jamaica Information Service, 25 May, 1989).

[13] John Hearne, "Manley—a month after," (*Daily Gleaner*, 13 March, 1989).

[14] Hearne, "Manley", *Daily Gleaner*.

[15] "P.J. defends super Ministry" (*Jamaican Weekly Gleaner*, 3 April, 1989).

[16] *Caribbean Update*, (July 1989).

[17] Wilmot Perkins, "Mutterings from Afar ," (*Money Index*, 21 March, 1989).

[18] "Wrong Moves" (*Jamaican Weekly Gleaner*, editorial, 6 March, 1989).

[19] "Manley should bite the bullet now—Buck," (*Jamaican Weekly Gleaner*, 3 April 1989).

[20] Ian Boyne, "Will Manley Squander his second chance?" (*Daily Gleaner*, 21 February, 1989).

[21] Wilmot Perkins, "Mutterings from Afar," (*Money Index*, 6 June, 1989).

[22] Manley, "Swearing-in Speech," February, 1989.

[23] Quoted in "This will be a tight financial year—Manley," (*Jamaican Weekly Gleaner*, 1 May, 1989).

[24] Michael Manley, *Prime Minister's Broadcast to the Nation*, (Jamaica: Jamaica Information Service, 23 April 1989).

[25] Personal Interview with Hon. G. Arthur Brown (former Governor, Bank of Jamaica, August, 1990).

[26] Personal Interview with Michael Manley, July 1989.

[27] Quoted in Joseph Treaster, "Mellow Manley Steers Jamaica to Quiet Days," (*The New York Times*, 23 July, 1989).

[28] Quoted in *Caribbean Update*, August 1989.

[29] Quoted in Treaster, "Mellow Manley Steers Jamaica to Quiet Days," *The New York Times*.

[30] Wilmot Perkins, "Mutterings from afar," (*Money Index*, 17 October, 1989).

[31] Personal Interview with Rt. Hon. Edward Seaga (Leader of the Opposition, August 1991).

[32] Mark Ricketts, "Devaluation? NONSENSE! this is madness..." (*Jamaica Record*, 5 November, 1989).

[33] P.J. Patterson, *Speech at Press Conference*, (Personal Transcript recorded by the Author, March 1992).

[34] Carl Stone, "Rethinking economic policy," (*Daily Gleaner*, 15 January, 1990).

[35] Michael Manley, *The Challenge of the Nineties: Facing Economic Reality, Broadcast to the Nation* (Jamaica: Jamaica Information Service, 28 January, 1990).

[36] P.J. Patterson, *Budget Presentation* (Jamaica: Jamaica Information Service, 31 May, 1990).

[37] *Jamaica Five-Year Development Plan* (1990-95) (Jamaica: Planning Institute of Jamaica, July 1990), v.

[38] Patterson, *Budget Presentation*, 31 May 1990.

[39] *Caribbean Update*, (February 1990).

[40] *Caribbean Update*, (March, 1990).

[41] Howard French, "All Forgiven, Jamaican Will See Bush Today," (*The New York Times*, 3 May, 1990).

[42] Interview with Michael Manley, October 1991.

[43] Dana Priest, "Bush Hails Jamaica's Manley, Once a Third-World Spokesman," (*The Washington Post*, 4 May, 1990).

[44] P.J. Patterson, "New Foreign Exchange Regime," (Jamaica: Jamaica Information Service, 12 September, 1990).

[45] Michael Manley, "Jamaica's New Economic Direction," (Jamaica: Jamaica Information Service, 16 September 1990).

⁴⁶ Michael Manley, "New Economic Measures and $100 million Social Security Programme," (Jamaica: Jamaica Information Service, 24 October, 1990).

⁴⁷ Michael Manley, "Christmas and New Year's Message," (Jamaica: Jamaica Information Service, January 1991).

⁴⁸ Michael Manley, *Budget Presentation*, (Jamaica: Jamaica Information Service, June 1991).

⁴⁹ Anne Shirley, "De-regulation or More Regulation," (*Investor's Choice*, November 1990).

⁵⁰ Wilmot Perkins, "Mutterings from Afar," (*Money Index*, 30 October 1990).

⁵¹ Interview with Michael Manley, October 1991.

⁵² Michael Manley, *Independence Message*, (Jamaica: Jamaica Information Service, August 1991).

⁵³ Interview with Michael Manley, October 1991.

⁵⁴ "Economy out of control—says Seaga" (*Daily Gleaner*, 12 September, 1991).

⁵⁵ Michael Manley, *Prime Minister's Broadcast to the Nation*, 9 September, 1991.

⁵⁶ Michael Manley, *Prime Minister's Broadcast to the Nation*, (Jamaica: Jamaica Information Service, 27 September, 1991).

⁵⁷ P.J. Patterson, *Address to Parliament* (Transcript in *Money Index*, 2 October 1991).

⁵⁸ "Foreign Exchange liberalisation—A bold new step," (*Enterprise*, PSOJ Publication, September/October, 1991).

⁵⁹ "Following up on that bold move," (*Investor's Choice*, November 1991).

⁶⁰ Wilmot Perkins, "Mutterings from Afar" (*Money Index*, 15 October 1991).

⁶¹ Personal Interview with Michael Manley, October 1991.

⁶² Michael Manley, "Jamaica is casting off the debt hook: with Bush's help, the hemisphere turns to free trade," (*The Jamaica Record*, 17 November 1991).

⁶³ Michael Manley, "Address to La Secretaría Permanente del Sistema Económico Latinoamericano," (Jamaica: Jamaica Information Service, February 1991).

⁶⁴ "Big hike in foreign exchange inflows since liberalization," (*Jamaican Weekly Gleaner*, 28 October 1991).

⁶⁵ Terry Smith, "A Struggle for the soul of the PNP," (*Daily Gleaner*, 12 January 1992).

⁶⁶ Smith, "A Struggle for the soul of the PNP," 12 January 1992.

⁶⁷ Carl Stone, "PNP's political management," (*Jamaican Weekly Gleaner*, 13 January 1992).

⁶⁸ "PM names think-tank team," (*Jamaican Weekly Gleaner*, 13 January 1992).

⁶⁹ Wilmot Perkins, *Straight Talk* (KLAS, January 1992, personal transcript of the author).

⁷⁰ Michael Manley, *Prime Minister's Broadcast to the Nation*, (Transcript in *Daily Gleaner*, 13 January, 1992).

⁷¹ "Below Expectations," (*Daily Gleaner*, 14 January, 1992).

⁷² Michael Manley, *Prime Minister's Broadcast to the Nation*, (Transcript in the *Sunday Record*, 29 March, 1992).

⁷³ Michael Manley, *The Search for Solutions: Excerpts from the Speeches and Writings of Michael Manley*, John Hearne, ed., (Canada: Maple Publishing House, 1976),167. Manley delivered these remarks to PNP delegates at the 36th Annual Conference in 1974 where he officially launched democratic socialism.

⁷⁴ Personal Interview with Rt. Hon. Michael Manley (former Prime Minister of Jamaica, June 1989).

⁷⁵ Manley, "Jamaica's New Economic Direction," 16 September, 1990.

⁷⁶ Paula Pilgrim, "The 52nd Annual Conference of the PNP," (*Caribbean Spectrum*, November/December 1990).

⁷⁷ *Policy Review Committee Report*, in PNP, "Report to the 52nd Annual General Conference," 80.

[74] Michael Manley, "The Compass," (Jamaica: PNP National Archives, 1991), 6.

[79] Quoted in Wilmot Perkins, "Mutterings from Afar," (*Money Index*, 13 November, 1990).

[80] Perkins, "Mutterings from Afar," November 1990.

[81] Personal Interview with Michael Manley, October 1991.

[82] PNP, "Principles and Objectives of the People's National Party," (Jamaica: Office of the Prime Minister, July 1991 Draft).

Chapter 7

[1] Norris McDonald, "Manley and the PNP's Economic Strategy," (*Money Index*, 13 November 1990).

[2] Trevor Munroe, *Jamaican Politics: A Marxist Perspective in Transition* (Jamaica: Heinemann Publishers (Caribbean) Limited, 1990), 277.

[3] McDonald, "Manley and the PNP," 13 November 1990.

[4] McDonald, "Manley and the PNP," 13 November 1990.

[5] Edward Seaga, "Farewell Tribute to Michael Manley," (Jamaica: House of Parliament, 26 March, 1992, personal transcript of the author).

[6] Wilmot Perkins, "Government with his Convictions Mothballed," (*Money Index*, 30 May 1989).

[7] Wilmot Perkins, "That Irresistible Logic," (*Money Index*, 1 August 1989).

[8] Perkins, "Government with his Conviction Mothballed," *Money Index*.

[9] Carl Stone, "Assessing the Manley legacy," (*Daily Gleaner*, 11 April 1992).

[10] Norman Washington Manley, *Manley and the New Jamaica: Selected Speeches and Writings 1938-1969* (Rex Nettleford, ed., London: Longman Caribbean, 1971), 381.

[11] Wilmot Perkins, "Mutterings from Afar," (*Money Index*, 21 March 1989).

[12] Wilmot Perkins, "Mutterings from Afar," (*Money Index*, 14 November, 1989).

[13] Michael Manley, *The Search for Solutions: Excerpts from the Speeches and Writings of Michael Manley* (John Hearne, ed., Canada: Maple Publishing House Company, 1976), 71.

[14] Personal Interview with Rt. Hon. Michael Manley (former Prime Minister of Jamaica, July 1989).

[15] Michael Manley, *The Politics of Change: A Jamaican Testament* (London: Andre Deutsch, 1974), 215.

[16] Personal Interview with Michael Manley, July 1989.

[17] Personal Interview with Michael Manley, October 1991.

[18] Personal Interiew with Michael Manley, October 1991.

[19] Wilmot Perkins, "Mutterings from Afar" (*Money Index*, 13 November 1990).

[20] Manley, *The Search for Solutions*, 64.

[21] Jean Marie Burgaud, *The New Caribbean Deal: The Next Five Years* (London: The Economist Intelligence Unit, Special Report No 240, March 1986), 57.

[22] Personal Interview with Edward Seaga, August 1991.

[23] Munroe, *Jamaican Politics*, 277.

[24] Personal Interview with Michael Manley, October 1991.

[25] Joan Nelson, "The Political Economy of Stabilization: Commitment, Capacity, and Public Response," (*World Development*, vol. 12, no. 10, 1984), 983.

[26] Carl Stone, *The Political Opinions of the Jamaican People, 1976-81* (Jamaica: Blackett Publishers, 1982), 17.

[27] Carl Stone, *Politics versus Economics: The 1989 Elections in Jamaica* (Jamaica: Heinemann Publishers (Caribbean) Limited, 1989), 69.

[28] Nelson, "The Political Economy of Stabilization," 997.

[29] "Is Michael Manley a saint or a sinner?" (*Euromoney*, August 1979), 95

[30] Personal Interview with Michael Manley, October 1991.

[31] Personal Interview with Michael Manley, October 1991.

[32] Manley, *The Search for Solutions*, 66.

[33] Personal Interview with Edward Seaga, August 1991.

[34] Rex Nettleford, "One Don, Don Juan (Options for National Leadership)," (*Money Index*, 13 November 1990).

[35] Allan Rickards, "Political Dishonesty," (*Money Index*, 22 October 1991).

[36] Headley Brown, *The Return of Instability (1989-92)* (forthcoming).

[37] Headley Brown, "The Manley Years and the Jamaican economy," (*The Financial Gleaner*, 27 March, 1992).

[38] Carl Stone, "Rating Manley and Seaga," (*Daily Gleaner*, 11 May, 1992).

[39] Edward Seaga, "JLP will beat any PNP leader," (*Jamaican Weekly Gleaner*, 30 March, 1992).

APPENDIX A: STATISTICAL PROFILE OF JAMAICA

Population (1990)	2.4 million
Urban	49%
Rural	51%
Population Growth Rate	0.9%
Life Expectancy	
Male	69
Female	72
Land Area (sq. ml)	4,411

Source: Quarterly Economic Report, July/September 1991, 52.

APPENDIX B: SELECT ECONOMIC INDICATORS (1989-1991)

FINANCIAL INDICATORS	1989	1990	1991*
Real GDP Growth Rate	6.5	4.8	0.2
Net Foreign Assets (J$M)	(4994)	(5072)	(8652)
Int'l Reserves (US$M)	170	(92)	54
Interest Rates (Avg. Lending Rate)	28.2%	31.6%	34.0%
Exchange Rate US$1=J$	7.2	7.5	11.8
Consumer Price Index % Change	17.2%	29.8%	80.2%
FISCAL ACCOUNTS			
Bauxite	265	555	-
Tax Revenue	6364	744	11,469
Total Receipts	8309	630	14,496
Government Surplus/Deficit	655	51	1448
Debt Servicing (as % of Total Expenditure)	42.7%	40.9%	23.5%
BALANCE OF PAYMENTS			
Exports (f.o.b.)	998	1158	1145
Imports (c.o.f.)	1820	1942	1800
Balance of Trade	(822)	(784)	(654)
Current Account Balance	(258)	(340)	(131)

Source: Economic and Social Survey and
Quarterly Economic Report. July/September 1991.
*Exchange rate, bauxite, and debt servicing figures from January-September 1991

APPENDIX C: GDP AT FACTOR COSTS BY ECONOMIC SECTOR
(1950, 1960, 1970)

Sector	1950		1960		1970	
	J$m	%	J$m	%	J$m	%
Agriculture	43.2	31.5	51.9	12.0	78.9	7.4
Mining	*	*	41.6	9.6	146.7	13.7
Manufacturing	15.8	11.5	58.7	13.6	139.8	13.0
Construction and installation	10.6	7.7	51.1	11.8	155.7	14.5
Electricity, gas and water	1.5	1.1	4.5	1.0	11.8	1.1
Transportation, storage and communication	10.0	7.3	33.4	7.7	62.9	5.9
Distribution	21.2	15.5	77.8	18.0	179.5	16.7
Financial institutions	2.8	2.0	16.2	3.8	43.6	4.1
Ownership of dwellings	8.3	6.1	13.5	3.1	104.7	9.8
Public administration	7.0	5.1	26.6	6.2	91.6	8.5
Miscellaneous services	16.6	12.1	56.3	13.0	57.1	5.3
Total	137.0	100.0	431.6	100.0	1072.3	100.0

*The mining sector was virtually non-existent in 1950.
Numbers may not add up to 100.0% because of rounding.

Source: Stephens and Stephens, *Democratic Socialism*, 23

APPENDIX D: JAMAICA: FISCAL INDICATORS (1972-1980)

	1972	1973	1974	1975	1976	1977	1978	1979	1980
Government Expenditures/GDP	25	26	33	38	46	41	40	45	44
Overall fiscal deficit/GDP	5	6	10	13	24	19	13	20	18
National external debt/GDP	9	11	13	16	18	18	32	33	30
National internal debt/GDP	18	18	18	18	25	44	44	45	43
External Debt Service/GDP	1.1	0.9	2.3	2.9	3.7	4.4	9.2	8.7	7.0

Increase over previous financial year	1972/73 -1973/74	1973/74 -1974/75	1974/75 -1975/76	1975/76 -1976/77	1976/77 -1977/78	1977/78 -1978/79	1978/79 -1979/80
a. Central government expenditures	23	61	36	27	23	-1	27
b. Central government revenues and capital development fund	22	48	24	-5	58	8	30
c. Overall fiscal deficit	26	108	66	88	-16	-11	77

Source: Sharpley, *Jamaica, 1972-80, 126*

APPENDIX E: SELECT SOCIAL INDICATORS (1970-1980)

	1970	1971	1972	1973	1974	1975	1976	1977	1978	1979	1980
GDP per capita (J$1974)	1055	1082	1163	1155	1091	1070	987	953	946	919	867
Net Migration (000's)	23.0	31.5	11.2	10.2	12.9	12.5	220	21.1	17.8	21.0	24.3
Migration Rate	46%	60%	21%	21%	27%	26%	48%	46%	39%	47%	53%
Wage/Salary as % of Private Consumption	83	80	79	86	80	84	81	82	82	80	77
Unemployment %	-	-	23.2	21.9	21.2	20.7	22.4	24.2	24.5	27.8	27.5
Infant Mortality	32.5	27.9	30.9	31.4	25.9	23.5	20.3	15.1	14.6	12.4	-
% Public Exp. on Education/Health as % Total Government exp.	26	21	24	27	27	27	26	21	24	21	19

Source: Levitt, The Origins and Condequences of Jamaica's Debt Crisis, 12.

APPENDIX F: COMPOSITION OF EXPORTS OF GOODS AND SERVICES (1980-1988)

	1980	1981	1982	1983	1984	1985	1986	1987	1988
Total Exports	963	974	768	686	702	568	590	706	833
Domestic Export	941	965	746	673	687	527	565	687	803
Major Traditional	800	811	568	488	511	343	367	430	510
Bauxite/Alumina	735	760	514	424	444	291	295	336	417
Sugar	54	47	49	57	66	50	62	74	77
Banana	11	4	5	7	2	4	9	19	15
Other Traditional	26	32	34	33	36	30	37	37	47
Coffee	5	6	8	8	9	8	7	9	11
Rum	10	11	11	8	9	9	10	10	13
Non-Traditional	115	122	144	152	140	154	161	220	246
Garments	7	7	17	13	32	36	53	103	n/a
Services	399	428	476	525	607	655	818	920	881
Tourist Earnings	241	284	336	399	407	407	516	595	527
Other Services	158	144	140	126	200	248	302	325	324

Source: Levitt, The Origins and Condequences of Jamaica's Debt Crisis, 19.

PERSONAL INTERVIEWS

Name	Organisations	Date of Interview
Donald Banks	Chairman, NCB Bank Ltd. Member, Economic Advisory Council	November 1991
Richard Bernal	Jamaican Ambassador to the United States	December 1991
G. Arthur Brown	Former Governor, Bank of Jamaica Member, Economic Advisory Council Member, Council of Advisors on Government Structure	August 1990
Horace Clarke	Former PNP Minister Member of Parliament	March 1992
D.K. Duncan	Former PNP Minister Member, New Beginning Movement	November 1991
Omar Davies	Director-General, Planning Institute (PIOJ) Economic Adviser, Ministry of Finance Government Negotiating Team with Bilateral and Multilateral Agencies	August 1990
Carlton Davis	Executive Director, Jamaica Bauxite Institute (JBI) Chairman, National Housing Trust	August 1990
Errol Ennis	PNP Minister of State Member of Parliament	November 1991
Florizel Glasspole	Former Governor-General of Jamaica	March 1992
Bruce Golding	Chairman, Jamaica Labour Party Former JLP Minister Member of Parliament	August 1990
Lloyd Goodleigh	President, National Worker's Union Member, Jamaican Senate	November 1991
Hugh Hart	Former JLP Minister	August 1990

Michael Henry	Member of Parliament Former JLP Minister of State	April 1992
Glen Holden	United States Ambassador to Jamaica	October 1991
Dennis Lalor	President, Private Sector Organisation of Jamaica (PSOJ)	November 1991
Delroy Lindsay	Former Executive Director, Private Sector Organisation of Jamaica (PSOJ)	October 1991
Beverly Manley	Former President, PNP Women's Movement	November 1991
Douglas Manley	Former PNP Minister Member of Parliament	March 1992
Michael Manley	Former Prime Minister of Jamaica October 1991	June 1989
Dennis Morrison	Economist, Jamaica Bauxite Institute	August 1990
Trevor Munroe	General Secretary, Worker's Party of Jamaica (WPJ) Member, New Beginning Movement	November 1991
Dwight Nelson	Island Supervisor, Bustamante Industrial Trade Union Member, Jamaican Senate	November 1991
Rex Nettleford	Chairman, Council of Advisers on Government Structure and Function	January 1992
P.J. Patterson	Prime Minister of Jamaica	March 1992
Wilmot Perkins	Journalist, *Money Index* Radio Host, *Straight-Talk*	November 1991
Robert Proctor	Political Affairs Director, United States Embassy in Jamaica	October 1991
Paul Robertson	PNP Minister Member of Parliament	January 1992
Edward Seaga	Leader of the Opposition Former Prime Minister of Jamaica	August 1991
Dudley Stokes	Former Editor, Gleaner Publications	January 1992
Ronald Thwaites	Convener, New Beginning Movement Chairman, Micro-Investment Development Agency (MIDA) Radio Host, *The Public Eye*	January 1992

BIBLIOGRAPHY

BOOKS, DISSERTATIONS, AND PAPERS

Ashby, Timothy, *Missed Opportunities: The Rise and Fall of Jamaica's Edward Seaga* (Indiana: Hudson Institute, 1989).

Augier, F.R., S.C. Gordon, D.G. Hall, and M. Reckord, *The Making of the West Indies* (London: Longmans, 1960).

Ayub, Mahmood, *Made in Jamaica: The Development of the Manufacturing Sector* (Washington D.C.: World Bank Occasional Paper, no. 31, 1980).

Bakan, Abigail, *Ideology and Class Conflict in Jamaica* (Montréal: McGill-Queen's University Press, 1990).

Behrman, Jere and Anil Deolalikar, *Health, Nutrition and Macroeconomic Adjustment with a Human Face; the Analytical Basis for the UNICEF: Advocacy and Case Comparison* (Philadelphia: University of Pennsylvania, mimeographed, 1989).

Beckford, George, *Persistent Poverty: Underdevelopment in the Plantation Economies of the Third World* (New York: Oxford University Press, 1972).

_____, and Michael Witter, *Small Garden...Bitter Weed: Struggle and Change in Jamaica* (Jamaica: Maroon Publishing House, 1980).

Bell, Wendell, *Jamaican Leaders: Political Attitudes in A New Nation* (Berkeley: University of California Press, 1964).

Black, Clinton, *History of Jamaica* (Jamaica: Longman Caribbean, 1983).

Boyd, Derick, *Economic Management, Income Distribution, and Poverty in Jamaica* (New York: Praeger Press, 1988).

Brown, Headley, *The Return of Instability (1989-92)* (forthcoming, 1993).

Burgaud, Jean-Marie, *The New Caribbean Deal: The Next Five Years* (London: The Economist Intelligence Unit, Special Report No. 240, March 1986).

Chen-Young, Paul, *An Economic Evaluation of the Tax Incentive Programme in Jamaica* (Unpublished Doctoral Dissertation, University of Pittsburgh, 1966).

Cowan, L. Gray, *Privatization in the Developing World* (Connecticut: Greenwood Press, 1990).

Dell, Sidney and Roger Lawrence, *The Balance of Payments Adjustment Process in Developing Countries* (Oxford, Pergamon Press, 1980).

Downie, Winsome, *Democratic Socialism: The Jamaican Experiment* (Unpublished Doctoral Dissertation, Columbia University, 1985).

Eaton, George, *Alexander Bustamante and Modern Jamaica* (Jamaica: Kingston Publishers Ltd., 1975).

Edie, Carlene, *Democracy by Default: Dependency and Clientelism in Jamaica* (London: Lynne Reinner Publishers, 1990).

Eisner, Gisela, *Jamaica 1830-1930: A Study in Economic Growth* (Manchester, England: Manchester University Press, 1961).

Gauhar, Altaf, ed., *Talking about Development* (London: Third World Foundation for Social and Economic Studies, 1983).

Girvan, Norman, *Corporate Imperialism: Conflict and Expropriation* (New York: Monthly Review Press, 1976).

Gray, Obika, *Radicalism and Social Change in Jamaica, 1960-72* (Knoxville, Tennesee: The University of Tennessee, 1991)

Grosh, Margaret, *Social Spending in Latin America: The Story of the 1980's* (Washington D.C.: World Bank Discussion Papers 106, 1990).

Hall, Douglas, *Free Jamaica, 1838-1865* (New Haven: Yale University Press, 1959).

Hoffman, Linda, *Politics of the Manley Regime in Jamaica, 1972-80* (Unpublished Doctoral Dissertation, University of Wisconsin-Madison, 1983).

International Bank for Reconstruction and Development, *The Economic Development of Jamaica* (Johns Hopkins Press: Baltimore, 1952).

Jefferson, Owen, *The Post-War Economic Development of Jamaica* (Jamaica: Institute of Social and Economic Research, 1972).

Kaufman, Michael, *Jamaica Under Manley: Dilemmas of Socialism and Democracy* (London: Zed Books, 1985).

Keyes, Bill, *The Caribbean Basin Initiative: A Major Step Toward Strong Free Market Economies* (Washington D.C.: Council for Inter-American Security Educational Institute, 1982).

Kuper, Adam, *Changing Jamaica* (London: Routledge & Kegan Paul, 1976).

Lacey, Terry, *Politics and Violence in Jamaica* (Manchester: Manchester University Press, 1977).

Leeds, Roger, *Privatization in Jamaica: Two Case Studies* (Massachusetts: Kennedy School of Government, Center for Business and Government, 1987).

Levi, Darrell, *Michael Manley: The Making of a Leader* (Jamaica: Heinemann Publishers (Caribbean) Ltd., 1989).

Levitt, Kari, *The Origins and Consequences of Jamaica's Debt Crisis* (Jamaica: Consortium Graduate School of Social Sciences, 1991).

Long, Frank, *Employment effects of Multinational Enterprises in Export Processing Zones in the Caribbean* (Washington, D.C., International Labor Office, Working Paper no. 42, 1986).

Looney, Robert, *The Jamaican Economy in the 1980's: Economic Decline and Structural Adjustment* (Colorado: Westview Press, 1987),

Manley, Michael, *Jamaica: Struggle in the Periphery* (London: Third World Media, 1982).

_____, *The Politics of Change: A Jamaican Testament* (London: André Deutsch, 1974).

_____, *The Poverty of Nations: Reflections on Underdevelopment and the World Economy* (London: Pluto Press, 1991).

_____, *The Search for Solutions: Excerpts from the Speeches and Writings of Michael Manley*, John Hearne, ed., (Canada: Maple House Publishing, 1976).

_____, *Up the Down Escalator: Development and the International Economy: A Jamaican Case Study* (London: André Deutsch, 1987).

_____, *A Voice at the Workplace* (London: André Deutch, 1975).

Manley, Norman, *Manley and the New Jamaica: Selected Speeches and Writings (1938-1968)*, Rex Nettleford, ed., (London, Longman Caribbean Ltd., 1971).

Munroe, Trevor, *Jamaican Politics: A Marxist Perspective in Transition* (Jamaica: Heinemann Publishers (Caribbean) Ltd., 1990).

_____, *The Politics of Constitutional Decolonization: Jamaica, 1944-62* (Jamaica: Institute of Social and Economic Research, 1972).

Nelson, Joan, ed., *Economic Crisis and Policy Choice: The Politics of Adjustment in Developing Countries* (Princeton: Princeton University Press, 1990).

Nettleford, Rex, *Mirror, Mirror: Identity, Race and Protest in Jamaica* (Jamaica: Collins and Sangster, 1971).

Palmer, Ransford, *The Jamaican Economy* (New York: Praeger Press, 1968).

Payne, Anthony, *Politics in Jamaica* (London: C. Hurst & Co., 1988).

_____, and Paul Sutton, eds., *Dependency under Challenge: The Political Economy of the Commonwealth Caribbean* (Manchester: Manchester University Press, 1983).

Post, Ken, *Arise Ye Starvelings: The Jamaica Labour Rebellion and its Aftermath* (The Hague: Martinus Nijhoff, 1972).

_____, *Strike the Iron* (The Hague: Martinus Nijhoff, 1981).

Ragatz, Joseph, *The Fall of the Planter class in the British Caribbean* (New York: Octagon Books, 1971).

Ranston, Jackie, *From We Were Boys: The Story of the Magnificent Cousins Manley and Bustamante* (Jamaica: Bustamante Institute of Public and International Affairs, 1989).

Socialist International, Committee on Economic Policy, *Global Challenge: From Crisis to Cooperation: Breaking the North-South Stalemate* (London: Pan Books, 1985).

Stephens, Evelyne Huber and John Stephens, *Democratic Socialism in Jamaica: The Political Movement and Social Transformation in Dependent Capitalism* (London: MacMillan Press, 1986).

Stone, Carl, *Class, Race and Political Behavior in Urban Jamaica* (Jamaica: Institute of Social and Economic Research, 1973).

_____, *Democracy and Clientelism in Jamaica* (New Jersey: Transaction Books, 1980).

_____, *The Political Opinions of the Jamaican People (1976-81)* (Jamaica: Blackett Publishers, 1982).

_____, *Politics versus Economics: The 1989 Elections in Jamaica* (Jamaica: Heinemann Publishers (Caribbean) Limited, 1989).

_____, and Aggrey Brown, eds., *Essays on Power and Change in Jamaica* (Jamaica: Jamaica Publishing House, 1976).

Weiss, John, *Industrial Policy in the 1980's* (United Kingdom: University of Bradford, Occasional Paper no. 13, 1989).

Williams, Eric, *Capitalism and Slavery* (London: André Deutsch, 1964).

_____, *The Negro in the Caribbean* (Washington: Panaf Publications, 1942).

ACADEMIC AND JOURNAL ARTICLES

Ahiram, E., "Income Distribution in Jamaica, 1958," (*Social and Economic Studies,* vol. 13, no. 3, 1954), 333-369.

Ambursley, Fitzroy, "Jamaica: the Demise of "Democratic Socialism," (*New Left Review,* vol. 128, 1980), 76-87.

Berger, Peter, "Can the Caribbean Learn from East Asia?", (*Caribbean Review,* vol. 13, no. 2, 1984), 7ff.

Best, Lloyd, "A Model of a Pure Plantation Economy," (*Social and Economic Studies,* vol. 17, no. 4, 1968), 283-326.

Bonnick, Gladstone, "Jamaica: Liberalization to Centralization, and Back?" in Arnold Harberger, ed., *World Economic Growth* (San Francisco: Institute for Contemporary Studies, 1984).

Boyd, Derick, "The Impact of Adjustment Policies on Vulnerable Groups: The Case of Jamaica, 1973-1985" in Giovanni Cornia, Richard Jolly, and Frances Steward, eds., *Adjustment with a Human Face* - Vol II (Oxford: Clarendon Press, 1988).

Braveboy-Wagner, Jacqueline Anne, "The Politics of Developmentalism: U.S. Policy Toward Jamaica," in H. Michael Erisman, *The Caribbean Challenge: U.S. Policy in a Volatile Region* (Colorado: Westview Press, 1984).

Campbell, Horace, "Rastafari: Culture of Resistance," (*Race and Class,* vol. 22, no. 1, 1980), 1-22.

Davies, Omar, "An Analysis of Socio-Economic Developments in Jamaica 1980-85," in Judith Wedderburn, ed., *A Caribbean Reader in Development* (Jamaica: Friedrich Ebert Stiftung, 1986).

Garrity, Michele and Louis Picard, "Organized Interests, the State, and the Public Policy Process: An Assessment of Jamaican Business Associations," (*The Journal of Developing Areas,* vol. 25, April 1991), 369-94.

Girling, Robert and Sherry Keith, "The Planning and Management of Jamaica's Special Employment Programme: Lessons and Limitations," (*Social and Economic Studies,* vol. 29, no. 2, 1980), 1-34.

Norman Girvan, Richard Bernal, and Wesley Hughes, "The IMF and the Third World: the Case of Jamaica, 1974-80," (*Development Dialogue,* vol. 2, 1980), 113-52.

Goldstein, Morris and Mohsin Khan, "Effects of Slowdown in Industrial Countries on Growth in Non-oil Developing Countries," (Washington, D.C.: IMF Occasional Paper 12, 1982).

Goodsell, James, "Free Enterprise in Jamaica: Caribbean Lazarus," (*Journal for the Institute for Socioeconomic Studies*, vol. 8, no. 3, 1983), 39-51.

Hart, Keith, "Informal Income Opportunities and Urban Employment in Ghana," (*The Journal of Modern African Studies*, vol. 11, no. 1, 1973), 61-89.

Headley, Bernard, "A Contest that Became a Referendum," (*Caribbean Review*, vol. 15, no. 3, 1987), 13.

_____, "Behind a Manley Victory in Jamaica," (*Monthly Review*, February 1987), 17-30.

_____, "Mr. Seaga's Jamaica: An Inside Look," (*Monthly Review*, September 1985), 35-42.

Herbst, Jeffrey, "The Structural Adjustment of Politics in Africa," (*World Development*, vol. 18, no. 7, 1990), 949-958.

Hillman, Richard, "Legitimacy and Change in Jamaica," (*The Journal of Developing Areas*, vol. 13, 1979), 395-414.

Jacobs, H.P., "The Self-Governing Movement" found in A. L. Hendrics and Cedric Lindo, eds., *Independence Anthology of Jamaican Literature* (Jamaica: Arts Celebration Committee of the Ministry of Development and Welfare, 1962).

Jamaica: Adjustment Under Changing Economic Conditions (Washington, D.C.: World Bank, April 26, 1989).

Jameson, Kenneth, "Socialist Cuba and the Intermediate Regimes of Jamaica and Guyana," (*World Development*, vol. 9, no. 9/10, 1981), 871-88.

Johnson, Janis and Robert Rankin, "Interviewing Michael Manley: The Role of the Opposition in Jamaica," (*Caribbean Review*, vol. 11, no. 3, 1982), 26-29.

Kincaid, G. Russell, "Conditionality and the Use of Fund Resources," (*Finance and Development*, vol. 18, no. 2, 1981), 18-21.

_____, "Fund Assistance to Jamaica," (*IMF Survey*, December 15, 1980), 378-82.

Kirton, C. and M. Figuorea, "State Trading: A Vital element in Caribbean Economic Development," in Carl Stone and Aggrey Brown, eds., *Perspectives on Jamaica in the Seventies* (Jamaica: Jamaica Publishing House, 1981).

Kohli, Atul, "Politics of Liberalization in India," (*World Development*, vol. 17, no. 3, 1989), 305-28.

Krueger, Anne, "Problems of Liberalization," in Arnold Harberger, ed., *World Economic Growth* (San Francisco: Institute for Contemporary Studies, 1984).

Levitt, Kari, "Jamaica: Manley's Defeat—Who's Responsible?" in Jill Torrie, ed., *Banking on Poverty* (Toronto: Between the Lines, 1983).

Lewin, Arthur, "The Fall of Michael Manley: A Case Study of the Failure of Reform Socialism," (*Monthly Review*, vol. 13, no. 9, 1982), 49-60.

Lewis, W. Arthur, "An Economic Plan for Jamaica," (*Agenda*, vol. 3, no. 4, 1944), 154-63.

_____, "Economic Development with Unlimited Supplies of Labour," (*Manchester School of Economic and Social Studies*, vol. 22, 1954), 139-91.

_____, "The Industrialization of the British West Indies," (*Caribbean Economic Review*, vol.. 2, 1950), 1-61.

Nelson, Joan, "The Political Economy of Stabilization: Commitment, Capacity, and Public Response," (*World Development*, vol. 12, no. 10, 1984), 983-1006.

_____ "The Politics of Adjustment in Small Democracies: Costa Rica, the Dominican Republic, Jamaica," in Joan Nelson, ed., *Economic Crisis and Policy Choice: The Politics of Adjustment in Developing Countries* (Princeton: Princeton University Press, 1990).

Panton, David, "Dual Labour Markets and Employment in Jamaica: A Modern Synthesis," (*Social and Economic Studies*, forthcoming 1993).

Payne, Anthony, "Jamaica: the 'Democratic Socialist' Experiment of Michael Manley," in Anthony Payne and Paul Sutton, eds., *Dependency under Challenge: The Political Economy of the Commonwealth Caribbean* (Manchester: Manchester University Press, 1983).

_____, "Orthodox Liberal Development in Jamaica: Theory and Practice," (*Third World Quarterly*, vol. 16, no. 3, 1988), 1217-38.

Rao, Mohan "Aspects of Jamaican Agriculture," (*Social and Economic Studies*, vol. 39, no. 1, 1990), 161-201.

Reid, Stanley, "An Introductory Approach to the Concentration of Power in the Jamaican Corporate Economy and Notes on its Origin," in Carl Stone and Aggrey Brown, eds., *Essays on Power and Change in Jamaica* (Jamaica: Jamaica Publishing House, 1977).

Robinson, Roger and Selde Schmitz, "Jamaica: Navigating through a Troubled Decade," (*Finance and Development*, vol. 26, no. 4, 1989), 30-33.

Seaga, Edward, "Government Policy and the Economic Turnaround," (*Atlantic Economic Journal*, vol. 10, no. 3, September 1982), 1-7.

Sharpley, Jennifer, "Jamaica, 1972-80," in Tony Killick, ed., *Developing Country Experiences and the IMF* (New York: St. Martin's Press, 1984).

Smith, M.G., "The Plural Framework of Jamaican Society," (*The British Journal of Sociology*, vol. 12, no. 3, 1961), 249-62.

Stephens, Evelyne Huber and John D. Stephens, "Manley Prepares to Return: PNP Options in Today's Jamaica," (*Caribbean Review*, vol. 6, no. 2, 1988), 16ff.

Stone, Carl, "Democracy and the State: The Case of Jamaica," (*Journal of Commonwealth and Comparative Politics*, vol. 29, no. 2, 1981), 115-33.

_____, "Democracy and Socialism in Jamaica, 1962-1979," in Omar Davies, ed., *The State in Caribbean Society* (Jamaica: University of the West Indies, Monograph no. 2, 1986).

_____, "The Jamaican Reaction: Grenada and the Political Stalemate," (*Caribbean Review*, vol. 12, no. 4, 1983), 31ff.

_____, "Jamaica's 1980 Elections: What Manley Did Do; What Seaga Need Do," (*Caribbean Review*, vol 10, no. 2, 1981), 5ff.

_____, "Running Out of Options in Jamaica: Seaga and Manley Compared," (*Caribbean Review*, vol. 15, no. 3, 1987), 10ff.

_____, "Seaga is in Trouble: Polling the Jamaican Polity in Mid-Term," (*Caribbean Review*, vol. 11, no. 4, 1982), 5ff.

_____, "Tenant Farming Under Capitalism," in Carl Stone and Aggrey Brown, eds., *Essays on Power and Change in Jamaica* (Jamaica: Jamaica Publishing House, 1976).

St. Pierre, Maurice, "The 1938 Jamaica Disturbances, A Portrait of Mass Reaction Against Colonialism," (*Social and Economic Studies*, vol. 27, no. 2, 1978), 171-98.

Tidrick, Gene, "Wage Spillover and Unemployment in a Wage-Gap Economy: The Jamaican Case," (*Economic Development and Cultural Change*, vol. 23, no. 2, 1975), 306-24.

Van Horne, Winston "Jamaica: Problems of Michael Manley's Politics of Change, 1972-1980," (*Journal of Caribbean Studies*, vol. 2, no. 2/3, 1981), 210-227.

_____, "Jamaica: Why Manley Lost," (*The World Today*, vol. 37, no. 11, 1981), 428-34.

Whitehead, Laurence, "Political Explanations of Macroeconomic Management: A Survey," (*World Development*, vol. 18, no. 8, 1990), 1133-46.

Witter, Michael, "Exchange Rate Policy in Jamaica: A Critical Assessment," (*Social and Economic Studies*, vol. 32, no. 4, 1983), 1-50.

SPEECHES, BROADCASTS, ESSAYS AND OTHER DOCUMENTS

Economic and Social Progress in Latin America (1991), (Washington D.C.: Inter-American Development Bank, October 1991).

Economic and Social Survey (Jamaica: Planning Institute of Jamaica, various issues).

Fisher, William, *Experiment in Development*: The U.S. Business Committee on Jamaica (U.S. Business Committee on Jamaica, Inc., 1985).

IMF, World Bank, USAID, *Jamaica: A Medium-Term Assessment, Report of the Tripartite Mission* (Washington D.C.: IMF, 1986).

Jamaica Five-Year Development Plan (1990-1995) (Jamaica: Planning Institute of Jamaica, July 1990).

JLP, "Change Without Chaos, A National Programme For Reconstruction," (Jamaica: Jamaica Labour Party, 1980).

Manley, Michael, "Address to PNP Delegates, 36th Annual Conference of People's National Party," (PNP National Archives: Jamaica, 1974).

_____, "Address to La Secretaría Permanente del Sistema Económico Latinoamericano," (Jamaica: Jamaica Information Service, February 1991).

_____, "Address to the 12th Annual TransAfrica Town Dinner," (Jamaica: Jamaica Information Service, 10 June 1989).

_____, *Broadcast by the President of the People's National Party* (Jamaica: PNP National Archives, various dates).

_____, "Budget Presentation to Parliament," (Jamaica: Jamaica Information Service, various dates).

_____, "The Compass," (Jamaica: PNP National Archives, 1991).

_____, "The Drug Menace—Stamp out the Scourge," (Jamaica: Jamaica Information Service, 2 October, 1989). Speech delivered to the Inter-Ministerial Conference on Drugs.

_____, "Jamaica's New Economic Growth" (Broadcast to the Nation: Office of the Prime Minister, September 16, 1990).

_____, *Prime Minister's Broadcast to the Nation*, (Jamaica: Jamaica Information Service, various dates).

_____, "The Role of the State," (Jamaica: Office of the Prime Minister, 1991: Draft).

_____, "Speech Given at Vernon Arnett Party School Graduation: Kingston Campus," (Jamaica: August 1985).

_____, "Swearing-in Speech," (Jamaica: Jamaica Information Service, 13 February 1989).

_____, *Toward a Self-Reliant Economy: The Non-IMF Path* (Jamaica: PNP National Archives, March 25, 1980).

_____, "Testimony before Congress," delivered by Congressman Charles Rangel (Washington D.C.: Congressional Record, 17 October, 1990).

National Planning Agency, *Five Year Development Plan 1978-82* (Jamaica: Ministry of Finance and Planning, 1978).

PNP, "The Economy: Expanding Production for Nation Building"; "Human Resource Development: Harnessing People's Talents"; "The Physical Infrastructure: Laying the Foundations"; "The Framework: Entrenching Our Democratic Tradition" (Jamaica: PNP National Archives, four document series 1988).

PNP, "Our Achievements and Our Development Strategy," (Jamaica: PNP National Archives, 1984).

PNP, "Democratic Socialism: The Jamaican Model," (Jamaica: PNP National Archives, 1974).

PNP, "1989 Election Manifesto: A Programme for Taking Jamaica into the 21st Century," (PNP: National Archives, 1989).

PNP, "Principles and Objectives of the People's National Party," (Jamaica: PNP National Archives, 1978).

PNP, "Principles and Objectives of the Peoples National Party," (Jamaica: Office of the Prime Minister, July 1991 Draft).

PNP, "Report to the Annual General Conference," (Jamaica: PNP National Archives, various issues).

PNP, "Strategy for Development to lead Jamaica into the 21st Century," (*Daily Gleaner*, 25 October 1985).

PNP, "Thirteen Principles of Democratic Socialism," (Jamaica: PNP National Archives, 1974).

Private Sector Organization of Jamaica, "Exchange Rate Policy for Economic Growth and Development," (Jamaica: PSOJ, October 1987).

Quarterly Economic Report, (Jamaica: Planning Institute of Jamaica, various issues).

NEWSPAPERS AND MAGAZINES

The Banker
Canabusine$$
Caribbean Contact
Caribbean Insight
Caribbean Update
Courier
Daily Gleaner
Ebony
The Economist
Euromoney
Investor's Choice
Jamaica Weekly Gleaner
Jamaica Record
Latin American Weekly Report
Los Angeles Times
Money Index
The Nation
Newsweek
New York Times
Public Opinion
Rising Sun
Wall Street Journal
Washington Post

Printed in the United States
2769